READ THE BIBLE FOR A CHANGE

READ THE BIBLE
FOR A CHANGE

Understanding and responding to **God's Word**

RAY LUBECK

WIPF & STOCK · Eugene, Oregon

Wipf and Stock Publishers
199 W 8th Ave, Suite 3
Eugene, OR 97401

Read the Bible for a Change
Understanding and Responding to God's Word
By Lubeck, Ray
Copyright©2005 by Lubeck, Ray
ISBN 13: 978-1-60899-153-2
Publication date 1/1/2010
Previously published by Authentic Media and World Vision Press, 2005

Dear Reader,

World Vision invites you to share your response to
the message of this book by writing to World Vision Press at
worldvisionpress@worldvision.org or by calling 800-777-7752.

For information about other World Vision Press publications, visit us
at www.worldvision.org/worldvisionpress.

To my wife, **Tamara**, whose buoyant enthusiasm for this work, unflagging encouragement, selfless support, daily sacrifices, long-term patience, probing questions, persistent challenges, creative suggestions, clear-sighted critique, prayers, and faithful love have made this book possible and my life far richer.

Contents

Acknowledgments

This book is the product of many years of reflection, development, and refinement. Though my name is credited as its author, the ideas expressed in it have been generated through conversations and interaction involving many different parties who rightly deserve credit for that which is both good and helpful to the reader.

Thank you to Mickey Day, former professor at Multnomah Bible College. It was under his teaching, more than any other person's, that it first dawned upon me that reading the Bible and thinking can and should be attempted simultaneously. I consider his insights to have provided the spark that ignited my lifelong desire to study God's Word in a manner that it deserves.

To David Sanford and his team I owe a deep debt of gratitude. It was David who recognized the potential in my ideas to equip those who wish to study the Bible. He spearheaded the development of the *Starting Point Study Bible* (Zondervan, 2002), and convincingly impressed upon me the need to share my own discoveries with a larger audience of readers. It is in this study Bible that some of my own thoughts were first made available in print. He also invested a great deal of effort in pursuing a publisher on my behalf, pressing me firmly but kindly to develop my thoughts into a book-length text, and coached me through all the steps of becoming a first-time author. His confidence and enthusiasm have been a driving force behind all my efforts culminating in the book in your hands.

I would also like to recognize Tim Beals of World Vision for believing in this project, and being committed "above and beyond the call of duty" to its coming into print.

My colleagues at Multnomah Bible College and Biblical Seminary, especially those committed to our monthly faculty forum called *Hermeneuo*, have observed the development of some of these ideas, and have given very fruitful responses along the way. In this regard, Brad Harper, Domani Pothen, and Nate Baxter have provided loyal support while offering frank and stiff challenges. Likewise, I am grateful to my long-term associates in Westnomah, and especially to Gerry Breshears, for his remarkably keen alacrity and insight at 6 a.m. each week.

Vern Steiner, a kindred spirit, brought penetrating questions and outside-the-box suggestions at the perfect time to catalyze a much-needed paradigm shift in my own conceptual categories.

My thanks to Adam Rust and Bobby Grow for carefully going through earlier drafts: not only correcting typos, spelling, and grammar, but also offering stimulating comments, helpful suggestions, and questions. Jarod Tippy provided valuable assistance in creating the illustrations, an asset for all of us who are visual learners. Joel Roberts and Tim Burke were also instrumental in reading the manuscript and identifying many of its infelicities.

I am also indebted to the many hundreds of students and dozens of lab instructors who have field-tested the steps and strategies I present in this book throughout the Bible Study Methods courses I've taught at Multnomah Bible College. Their questions and insights have precipitated my thinking in countless ways and occasions.

And my deepest appreciation of all is reserved for Chip, Lani, Joel, and Tamara. The joy I find in their patience with me, in their love, and in our fellowship together extends well beyond my ability to express in words. May God continue to reward them as they each seek to follow him more closely.

Prologue

Forty pairs of widened eyes, together with one pair of narrowed ones, turned to fix upon me, or rather upon my head, which I quickly ducked down. I could feel the collective weight of everyone's gaze upon me. I sat in stunned silence. My own eyes shifted down to my lap, where my Bible lay opened to the passage from which my high school Sunday school teacher, an energetic and forceful matriarch within our conservative church, had just read. I could feel my ears redden and was grateful that the ears were covered under my long, brown hair which curled down to my shoulder line. I liked it that my hair covered those embarrassing ears which, as a sophomore, I still had not grown into. However, it was that very hair that was the cause of my teacher's drilling, accusatory stare. The words from 1 Corinthians 11:14 seemed to hang in the air like icicles:

> Does not the very nature of things teach you that if a man has *long hair*, it is a *disgrace* to him . . . ?

As the "man" in the room with the longest hair by far, her attack was clearly pointed at my head, my hair, and my, well . . . *disgrace*. I was vaguely aware that she was now explaining what this passage was about, about the *unnaturalness* of men with long hair, and how important it was for this passage to be applied today by anyone claiming to follow God. But I wasn't really paying close attention anymore. Instead, after the initial numbing, my brain shifted into overdrive; thoughts of shame, defensiveness, guilt, blame, unfairness, and excuse were careening around my consciousness. Forcing myself into distraction, a favorite coping mechanism of mine, I focused on the Bible in front of me. My eyes fell upon the part of the text immediately after the accusing passage, the rest of the sentence that she hadn't read:

. . . but that if a woman has long hair, it is her glory?

Not daring to look up, I couldn't help picturing her own hair, certainly not more than two inches in length anywhere on her head. *Well, she's certainly not too "glorious" herself*, I thought. My eyes skipped back to the verse before:

Judge for yourselves: Is it proper for a woman to pray to God with her head uncovered? (14:13)

At this, my own eyes widened. *Hey! She already opened the class in prayer. And she's not wearing any kind of hat at all!* I went back to the beginning of the chapter with genuine interest, reading my way up to verse 6:

If a woman does not cover her head, she should have her hair cut off; and if it is a disgrace for a woman to have her hair cut or shaved off, she should cover her head.

My perverse humor kicked in at this point. I ducked my head further to ensure that my smirk was hidden as I imagined what this four-foot ten-inch dynamo would look like bald.

Then one of those moments occurred which seems to stand as a defining moment in life, a crossroads event which has continuing consequences for life. *I know,* I thought, *she put me on the spot in front of all my friends with her attack but I can regain a measure of respect. I'll simply raise my hand and ask her why she doesn't obey the Bible either.* My hand started up, got to about shoulder height, and then, for some reason that I cannot pinpoint to this day, I let it drop. I let my hand drop; I let the issue drop. I didn't chicken out, I just decided, for some urgent but completely unidentifiable reason, not to push it right then.

Ever since, I've been thankful that the Holy Spirit vetoed my intent that morning. You see, about ten years later, I ended up marrying her granddaughter. By then my hair was shorter, though it had nothing to do with her lesson that morning. To her dying day, I never brought it up again. But I've always been glad that I chose not to battle her or publicly challenge her inconsistency—it would have made for a very awkward way to begin a relationship with future in-laws!

— — — — — — — — — — — — — — — — — — —

But in another sense, I never did let it drop. The unfairness and the selectivity she showed when using her Bible bothered me. I'm pretty sure that if I had spoken up to challenge her, she would have claimed that the requirement that women wear head coverings was something that only related to the first century and was *no longer binding upon people today*. Whether or not a woman wears a hat nowadays simply doesn't mean what it did during the first century in that ancient culture. But if so, wouldn't the same argument apply to the long hair issue in the same passage? And more importantly, why couldn't that argument be used by anyone on *any* passage they simply don't want to obey? I came away from that Sunday school class filled with questions, ones which have stayed with me for many years.

- Who gets to decide which verses from the Bible are to be obeyed and which can be safely ignored?
- Are some of God's commands just relevant to ancient, far away people and not really God's Word to us today?
- Are there any reliable guidelines for deciding?
- How can anyone be sure?
- Is it just me, or does this sound like some kind of now-you-see-it, now-you-don't interpretative game?
- Is obeying God's Word something as simple as picking and choosing for ourselves which verses we prefer to obey, or that we want others to obey?
- If it is just a matter of our own preferences, then how can God hold us accountable for whether or not we've obeyed it?
- Why is it that people seem to know better how to apply the Bible to others than to themselves?

At the time I knew nothing about terms like hermeneutics, exegesis, epistemology, interpretive horizons, or illocution. Though I lacked the technical vocabulary which I have since gained, the questions bouncing around my sixteen-year-old brain continued to tumble through my thinking during the rest of my educational pilgrimage—through high school, into my studies in Bible college, through my graduate and seminary work, and ultimately through my doctoral program.

— — — — — — — — — — — — — — — — — —

Several key realizations have revolutionized my Bible reading quest. The first realization is the importance of looking at the big picture—seeing the much larger contexts of the particular passage that I'm reading.

Two recent developments in interpretive theory (*hermeneutics*) have contributed to a renewed interest in this: "Bible as Literature" courses (which have become popular in public high schools and colleges) and "canon[ical] approaches" to the Bible. Without getting bogged down in the history or details of these, there is a fundamental insight they share: we must read biblical books as a whole, not in isolated passages.

While all of us would agree in principle that it's best to read things in context, conservative Bible readers have a very poor track record in practicing it. Looking for spiritual gems in short passages or single verses seems to be the norm for us, both in preaching and in personal devotional reading. I believe, along with a growing number of others, that we must take seriously the importance of getting the big idea(s) of biblical books.

A second realization is the importance of recognizing the literary style of the passage we're reading. This includes identifying the literary categories to which it belongs (its type and genre), as well as other techniques and patterns the author may be using (its forms).

A third realization that has changed my approach to the Bible is the conviction that my goal in interpreting the Bible is not to see what I can *get out of* the text, but is to seek to identify and understand what God has *put into* the text. I am to recognize, to re-think, and to follow God's own thoughts, which through inspiration he has communicated via a human author. I can only submit to God's voice if I am listening for his intent. I cannot hijack the text to serve my own selfish desires, whether by accident or purposefully.

A fourth realization is that there are universal and eternal qualities about God's Word that make it different from any other ancient piece of literature. We don't read Bible stories just because they tell historically reliable facts about events of the past. Nor do we read biblical poetry just because it is aesthetically pleasant. Neither do we read the epistles in order to see what people said to one another in ancient letters. The Bible has an enduring quality, certain timeless truths and insights, which can be shared by all people, of all time periods, living everywhere. Learning how to identify these life-changing realities is a crucial element in successfully following the Bible.

A final realization is that responding to the Bible correctly involves more than understanding it, more even than obeying it. It also involves what I call *following* it. Not every passage is intended to tell us what to do. Many biblical passages do other things—teach, encourage, challenge, comfort, convict, bless, warn and so on. The Pharisees' biggest mistake was assuming that the chief purpose of the Bible was to lay down the rules for proper behavior. Well-intentioned Bible readers today can easily make the same mistake when they view the entire Bible as "this is what you're supposed to do."

In retrospect, I realize that my main reason for challenging my Sunday school teacher in class that day wasn't merely revenge. Nor was I moved by defiance or typical adolescent arrogance. Rather, I was searching for honest answers to questions such as those above that, frankly, do not require a doctoral degree to answer satisfactorily. In this book, I will try to share with you in simple terms the exciting insights that I've discovered in my own quest for finding God's truth in his Word.

After reading this book, you can expect the following:

- You will be able to quickly recognize the author's style of writing in any biblical passage.

- By knowing the style, you will learn to ask and explore the most fruitful questions to get at the meaning of the passage.

- You will see the importance of locating each particular passage within the entirety of the book and beyond.

- You will value not just reading the Bible, but what it really means to *follow* it, involving your heart, mind, imagination, and emotions in the process. This is the point of the book: to read the Bible *for a change*.

- If you begin practicing these steps for yourself, you will embark on a lifetime quest of Bible reading that will enable you to see for yourself how exciting it is when we read it on its own terms rather than on ours.

CHAPTER ONE

Come, Follow Me

Reading as Following

By definition, Christians are people who follow Christ. What does it mean to "follow" Jesus Christ? At the simplest level, it means that we accept what he has taught as accurate and truthful. Beyond that, we also embrace these teachings as the guidelines for our lives. We use his life as the pattern for our own, and learn from all the instruction he left to us. We do this by putting into practice that which he stood for.

But how do we know what he stood for? Virtually everything we need to know about Jesus is communicated to us in God's Word, the Bible. It is in the Bible that we discover who Jesus is, why he came, what he did, what he taught, what he was willing to sacrifice his life for, and the plans that he has for those who know and love him.

Once when he was confronted by a Pharisee, a self-appointed "expert" on the commands given to Moses, Jesus got to the heart of the matter. In response to the question, "Which is the greatest commandment in the Law?" Jesus answered,

> "'Love the Lord your God with all your heart and with all your soul and with all your mind.' This is the first and greatest commandment. And the second is like it: 'Love your neighbor as yourself.' All the Law and the Prophets [i.e., the Bible] hang on these two commandments" (Matthew 22:37-40).

There are two interesting points in Jesus' response here. The first is that the chief purpose of the Bible is to foster loving relationships with God and other people. The Bible's primary purpose is not about governing our behaviors or restricting our desires. It is certainly not for enforcing our own preferences upon others. Rather, its focus is upon love, and on how we can grow in our understanding and expression of love. Bible reading truly accomplishes its intention only when we become more aware of how much we are loved and so become more loving. The significance of our Bible study and teaching should center on the building of relationships with God and others.

The second issue is the centrality of God's Word itself. In this passage, as well as in many others, Jesus connects his own teaching to what has already been taught in previous Scriptures. Jesus' teaching and his exemplary pattern of living are clearly grounded in a much larger story, the one which begins with the words, "In the beginning" (Genesis 1:1). Jesus' life was lived in an intentional and strategic way in which he made continual reference to this larger plan laid out throughout the Bible. His origin, his values, his relationship with humanity, his relationship with the Father and the Spirit, his purpose, his authority, and his destiny were all related to living out ("fulfilling") the Scriptures. He clearly did not come to set aside the Bible or to establish himself above it or as independent from it.

Instead we find him drawing on it by assuming its truthfulness, its authority, and its power to convince, refute, and change people's lives. He resisted temptation by quoting Scripture (Matthew 4:1-11); he taught in the synagogue from the Scripture (Luke 4:16-22); he countered his opponents' arguments by appealing to Scripture (Mark 12:24-27); he explained his mission on earth in terms of Scripture's teaching (Matthew 21:42-44); and he defended the Bible's ongoing relevance and validity. All four gospel accounts both directly quote and draw innumerable parallels from previous Scripture, demonstrating how the entirety of God's Word points to Christ (Matthew 5:17-19; Mark 4:10-12; Luke 24:25-27, 44-47; John 5:39-47).

SIMPLY PUT, WE CANNOT TRUTHFULLY SAY THAT WE ARE FOLLOWERS OF JESUS IF WE NEGLECT OR REFUSE TO OBEY WHAT THE BIBLE TELLS US, OR IF WE USE IT IN SELF-SERVING WAYS THAT ARE NOT WHAT GOD ORIGINALLY INTENDED.

For believers to "follow Jesus" implies, among other things, adopting the same attitude toward God's Word as Jesus had. Becoming like Christ involves accepting his example as one who reads the Bible. It means defining ourselves and our purpose in life in light of the Bible. Following Christ also means practicing what the Bible says. Simply put, we cannot truthfully say that we are followers of Jesus if we neglect or refuse to obey what the Bible tells us, or if we use it in self-serving ways that are not what God originally intended.[1]

God speaks to us in the Bible. At the very least it is rude not to listen to someone else when they speak. When that someone else is the all-powerful God over all space and time in the entire cosmos, it is utterly foolish not to listen. When that someone is the most perfect lover ever, indeed the one who created love itself, and who further both proclaims and demonstrates his love for *us* in his Word—including me personally—it is absurd to not listen. But to claim to follow him while refusing to listen to what he is saying is delusional. If we do not submit to him, either through stubbornness, ignorance, or neglect, then we have no right to identify ourselves with him; in practice, we are actually opposing him. Loving God necessarily means obeying his Word: "This is love for God: to obey his commands" (1 John 5:3).[2]

It is crucial for our faith and growth that we become increasingly skilled at learning to read the Bible well. But in one very important sense we should not strive for gaining mastery over the text of the Bible at all. This is because we are not its master, but rather the reverse; the Bible is to have mastery over our own lives, even to the point of calling upon us to sacrifice our petty interests to its higher and nobler demands.[3] This book seeks to offer you help in how to *receive* the Bible on the right wavelength,[4] in the way that God intended it, and consistent with his purposes.

What happens when we read and use Scripture in ways that are different from what God had in mind? Others have wisely pointed out that when people quit believing in God, they don't believe in nothing, they believe in anything.[5] That is also precisely the case with his Word. When we no longer turn to God's Word in order to listen for God's own intentions, what happens is that even if we continue to use the Bible, we replace God's purposes with our own. We may use the Bible to underwrite and give authority to our own opinions or to the topics which interest us, or to criticize others with whom we disagree.[6] Or perhaps we believe that the Bible is too hard to understand or that it isn't really relevant to our contemporary world, and so we replace it with other "authorities"[7]: new fads in church ministry; insights drawn from the fields of social science and psychotherapy; devotional writers and speakers who may not be very biblical but who can effectively pull at the heartstrings of our emotions; or recognized "stars" (from the worlds of sports, entertainment, politics, or Christian ministry).[8] The net result is that many people who claim to be Christian neither know the Bible, nor sense any particular need to learn it. We are no longer convinced that it is essential for living a Christian life.

A starting point in this book is that reading, understanding, receiving, responding appropriately, and practicing the Bible—or more simply, *following* the Bible—is essential to the experience that God intends for us as Christians. I recognize that for many, reading is a means to an end. In a busy world, we move from one place to another, and reading, like driving a car or taking a bus, is simply what is needed to get from point A to point B. We often read because we need to know how to fix the plumbing, prepare a particular meal, pass an exam in school, learn about last night's game, find out what is happening in the Middle East, and acquire other information necessary for living better or satisfying our curiosity.

But another way to approach reading, and especially reading the Bible, is to view it as a departure on a journey. We recognize that we are leaving the familiar but vaguely unsatisfying world in which we live our daily lives, on a quest to find a better country.

FOLLOWING THE BIBLE IS ESSENTIAL TO THE EXPERIENCE THAT GOD INTENDS FOR US AS CHRISTIANS.

As those who voluntarily undertake this journey, seeking not to impose themselves upon its world but to discover its riches, we are not disappointed. In willingly choosing to read the Bible, we are transported to another world, filled with strange phenomena like miracles, angelic announcements, prophets who speak the very words of God, and earth-shaking appearances by God, yet also with people who are surprisingly similar to ourselves. When we put the Book down, we return home to our "normal" world, but we have been *changed* through the experience of our cross-cultural encounter. We have encountered new ways of thinking and different perspectives on what is real, and now we return with these treasured souvenirs of our travels. Our minds have been opened to new possibilities and enticing alternatives to our ways of living. We begin to question the status quo thinking and habits which, due to their very familiarity, we have never before challenged. We learn that the near horizons of our natural world are not the outer boundaries of reality, but only the borders into the vaster, mind-stretching and soul-liberating world of the supernatural. When we read the Bible in this way, with eyes of faith, we not only see this more fantastic country, we also see this too familiar "normal" world in fresh and new ways.[9]

This kind of mind transformation is supposed to be the norm for growing Christians: "Do not conform any longer to the pattern of this world, but be transformed by the renewing of your mind" (Romans 12:2; cf. 2 Corinthians 5:16). Indeed, if the metaphor can be stretched a little further, the more time we spend in this other world, seen through not merely reading but inhabiting this world of the Word, and the deeper we invest ourselves in it, the more we identify with its values, priorities, and customs as opposed to those of the world we see only with our eyes. Taking up the Bible in our hands in this way, and with these expectations, we now stand on the threshold of an epic adventure of life change.

Calvin Miller, in his poetic rendition of the life of Christ, says that "the world is poor because her fortune is buried in the sky, and all her treasure maps are of the earth."[10] The only treasure map that could help is one from heaven itself, the Bible, which plots for us a course to a heavenly realm, a place where we can gain sufficient altitude to see and understand the world from a better, clearer perspective. It is overwhelmingly rewarding for those who are willing to venture out in their thinking, and to take up the risks associated with treasure seeking. And that treasure is nothing less than a living encounter with the overwhelming, awe inspiring, and fascinating mystery[11] of the person of God.

I should warn the reader that learning to study the Bible with these goals in mind is not a simple task—at times the effort may seem difficult, complicated, or exhausting. But having observed literally hundreds of students who have come to embrace, more or less firmly, the methods I suggest in this book, and having seen the life change that has taken place during their engagement with God's Word as they do so, I am convinced that it is very possible. It would be unfair and unrealistic to promise that if you are seriously committed to adopting the methods for studying the Bible set forth in this book, then your Bible reading will become effortless or consistently exhilarating. But I believe that it is realistic to promise that if these methods become part of your regular pattern for following the Bible, then you will begin to see for yourself things in the Scriptures which you have never seen before, while gaining confidence that your interpretations are more accurately reflecting what God himself has communicated to us through his Word.

I am aware that any book which deals with the how-to's of studying the Bible can easily deteriorate into a checklist of to-do's, leading to life-sapping, outward performance and all the problems associated with legalism. I am not altogether certain how to prevent this from happening. Some ingredients for effective Bible study cannot be reduced to steps or methods. They deeply affect our ability to follow the Bible. They are foundational (logically and spiritually) to all the rest of the reading strategies that I explain in the rest of the book. But they are so important that they cannot go without mentioning, and so I set them out here. Our capacity to respond rightly to God's Word is influenced by the following factors.

Natural abilities

God has gifted some people with special abilities in thinking processes. One of these is good memory. While all of us are urged to remember the things of God,[12] some people possess better skills in memorizing Scripture, remembering contexts, and associating chapter and verse references. Second, some have an eye for details and simply notice more, and more quickly, when they read. A third of these aptitudes is the ability to see relationships. Most intelligence tests have one or several sections that assess a person's ability to recognize patterns and draw analogies. Nearly everyone profits from coaching in this, yet some are more naturally adept at this. A fourth skill that some naturally possess in greater measure is good judgment in evaluating options. Critical thinking involves the ability to identify both the strengths and weaknesses of various interpretations. Again, some people intuitively sense which interpretive option seems best to account for all the information.

Learned Knowledge

A second factor in how well we can read the Bible is the information that can be learned by virtually anyone. One example is knowledge of language: how languages work, communication theories, grammar, syntax, and semantics. Another is becoming adept in the language of the Bible that is used by the reader. Obviously someone reading the Bible in English will need to know the vocabulary used in the translation. Learning English grammar and syntax (how the sentences are structured to communicate meaning) will also aid Bible readers in following the flow of thought in certain kinds of biblical passages. This knowledge may have special value when studying the discourse section of the Bible (more on this later). Knowledge of the original languages of the Bible, primarily Hebrew and Greek, can be also very beneficial, provided one recognizes the limits of his or her abilities in the nuances and subtleties of these languages.

Learning fundamentals of logic and reasoning can enable the reader to understand more precisely how a biblical author is making his point.[13] It is also important to learn the different styles of writing that an author may employ: the literary types of narrative, poetry, and discourse, as well as literary genres such as epistle, prophecy, and wisdom, along with many different literary forms such as parallelism, diatribe, genealogy, and chiasm. Each of these literary patterns communicates truth differently, so awareness of how they function will help us in the quest for discovering biblical truth. There are also rhetorical devices that the author may be employing such as irony, comparison, and appeal to other sources or authorities.

Learning about biblical and theological concepts can open the reader's eyes to features in the Bible that might otherwise be overlooked. The same is true for learning about biblical characters, events, objects, and places. The more familiar we are with these, the easier it will be to recognize commonalities between passages.

Attitudes

A third category of qualities that shapes our ability to see and receive the Scriptures accurately has to do more with our hearts. Coming to the text with an attitude of *humility* is needed for readers to accept realities about themselves, about others, about God, about the vast gulf that exists between humanity and God, and about the far reaching, damaging consequences of sin in our lives.

Reading the Bible with *sincerity* means that the reader adopts a position of openness to the Holy Spirit and the willingness to be teachable, especially when the reader's own sinfulness is exposed by reading the Scriptures. Sensitivity to the Holy Spirit is certainly not a "step" in learning to follow the Bible, but without it our Bible reading can be lifeless and misguided.

As we encounter God through his Word, the appropriate response involves *devotion* and *awe*——we should be drawn to the source of all goodness (James 1:17) and, paradoxically, simultaneously overwhelmed at the prospect of coming before one who is infinitely greater than ourselves, beyond all understanding.

Reading the Bible should start from, and end with, *love for God*. This is the first and greatest commandment. We are called upon not only to reflect on God, but also to draw into deeper, more intimate relationship with him.

Related to this is a *passion* to know God and to follow him as the Bible teaches. This is a crucial inward aspect that has to do with our motives for reading the Bible that transcend a sense of obligation or self-serving goals in favor of a desire for God himself.

NO AMOUNT OF ADVICE ON BIBLE READING TECHNIQUE CAN COMPENSATE FOR HEARTS AND MINDS THAT ARE NOT WILLING TO HUMBLY FOLLOW GOD.

An old maxim says that we see only what we're looking for. If that is the case, then *appreciation* and *respect for the Bible* will also affect what we're able to see. If we believe that the Bible is the product of ancient and therefore primitive cultures, lacking the literary or theological sophistication of today, then we probably will not recognize the features that are there. On the other hand, if we think that because God is the ultimate author, and thus the Bible should set the standard of excellence for human communication, than we are more likely to look for and see a high degree of literary sophistication.

Our expectations will also be affected by our *prayerfulness*. Once again, prayer is not a reading method per se, but without it our hearts are not tuned to receive God's Word on the right wavelength.

All that I share in the rest of this book rests on the characteristics outlined above. I begin this book with two convictions. The first is that no amount of advice on Bible reading technique can compensate for hearts and minds that are not willing to humbly follow God. Such readers simply will not receive God's Word in the way it is intended. Isaiah was commissioned to deliver a message to this kind of people: "Be ever hearing, but never understanding; be ever seeing, but never perceiving" (Isaiah 6:9).

The second conviction is more optimistic. I am certain that if willing readers will draw upon the following methods and strategies for following the Bible, then they stand on the threshold of a new dynamic of experiencing God. What lies ahead is the very real potential, not only for a different way of Bible reading, but also for a changed life.

CHAPTER TWO

Knowing Your Type
Literary Categories in the Bible

On the first day of football practice in 1965, the coach came striding into the locker room, held up a ball and announced to his NFL players, fresh off a third place finish in the league the year before, "Gentlemen, this is a football." This football legend, former Green Bay Packers coach Vince Lombardi, was trying to make an unforgettable point: they needed to start over by getting back to the basics. This strategy must have worked, since his team went on to win the NFL championship for the next three years in a row, including the first two Super Bowls.[1]

I also want to begin at the most basic level, by stating the obvious: the Bible is a book. In some ways it is just like any other book—it is written communication from an author to an intended reading audience, expressing ideas and values through a text. An important but easily overlooked consequence of this fact is that we should therefore read it in the same ways that we read other literature. It doesn't use magic, supernatural language, spiritual sentence structure or divine literary categories. It is best interpreted and understood when we use the normal conventions of communication.

On the other hand, there are at least three differences between the Bible and most other texts.

- Difference 1: It is God's Word. It is not merely a book about God written by people long ago, expressing their perspectives on what he is like. Instead, the ultimate author of the Bible is God himself, who guided many human authors (2 Peter 1:20-21) to communicate "God-breathed" thoughts (2 Timothy 3:16).

The Bible is a book given to us by God who used the different personalities of human authors to communicate his message to humanity. This cannot be said of any other book. In this sense, the Bible stands in a category all by itself. The doctrinal statement of the Evangelical Theological Society begins this way: "*The Bible alone*, and the Bible in its entirety, is the Word of God written. . . ."[2] The Bible tells us about God, about ourselves, about the world, and about God's plan for us in the world.

- Difference 2: The Bible is one book, yet it is made up of many different books. It is unlike the Qur'an or the book of Mormon, each of which are the work of only *one* human author. It is also unlike an anthology of completely different authors, because the many different biblical authors were still writing with a unity of purpose, characters, plot, and system of faith. The human authors of the Bible, living centuries apart from one another, reflect a cohesiveness and coherence that has no parallel in world literature. Once again, the Bible stands alone.

- Difference 3: The Bible contains many different styles of writing. Woven into a master storyline are songs, prayers, speeches, laws, birth records, letters, and much more. The positive side of this is that there is something interesting for everyone—God has accommodated a broad spectrum of literary tastes. The challenge is that, in order to become good at reading the entire Bible, we must learn to recognize and adjust our expectations to fit each literary style we encounter. Once again, the unity that emerges throughout the stylistic diversity is without equal in other books. This feature is the focus of this chapter.

Suppose you need to buy a couple of items and have chosen to do your shopping at a department superstore. You need a graduation card for a relative, some salsa, a 3/8" drill bit, and a couple of dishtowels. As you walk into the store, you are confronted with thousands of square feet of merchandise. You could spend hours wandering up and down each and every aisle looking for the items on your list.

For efficiency, you need to know how the store is organized. Products are not arranged according to size, color, price, or alphabetical order. Instead, the superstore is divided into main departments. For the greeting card, you'll need to go to the stationery department; for the salsa, to the grocery department. For the drill bit, you'll head to the tool department; for the towels, to the household department.

But there's actually more to it than that. Within the stationery department, you stick to the aisles with cards rather than wrapping paper, designer stationery, stickers, etc. Within the cards section, you don't have to begin with the first card on the top shelf of the first aisle. Instead, you look for little signs that identify the category of cards that are found in each section. You quickly scan past "Friendship——Humorous" and "Anniversary——Wife" until you spot "Graduation."

If you know where the card section is located before entering the store, then within a matter of a few minutes you can find the item you're looking for. The same shopping "strategy" is used for your other items as well, so that you can reasonably expect to find everything fairly quickly.

Who decided how department stores are organized? Is there a national law written into the Constitution that requires all stores to operate in this way? What school course teaches students how to shop in a department store? While there aren't any "laws" per se, these conventions are developed by our society in order to make our lives easier. We do it this way because . . . well, because that's how we do it.

Does it take a lot of practice and experience to learn how these stores are organized? Yes! From the time that we rode in our parents' shopping carts as small children, these conventions were imprinted onto our brains. But we never think of this as a hindrance to our shopping experience. The fact that all department stores "work" this way makes it easier for us to shop, even in stores we have never visited before, including those in "foreign" states. Nobody complains about department stores having so many "rules" which stifle human freedom and artistic expression. In order to be an efficient shopper, you need to know where to find the items you need.

The first step to finding a desired item is to find the correct store department. The same is true when we shop for a book. In a large bookstore, we find that the books are organized. Depending on whether you wanted a Cajun cookbook, a classic novel, a text on music history, a science fiction thriller, a book of William Blake's poetry, or a book of your favorite comic strip, you would look in different sections of the store.

But let me take this illustration a step further. If you were to buy one of each of these kinds of books and take them home, a similar mental process takes place as soon as you pick up the first book to read. Few people settle down on their couch with a cup of hot chocolate or a latte in order to enjoy an evening of reading a Cajun cookbook. Nor would you be likely to underline, take notes on, and study the science fiction thriller. Each of these books allows for, and requires, a different kind of reading. We don't read comic books with the same attention or expectations as we do with evocative poetry. The details we pay attention to and what we expect the book to do for us are different in each case. I am no expert in neurobiology, but I would suppose that different types of books even produce different brain wave patterns, triggering neural reactions in different parts of the brain.

We could go so far as saying that each book tells the truth, but it does so in an entirely different way, or rather, that it tells different kinds of truth altogether. A science fiction thriller may tell truth about certain possibilities that exist, given current cutting-edge experimental physics. A classic novel may tell the truth by portraying its characters in a way that offers us fresh insight into human values and behavior.

HOW WE READ ANY PIECE OF LITERATURE DEPENDS COMPLETELY ON WHAT KIND OF LITERATURE IT IS THAT WE THINK WE ARE READING.

A Cajun cookbook tells us truth by giving us proportions of ingredients and steps for combining and cooking them with the result of delicious food (providing we like Cajun flavors). A music history textbook informs us with facts about people, events, musical styles and instruments, and how they all interrelate to form movements. Comic strips strike us as funny because they stretch, distort, and bend familiar traits and realities that we recognize. And William Blake's poems offer us startlingly different ways of seeing the world around us, a system of metaphors that can alter our perceptions.

The point is that how we read any piece of literature depends completely on what kind of literature it is that we think we are reading.[3] How does this relate to Bible reading? Let me show you three aspects:

- Every piece of literature belongs to a particular **category**, and therefore has a particular form.[4] A personal letter has one form, a shopping list another, and a newspaper editorial another. Even e-mail messages have their own form, often omitting any capital letters.

- The category we think we are listening to or reading influences the way we understand it.[5] I have shown a number of audiences a short clip from an animated film. The episode brings up several very weighty philosophical points about the nature of reality, and uses a great deal of irony before ending tragically. But since it is animated, I consistently find that audiences laugh right up to the end, and then sit in stunned confusion. Clearly their minds have difficulty putting philosophy and tragedy together with the art of animation, something they normally reserve for "cartoons." In their minds, animated movies are supposed to be funny; a clip with a main character needlessly dying short circuits all their mental wiring.

- The Bible, a book made up of many books, contains **many** different styles of writing, so we must properly recognize the literary categories of each passage we read in order to understand it correctly.

The starting point in reading the Bible is identifying the literary **type** of the passage being studied. What we should look for and how we should respond as we study any particular biblical passage depends on which literary type we are investigating. And the more we understand how these different features work, the better we will be able to follow the message that God has inspired in the text, the truth he has revealed to us. C. S. Lewis made this same point:

WHAT WE SHOULD LOOK FOR AND HOW WE SHOULD RESPOND AS WE STUDY ANY PARTICULAR BIBLICAL PASSAGE DEPENDS ON WHICH LITERARY TYPE WE ARE INVESTIGATING.

> The first qualification for judging any piece of workmanship from a corkscrew to a cathedral is to know *what* it is——what it was intended to do and how it is meant to be used. . . . The first thing is to understand the object before you: as long as you think the corkscrew was meant for opening [cans] or the cathedral for entertaining tourists you can say nothing to the purpose about them.[6]

A chain saw is meant to cut wood, but does a very poor job of cutting other things——fabric for a dress, paper dolls, or melon balls. In the same way, the Bible is a book, but a particular kind of book meant for specific purposes. We misuse it if we utilize it as a coloring book, a textbook for science or grammar, or entertaining fiction. As a whole, the Bible belongs in a literary category all by itself——it is *revelation* (or "proclamation"). It announces a message from God to us, giving us insight into reality that we would not otherwise have. It also demands a personal response on our part, and we will stand before God to give an account of ourselves for whether or not we have followed it.

Every communicator, from a child protesting to her parents that she has been wronged by her brother, to a politician seeking votes, to a biblical author presenting a God's-eye view of human pride, employs logical, rhetorical, and literary "tricks" strategically designed to persuade. What we choose to highlight or skip, how we present the facts, what style and tone we use, are all intended to present our points as convincingly as we can.[7] Each biblical author seeks to make a case, to "score points," by building an argument as effectively as possible.

The effectiveness of the message of a biblical book will depend, in part, on which type of literature the author selects in order to communicate those ideas.[8] Within the "mega-category" of the entire Bible as revelation, there exist three major types of literature in the Bible.

- NARRATIVE: Narrative is a text that makes its point primarily by telling a story.
- POETRY: Poetry is a text where normal language is modified to intensify its impact. Various poetic devices are used that affect how sentences are structured, and there is usually a high concentration of figures of speech (word pictures).
- DISCOURSE: Discourse is a text that presents a logical sequence of ideas.

Each book of the Bible falls into at least one of these types. Some books may contain more than one type, but normally any given passage or chapter fits most closely with only one of these. Each of these types has distinguishable features that are fairly easy to recognize once you know what you're looking for. So which of these three types is most common in the Bible? Based on a chapter-by-chapter comparison, I have found that the Bible contains 502 chapters of narrative, 387 chapters of poetry, and 272 chapters of discourse.

Literary Types in the Bible

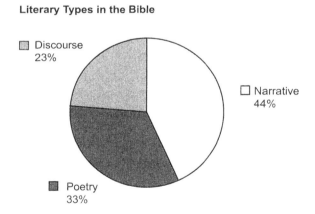

One of the most important factors in how well we interpret the Bible is whether or not we correctly identify which type of literature we are reading in any given passage. If we misunderstand the text at this level, the rest of our study will also be flawed.

Why is that the case? One way to illustrate this is by looking at games. Every game has a set of rules. Certain kinds of activities and movements are allowed, others are considered illegal. Is it a good thing for someone to grab the ball and run with it? In football, it is not only a good idea, it's a key component in succeeding at the game, providing you know which direction to run. But in basketball it is almost always illegal (with one exception—a player can run along the end line out of bounds after the opponent has scored), being penalized with a loss of possession of the ball. In volleyball it is not only illegal, but the other team will score a point.

In football, your team loses possession of the ball when it is kicked, but if the kick is performed under a certain set of conditions, it may earn points for your team. In basketball, kicking the ball will lose your team possession of the ball, with no opportunity to score. In soccer, most of the play centers on participants kicking the ball.

If you're playing a game with a deck of playing cards, you must first identify which game you're playing before you can determine whether or not you've got a good hand. In the game of spades, you play in such a way as to earn as many points as possible, while in hearts you play to earn as few points as possible. The queen of spades has a completely different value and function depending on which of those two games you're playing. Put another way, the queen of spades means something different, based upon which game you're playing.

THE WAY THAT WE "PLAY THE GAME" OF FOLLOWING THE BIBLE STARTS WITH KNOWING WHICH GAME WE'RE PLAYING.

Learning to play games well involves mastering the rules, then exploiting possibilities within those rules in order to maximize your chances for success. Skills or talents appropriate for one game, like being able to hit a small ball with a stick in the game of baseball, may not transfer over directly to another game, such as water polo.

How does this relate to Bible study? The way that we "play the game" of following the Bible starts with knowing which game we're playing. The "game" of narrative has different rules than the "games" of poetry or discourse. Someone attempting to find discourse elements in a narrative will most likely be asking the wrong questions, missing important ideas, and "discovering" things that weren't intended by the author at all.

Or, to change the illustration, think of a toolbox. If a craftsman is heading off to a job, the tools that are in the toolbox depend on the craftsman's trade. A carpenter, a plumber, and an electrician all use tools from their toolboxes, but the tools they carry in them are different. A pipe wrench is a heavy and clumsy tool for doing woodwork. While certain tools like a screwdriver may be found in all three toolboxes, the nature and materials of their job dictate which are the most appropriate tools to have available on the job site.

So it is for the Bible reader. The nature of biblical narratives requires one toolbox (a set of reading skills), while biblical poetry requires another toolbox, and biblical discourse a third. For example, looking for words that indicate logical relationships between sections ("yet," "for this reason," "nevertheless," "therefore," etc.) is highly significant when reading discourse but largely irrelevant when reading biblical narratives, because they almost never occur there. The inherent logic of biblical narrative does not depend upon these kinds of words, so looking for them will not only be a waste of time, but may interfere with seeing the logic in the passage.

Chapters 8, 9, and 10 of this book explain the unique characteristics of each of these types of biblical literature, and what to look for in each one. Chapters 11, 12, and 13 provide examples of how this works when studying a particular passage.

In addition to the three major literary types in the Bible, there is another level of unique literary characteristics found in the Scriptures. This is the level of genres. A genre is a recognizable category of writing that follows certain rules or patterns. It is like a type, except that it fits under the larger umbrella of literary type. Every passage of Scripture not only belongs to one of the three types, but also belongs to one (occasionally more than one) genre of literature.

There are seven genres in the Bible. These are described in much more detail in the Appendix, but here is a quick survey of them.

- **Apocalyptic**: Apocalyptic employs a style of writing that is highly symbolic, concerning end-of-the-world events. It incorporates angelic messages, visions, mysterious numbers, and concerns the fate, not just of Israel or the Church, but also of the whole heavens and the earth. It depicts all the forces of evil as pitted against God and those who are aligned with him.

- **Epistle**: The epistles are letters written by leaders of the early church to churches or individuals. Just as modern letters follow a predictable pattern, whether business letters or personal letters, so biblical epistles have a predictable format.

- **Gospel**: The gospels tell the story of the earthly life and ministry of Jesus, his preaching, miracle working, fulfillment of earlier biblical passages, death, resurrection, and the establishment and growth of the early church.

- **Prophecy**: Biblical prophecy is any writing in which the author speaks on behalf of God. Contrary to many people's use of the term prophecy, it most often is not about the future. Instead, the genre of prophecy includes anytime the author either directly says or implies, "Thus says the Lord . . . ." Prophecy is used to communicate God's commands, accusations of sin, calls to repentance, threats of punishment, comfort, and promises of future blessings.

- **Psalms**: Psalms are poetic songs, found in a number of places besides just the biblical book of Psalms. They are always poetic, they are frequently prayers to God, and they express praise, thanksgiving, and lament (grief), both of individuals and a larger group.

- **Story**: Stories record an event or series of events that have taken place. The features of story overlap with narrative (more on this later).

- **Wisdom**: Wisdom literature offers insights on how to live. The human authors have gained these perspectives by observing patterns within the world around them. Readers of wisdom literature discover insights, values, perspectives, and skills for godly success that emerge from the fear of the Lord.

The relationship between type and genre, as I use these terms, may seem at first a bit confusing. I use the terms type and genre in a more specific and technical way than most who have written in this area. Many use these two terms interchangeably, but I find it helpful to distinguish them. In my view, types are the biggest and broadest category, with genres being more specific.

Sometimes several types and genres may occur within a single biblical context. For example, 1-2 Samuel is an extended narrative that is predominantly story, featuring the careers of three individuals: Samuel, Saul, and David. But this two-volume narrative also has several sections embedded within it that are poetic psalms (1 Samuel 2:1-10; 2 Samuel 1:19-27; 22:2-51).

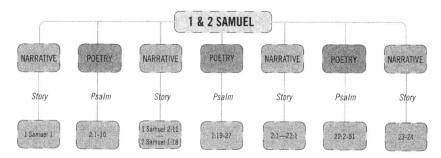

There is not a direct relationship between types and genres. For example, the type of narrative may coincide with any of the seven different genres. The same is true for poetry and discourse (see examples in the tables following).

Type	Genre	Example
Narrative	Apocalyptic	Daniel 8
	Epistle	Acts 15:23-28
	Gospel	Matthew
	Prophecy	Haggai
	Psalm	Psalm 105
	Story	Esther
	Wisdom	Job 1-2

Type	Genre	Example
Poetry	Apocalyptic	Revelation 19:1-8
	Epistle	Romans 11:33-36
	Gospel	Luke 1:68-79
	Prophecy	Isaiah 5
	Psalm	Psalms
	Story	Judges 5
	Wisdom	Proverbs

Type	Genre	Example
Discourse	Apocalyptic	Zechariah 8
	Epistle	1 Thessalonians
	Gospel	Matthew 24-25
	Prophecy	Isaiah 40-66
	Psalm	Deuteronomy 32
	Story	Galatians 1:13-2:21
	Wisdom	Ecclesiastes

Some of the features and characteristics to look for when reading these types and genres overlap. The clearest case of this is with narrative and story—all stories are narratives, though narratives can also display their characteristics with other genres as well. One way to think about this is to consider games once again. If someone has grown up playing baseball, then making the transition to softball is made easier, because the majority of the rules, as well as the skills required to play the game well, apply to both. The genre of story is to the type of narrative what the game of softball is to the game of baseball.

In some instances, a passage may reflect more than one type or genre simultaneously. Deuteronomy is an interesting case in point. The entire book is set within a narrative framework, beginning with clearly narrative elements (1:1-5). However, starting at 1:6, Moses begins a speech, that is, an extended discourse, that will extend for over thirty chapters—nearly the entire book (quite a sermon!). But his discourse is actually introduced by Moses telling the Israelites about their collective history for the last forty years. This historical prologue (1:5-4:49) is told in narrative form. Only when the reader comes to 5:1 does the discourse really start looking and sounding like a discourse. And, as if that isn't enough, Moses then ends his discourse with a psalm (32:1-43), that is, with poetry. And the book itself ends with . . . a chapter of narrative (34)! Why is it important to know this? Because to study the book of Deuteronomy as a whole, you need to bring to the job site all three of your toolboxes.

There is one more level of literary patterning that we can distinguish. It takes place within smaller sections of text, anywhere from a single phrase up to a chapter or more. This third level deals with the forms of biblical literature.[9] I have identified many of these, defining and giving examples of them, in the Appendix. These forms include, for example, Announcement of Birth, Blessing, Chronicle, Covenant, Dialogue, Exhortation, Farewell

Address, Genealogy, History, Lament, List, Miracle, Oracle, Parable, Proverb, Quotation, Satire, Thanksgiving, Travel Log, Treaty, and Woe.

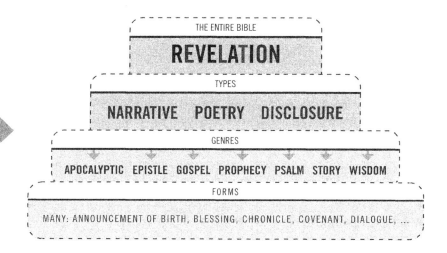

If you're feeling a little overwhelmed at this point, let me reassure you. It is vitally important to recognize the literary type of the passage you're reading in the Bible. The purpose for doing this is so that you will know what to look for as you read, and that will be different for each of these three major types. Once you have gained practice in doing this fairly simple skill, which will be explained in chapters eight through ten of this book, then you can consider the more advanced step of becoming familiar with the various genres and forms. You may actually begin seeing patterns and relationships between passages for yourself, and identify forms not even listed in the Appendix.

Learning to recognize and follow these literary patterns, once you're aware of them, is not a matter of memorizing "rules." Like learning how superstores are organized, you'll intuitively begin making the connections for yourself. And few athletes learn how to play a sport by sitting down to read the rulebook—you learn how to play a sport by playing it, over and over again, gradually learning through practice, trial and error, and a certain amount of coaching. Good players will eventually develop some of their own unique tactics and skills. This book is not intended to list the "facts" of Bible study for you to master before you can read your Bible right. Instead, this book is intended to offer you some coaching tips, and will introduce you to a way of learning to see the Bible in new and exciting ways for yourself.

CHAPTER THREE

Three Things, Even Four
4-Step Bible Study

There are four steps to the method of Bible study proposed in this book. These four steps will help a reader to understand any passage, and they work with all three of the literary types that were introduced in the previous chapter—narrative, poetry, and discourse. Each of these four steps addresses a particular question which is important to how we read and follow the Bible

1. Seeing

Seeing asks the question, "What does it say?"

We all know how frustrating it can be when we're having a discussion with someone who isn't really interested in what we have to say. Their eyes may be on us, but they don't really see us. Instead, they are too busy with their own thoughts, most likely framing what they're planning to say next. When this happens, we feel that we are not being treated fairly. They're too preoccupied with whatever is on their own mind to pay attention and respond appropriately and sympathetically to the voice of another. We get their message to us loud and clear: *What you have to say doesn't matter.*

None of us like to feel that we've been dismissed, especially if we've not even been heard yet. So we end up concluding, usually correctly, that those kinds of people are self-centered. Respect for others demands that we give a genuine, listening ear to another person before we respond. In fact, part of growing toward maturity involves recognizing that it is *not* all about me, and learning to de-center myself in order to enter into the thought world of somebody else.

We should approach our study of the Bible with this same insight. In this case, God is speaking with us, and it is not merely mature to listen to him, but is the most sensible and worshipful thing to do as well. To read the Bible honestly, respectfully, and fairly, then, we look for what God is saying to us through the text. Rather than searching for meanings that we want to find, for what we "get out" of it, or for how we can use it to our advantage, we should listen closely to the voice of the other, listening for what God wants us to understand and responding cooperatively to his intentions.

How do we do this? By starting with the recognition that since the Bible is a book, we "listen" by reading his Word. We need to read in such a way that we see with acute concentration and with careful reflection. We read with eagerness and expectation, the way that lovers pay attention to all the details of letters that they have written to one another. And we read with a humility that is willing to set aside our own agendas in favor of the wisdom which is from above.

In Bible reading, this translates into carefully *seeing* the Bible. We give our utmost attention to what God has written to us and how he has chosen to say it. When reading biblical poetry, we show respect for the voice of the other by reading it as it was intended, as poetry—not as a message secretly encoded with an outline for preaching or writing papers. We show honor to God when we observe Scripture, down to the very words, thoughts, structures, arrangements, patterns, and literary styles. We look for what he is talking about rather than those things we want to see. Bible reading should be about receiving what God has given rather than "getting from" it what appeals to us.

BIBLE READING SHOULD BE ABOUT RECEIVING WHAT GOD HAS GIVEN RATHER THAN "GETTING FROM" IT WHAT APPEALS TO US.

There are two particular dangers to avoid in this first step of *seeing*. The first danger occurs when we don't pay close enough attention to the text as we read. Whenever this happens, we miss seeing all that God has intentionally put there, and so in effect we haven't heard all he has said. Our understanding is shortchanged when we under-read the text, whether through impatience, oversight, or neglect. The importance of being thorough can be seen in this story, based on a true account.

An English professor was lecturing on the need to define words more precisely. "Young man," he commanded a student, "define a mammal for me."

"A mammal, sir," the student replied nervously, "has a hard skeleton . . . uh, it's hairy . . . and, uh, provides milk."

The professor considered this, and fixed him with an icy stare. "So far," he snapped, "you haven't eliminated the coconut."[1]

We also don't want to make the mistake of inadequate description by bailing out too soon, before we have read earnestly and carefully. The Bible is a text so rich and full that we never need to worry about exhausting all that it has to offer, and time spent studying it will always be well rewarded with new insights.

The other danger is the opposite—when we "see" what isn't actually there. This occurs when we allow our minds or imaginations to supply surplus details that the text does not actually state. There is a valuable place for the imagination in Bible reading, one that I'll clarify in a later chapter, but it is not at this stage. Being respectful to the Bible's ultimate author requires that we don't "put words in his mouth" by adding our own thoughts, opinions, speculations, and perspectives that are not his.

Often we are unaware of when and how we do this. As we read, our minds are so busy connecting the dots that we invent dots that aren't really there at all. Sometimes we merely default to what others have told us in the past without looking carefully for ourselves. For example, it is common for us to "see" the three wise men that come to visit the infant Jesus in Matthew, chapter 2. In actuality, there is no indication in Matthew 2 (or any other passage) of the number of Magi. But we are so familiar at seeing *three* wise men in manger scenes and Christmas plays and so used to singing "We Three Kings," that it is natural for us to assume that the number three is correct. (Actually, the number three is an inference, based on the Magi each bearing only a single gift, one each of gold, frankincense, and myrrh.). We set ourselves up for errors when we begin to attach significance to or draw meaning from matters that aren't in the text at all. So learning to respect the Bible involves becoming increasingly aware of assumptions that we've made, and also making a serious attempt at reading the Bible over and over again as if for the first time.

2. Understanding

Understanding asks the question, "What does it mean?"

The second step in following the Bible involves processing all the information that we have identified in the first step of seeing. Our human brains are amazing organs of organization. They are constantly flooded with sensory input from all over our bodies and remarkably prioritize this data so that, even without thinking, we know what to think about. Our brains are constantly aware of the sounds around us, like air moving through the ventilation systems, cars driving by in the distance, birds singing outside, and the hum of electric lights. Our brains are aware of the feel of clothing covering various parts of our skin, of faint odors of aftershave, and of a myriad of familiar objects within the orbit of our peripheral vision, of our breathing rate and body temperature and digestive processes. But it filters out the vast majority of this information, allowing us to narrow the focus of our attention.

The same cognitive principles apply when we read. We don't ordinarily pay attention to the color of the ink, the font style, the texture of the paper, or the frequency of occurrence of particular letters. Our brain looks past these irrelevant details in order to focus on more important matters. Some thoughts occur to us in the process of reading so effortlessly that we are unaware of having to think. Other insights occur only through intense concentration. Understanding a text requires us to make connections and interpret the facts that we encounter.

Our understanding of the Bible, and what God is communicating to us through it, emerges and grows as the reader performs the following mental tasks.

- We watch for what the author is claiming to be true and important.
- We look for the author's main purpose for writing and the points the author is making.
- We trace the author's flow of thought in developing the main purpose and points.
- We fill in the "gaps" that exist in the text—guessing at the motives and intentions of the characters and *why* certain events take place.
- We develop interpretive theories that connect actions with consequences—"b" happened *because of* "a."
- We evaluate the validity of the author's arguments and how persuasive they are.
- We connect similarities and parallels as well as notice contrasts.
- We identify quotations, references, and allusions to other texts that the author is building on.
- We contemplate and unpack the metaphors and other figures of speech—for example, how is a disciple of Jesus like salt to the world?

Our understanding of the Bible will improve as we become more attentive to and skilled at thinking through these tasks consciously and deliberately. Or, to put it more simply, the step of understanding seeks to identify the author's meaning, looking especially at two questions: why and what. *Why* did the author write—what purpose is he trying to accomplish through writing this text? And *what* is he talking about—what ideas and values is the author promoting to me?

3. Sharing

Sharing asks the question, "What truths is it teaching?"

Unlike *Aesop's Fables*, the Bible never says, "and the moral of the story is . . . ." Nevertheless, every passage of the Bible is purposeful. 2 Timothy 3:16-17 states that "*All* Scripture is God-breathed and is useful for teaching, rebuking, correcting and training in righteousness, so that the man of God may be thoroughly equipped for every good work." The Bible shares with readers assertions of truth—this is the way that things really are. Often what it claims to be reliable truth is in tension with our perceptions of reality. In these cases, readers are called upon to walk by faith, and not by sight (2 Corinthians 5:7).

I've chosen the term "sharing" for this step for several important reasons, but first I want to be clear what I *don't* mean by this term. We commonly say that we "share" a secret, a concern, a prayer request, a song, or a thought, or a Bible verse. In each of these cases, sharing involves talking to other people about things that are on our mind. But when I use the term "share," I don't mean that this step occurs when we tell others about what we have learned from the Bible from steps one (seeing) and two (understanding). While this is certainly an appropriate thing to do, this is not what I have in mind in this third step of following Scripture.

Instead, the sharing that takes place has two dimensions. The first is identifying what truth(s) the biblical author is sharing with his readers for their own benefit. This is an intentional act on the part of the author, and his thoughts are communicated by means of the written text.

Meaning is established by the author's intended purpose. The message that he brings is the truth claims being offered—shared—through the text. The reader can only legitimately share in what the author has given by recognizing and receiving the message without distorting it.

Suppose a very young girl gives you a crayon drawing she has made. She tells you that it's a picture of her smiling because she's happy to be with you. You take it from her, turn it sideways, and begin drawing in many other lines over the top of and intersecting with hers, making it into a customized Harley-Davidson motorcycle. It would be entirely inappropriate to show it to someone else and say, "Look what this little girl has shared with me!" Because of the alterations you have made, it no longer represents what she has offered to you. In the same way, a reader of the Bible genuinely shares in what the biblical author has given when it is recognized and received it *as it was intended.*

The notion of sharing requires that we respect the purpose and function of the message in the manner that the author had in mind. Attributing to the Bible meanings that originate with us instead of the biblical author is a violation comparable to and just as real as "vandalizing" the girl's self-portrait into a Harley. I use the term "sharing," then, as a safeguard against turning the focus away from what the author has offered us in the text.

A second reason for using the term "sharing" has to do with reading the Bible with a larger community in mind instead of reading it individualistically. The message that the biblical author shares is not different from reader to reader, because it originates with the author, not the readers. Anytime someone claims something like, "Well, this is *my* meaning—you can have yours," they fail to realize that authors generate the purpose and intention of the text. While in a postmodern climate it might at first appear to be more tolerant, inclusive, and politically correct to allow everyone his or her own meaning, the fact is that the opposite is true.

When "truth" is decided by each individual's preferences, it creates differences and separation that threaten and ultimately destroy the possibility of unity and community. Acceptance and tolerance are faint and inferior echoes of the higher virtue of unity. The possibility for unity in Bible reading can only exist when all agree that it is the author who establishes the meaning of the text. Otherwise, we are nothing but competing special interest groups with no authority higher than ourselves.

Suppose a piano tuner is assigned a task of tuning one hundred pianos, which will be played simultaneously in a performance on a vast concert stage.[2] They must be tuned perfectly to one another, or the result will be an ear-grating racket. The piano tuner takes out his electronic tuning device that measures the precise frequency of each note, adjusting each string to the correct frequency.

But now suppose he puts the tuner away, and tunes the second piano to the first, and the third to the second. By the time he tuned the one hundredth piano to the ninety-ninth, there would be significant differences from the first piano, and the musical unity would be severely jeopardized. Instead, the piano tuner uses the same tuning device for every single piano. If the piano tuner has done a careful job, the variations would be so slight as to be indistinguishable. In the same way, Bible readers can only hope to achieve some amount of consensus regarding the Bible if they choose a standard higher than themselves.

"Sharing" emphasizes that the truth shared by the biblical author is not my own personal property but is something held in common with all other believers. The author has shared this truth with everyone, with *all* people of *all* times. The Bible has a universal quality to it, making it relevant to everyone. My second reason for selecting the term sharing, then, is to safeguard against privatizing the Bible. The Truth that the author shares with me as an individual reader is *not* intended for me independently of others. Instead, the shared truth is something I hold in common with all other careful readers of the Bible. I am to "share" it with others by recognizing that its truth does not hinge on me personally, but I am part of a much larger community which spans centuries and continents and cultures: the community of intended readers of God's Word. Following the Bible therefore requires that I respect the otherness of those within this larger reading community as well as the authorial other.

> WHEN "TRUTH" IS DECIDED BY EACH INDIVIDUAL'S PREFERENCES, IT CREATES DIFFERENCES AND SEPARATION THAT THREATEN AND ULTIMATELY DESTROY THE POSSIBILITY OF UNITY AND COMMUNITY. ACCEPTANCE AND TOLERANCE ARE FAINT AND INFERIOR ECHOES OF THE HIGHER VIRTUE OF UNITY.

This second facet of sharing with other readers also allows for, and actually requires, that my Bible following ought to be done in conversation with other believers. My own views may be tested by the check-and-balance of how the Bible has been read both by others in the past and by others today. It could correct my mistakes, open my eyes to interpretive alternatives, expose blind assumptions that I have made, protect me from doing "what is right in my own eyes," and give due respect for the positive values of tradition, orthodoxy, and historical theology. (The truth is, we're not as original as we may think, even in the theological errors that we make!) And it is humbling to realize that my reading of the Bible, as vitally important as it is to the health of my own soul, serves as only a single voice in this far bigger arena. Hopefully this realization will prevent me from adopting dogmatic attitudes where I believe I have the final answer to truth or some special corner on the Bible that all others have missed.

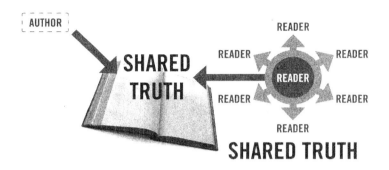

SHARED TRUTH

4. Responding

Responding asks the question, "So what?"

Whenever I choose to say or write something, I "mean" it, and I mean it in three ways. Actually, I'm not unique in this respect—whenever anybody communicates, they intend certain things at these three levels.[3]

- *Content:* they are talking about something. Sentences always have a subject, that is, a topic, and a main verb which is saying something about that topic. A paragraph is a unit of writing organized around a single thought. If we can't understand the point that someone is trying to make, or if they are deliberately talking in a way that has no point, then what has been said is literally meaning-less.

- *Purpose:* they are talking for some reason. However trivial it might at first appear, our communication always has some goal that motivates us. We are often unaware or only vaguely aware of what it is that we are trying to do when we communicate, but some function nevertheless underlies what we say. We talk in order to find out information, or to acknowledge a newcomer, or give advice, or to attract the attention of someone we admire. But even deliberately absurd nonsense fulfills some intended function, like irritating or amusing.

- *Response:* they are talking in order to get an appropriate response. They may expect me to perform some task for them, answer a question, smile and laugh, nod thoughtfully, shout back, "Sir, yes, sir!," act shocked or surprised, jump out of the way, express sympathy, or reply, "Why?"

Biblical authors are no different. They share *content* in the form of ideas, values, and truth claims. They are also *purpose*ful, although they do not state their purposes very frequently (e.g., 1 John 5:13). But the Bible also demands that we *respond*, and God will judge us on the basis of whether or not we have responded in the appropriate ways.

Some passages are there for me to obey. But surprisingly, a large amount of the Bible isn't telling me to do anything in particular. For example, how does a willing Bible reader obey the information about the materials and dimensions of the tabernacle (Exodus 35-40)? The killing of Sisera by Jael (Judges 4)? The genealogy and list of musicians in 1 Chronicles 6? The description of universal sinfulness in Psalm 53? The trumpet judgments of Revelation 8-9?

One of the shortcomings of focusing on "applying" the Bible is that it tends to create an expectation that the Bible's main (sole) purpose is to reform my actions. But there is an inward dimension to responding faithfully to God's Word as well. The author's intended purpose of some biblical passages is to offer comfort, or to instill hope, or to pronounce blessing, or to demonstrate God's character through telling us about his actions in the past, or to offer us promises. In each of these cases, the author wants to involve his readers.

We are urged to respond, although the appropriate response will not take the form of a sequence of steps or an action plan. We follow the Bible by turning to it for comfort in those passages where the author intends to offer comfort, or by experiencing a sense of well-being, courage, and joy from those passages where the author confers a blessing.

Perhaps another way of thinking about this is to imagine ourselves as being the ideal conversation partner. We not only pay full attention to what the speaker is saying, but we pick up on all the cues and clues, and we cooperate fully by affirming what is said, voicing enthusiastically and passionately our agreement, embracing every suggestion, and complying with every request or command. Bringing this to the Bible, I start by acknowledging that God is the perfect author. The communication only misfires when I am anything less than the ideal reader. Becoming an ideal Bible reader requires my entire being—heart, soul, mind, emotions, actions, and imagination. Only this kind of person can rightly be described as a follower of the Bible's author.

The method I'm proposing introduces certain techniques to help Bible readers get more out of the Bible. But the four steps that are the foundation to this way of reading the Bible will not succeed if we approach God's Word like technicians. Following the Bible does *not* entail doing something *to*, *upon*, or even *with* the text. A heightened respect for listening for the voice of God, the Holy "Other," requires that we are alert to the most finely nuanced details yet refrain from assigning our own meanings to it. This is the goal of step one, **Seeing**.

In the second step, **Understanding**, we seek to identify the author's purpose in writing, the main ideas he discusses, and what he says about those ideas. **Sharing**, the third step, involves coming to the Bible in order to receive what the author has given—our lives are enriched as we look to someone outside ourselves, one infinitely more qualified to tell us about reality. Sharing also means that I'm not preoccupied with myself while reading but am looking for how the author's message is intended for all humanity. I see myself as part of a larger community with whom and for whom I read.

And the fourth step, **Responding**, is where I imagine myself becoming the ideal reader, cooperating completely in the precise ways that would delight the divine Author. This kind of responding is a giving and yielding to one who urged his people long ago, "Take to heart all the words I have solemnly declared to you this day. . . . They are not just idle words for you—they are your life" (Deuteronomy 32:46-47).

CHAPTER **FOUR**

See for Yourself
Seeing

The first step to take in following the Bible is learning to *see* it carefully. I realize that anyone who has read the Bible has already "seen" it—the words on the page are seen. But I mean more than this.

Many people enjoy mystery or detective television shows or novels. The challenge or intrigue comes from observing the details given in the "text" of the show or book and making guesses at the identity and motive of the villain. In fact, in a sixty-minute television mystery show (less time for commercials), time is so limited that I have come to expect that every detail not only might be significant to uncovering the plot, but almost certainly is. A discarded glass, an overlooked stain, a missing button, a message left on an answering machine, a tool left behind, and an off the cuff comment are all important clues that point toward the culprit. Learning how to watch a television mystery, then, involves developing an eye for noticing things that others (including most of the characters) do not.

As we watch these television shows, we are actually coached in how to notice details and how to solve problems from those details by the lead character, the hero/ine (i.e., the protagonist) of the show. In most of these shows, there comes a moment near the end when the detective (or policeman, or doctor, or lawyer, or mystery novel writer) who is the main character gives us a second telling of the narrative we have just "seen." We are retold the same events, but this time we are given an interpretation of the details, with a commentary explaining the causes and effects and motives and factors which have been logically connected into a chain of events. In the retelling of the story, the protagonist shows us what we missed the first time around. We might remember "seeing" it the first time once we are given the reminder, but now we really "see" it in terms of its significance.

This second telling creates "Oh, yeah!" flashes of insight. In fact, in some episodes, not only does the protagonist (main character) retell the story, but actual footage is replayed as proof to the viewer—there, you see, it really was there the first time around (and you missed it!). This second version of the story, the one with all the important details highlighted and woven together into a coherent and convincing version, is actually a lesson in how we too can become more observant. If only we would notice the details of the world we live in the way that the protagonist does, then we too could solve the mysteries of our own lives. The second telling provides us with both the methods for learning how to see things more perceptively as well as giving us the reasons for why it is important to become a more observant person.

There are actually two variations of the murder mystery. The standard method begins with the discovery of a dead body, and then the viewer in effect walks alongside the main character, as if a silent partner, sifting and sorting the clues in order to piece together the most likely interpretation of what really happened at the time of the crime. In this scenario, the second telling by the main character at the end re-reveals what the viewer missed the first time.

In the second variation, the viewer actually sees the crime at the beginning of the show, and knows from the outset the answer to the problem of who did it—like looking at the answer to a math problem before trying to solve it. This is the first telling of the story. For the rest of the show, the viewer observes how the main character assembles the case for the second telling. Once again the protagonist points out to other characters in the drama those details that are significant, details that you, the viewer, may or may not have noticed. Watching the way that the main character develops the second telling of the story is precisely what captures and holds the viewer's interest.[1]

Learning to follow the Bible well requires that we first develop the same ability to notice details that the detective hero has. The Bible, unlike some novels, does not contain needless details that are merely ornamental. Things explicitly mentioned in the text nearly always have a pay-off— they contribute to the plot or argument being developed within the wider context. Bible scholars sometimes use the term "economy" or "reticence" to describe this feature of the Bible. We must assume everything matters. As we "see" the text, then, we are carefully scrutinizing it, sleuthing for clues in its details.

Seeing asks the question, "What does it say?" One way to approach this task, in keeping with the detective metaphor above, is to think of it as an interrogation. The basic questions to ask yourself when reading any passage of Scripture are the typical questions that come to mind: who, what, when, where, and how? Let's look at each of these questions in more detail.

1. Who?

- Does it say who wrote the book?
- What do you know about the implied author from this book, or other books?
- Under what conditions did the author write the book?
- To whom is the author speaking or writing?
- What are the circumstances of this first audience?
- Who are the characters involved in the book?[2]
- How are they described?
- Do any of the persons mentioned belong to a larger group of people, and, if so, what do you know about this group of people?
- Is the author quoting from or alluding to someone else from the past (earlier texts)?

2. What?

- Is the passage about events (narrative) or ideas (discourse, poetry)?
- What is the main idea being promoted in the book?
- What is the author saying about the main idea?
- What is the author saying about each of the characters?
- What is the overall plot (narrative)?
- What conflicts are presented in the text?
- How is the conflict resolved?
- What key events take place?
- What are the turning points?
- What other important themes are present?
- What images or illustrations does the author employ?
- What key words or phrases can you identify?

3. When?

- Does the passage say when the book was written?
- Does it describe the circumstances of its writing?
- What is the time frame of the events described in the book (narrative)?
- Does this time frame create a certain tone, mood, or atmosphere?[3]
- Does the text refer back to previous events?
- Does the text point toward future events?
- What words indicate time factors, sequences, or time changes (e.g., "whenever," "three days," "the next morning," "then," "tomorrow," "before," etc.)?

4. Where?

- Where was the author at the time of the writing of the book?
- Does the text indicate where the implied audience or initial readers of the book lived?
- Where does the action of the story take place (narrative)?
- What nations, regions, or cities are mentioned?
- What buildings, structures, or landmarks are referred to?
- Do these buildings or places have special theological significance (e.g., the temple, the wilderness, Babylon, Zion, etc.)?[4]

5. How?

- How would you describe the tone of writing?
- What literary type—narrative, poetry, or discourse—does the author employ?
- What genre(s) and forms are used?
- How does the author portray each of the characters?
- How does his characterization contribute to the message he is trying to get across?
- How would you describe the pace of the story (e.g., hurried, suspenseful, deliberate, jerky, etc.)?
- How does the pace affect the story impact and meaning?
- What figures of speech are used? What is their effect?

- What important words or phrases are repeated? Why?

- Are any motifs or type-scenes employed (i.e., expressions or situations which are found elsewhere in the Bible—e.g., miraculous birth to a previously childless couple, storm at sea, thunder and earthquake on a mountain, etc.)? If so, what is the significance of these parallels?[5]

- What kind of literary devices does the author use (symbols, parallelism, chiasm, inclusio, etc.)?

- What kinds of literary relationships exist in the passage (contrast, pivot, condition, result, etc.)?

- What strategies does the author employ to convince or persuade you as the reader?

The reason that we seek answers to these questions is so we can gather all the facts, the data, together before starting to assemble our second telling of the story. We have to have these details in front of us, that is, we have to become aware of them, before we can move to the next step. The retelling of the story, which I have referred to so frequently in this chapter, is the second step in the Bible study process, the step of understanding. But we simply are not prepared to do a good job of building the case if we have not first developed a keen eye for noticing the details of the text in front of us. We can't give a clear explanation of things that we haven't noticed for ourselves. We have to see before we can truly understand.

It's All a Matter of Interpretation
Understanding

Understanding is the second step of the four-step process of following Scripture. Understanding asks the question, "What does it mean?"

A person who just spouts off information like a fire hose with no one hanging on is not the kind of person that we consider to be wise. We may think that he is smart (or a know-it-all), but that's not the same thing as wisdom. When a person is talking, wisdom is displayed by knowing when to speak and how much to say (and not say), and most importantly, insight and clear thinking in what the person does say.

A wise person knows how to see patterns, connections, and relationships. It's not just that the wise person is factually correct. What the wise person says matters—it's relevant and it's important. "Facts are stupid things, until they are brought into connection . . . ."[1] The step of understanding involves seeing the *connections* between the Who-What-When-Where-How of the first step of seeing. How does all the information discovered through close attention to those details work together into a coherent whole, so that we are most likely to understand what the author has communicated to us through the text?

In fact, sometimes sermons and Bible studies or classes fail to generate any enthusiasm from the listeners, not because what is said about the Bible is wrong, but because so much of the information is unconnected—it is irrelevant to anybody's life. Speculations on historical backgrounds or parsing of Greek verbs or a list of five common interpretive variations are too frequently "stupid facts," simply because there is no real point in giving that information. There's no payoff in terms of how it actually affects people's lives.

Don't get me wrong. These things *may* be very significant clues (see the last chapter). But to build on my illustration from the last chapter, the detective who provides the explanation—the second telling of what happened—in a murder mystery television show never includes details that have no bearing on the case that he has built. Instead, the lead character selects, arranges, connects, and presents the facts in a way in which everything has been accounted for and which makes complete sense. All the different things that actually matter have been connected together into an integrated whole. So it is with understanding the Bible. Once we have seen all that we can in a text (the first step), we now need to give the most complete, clear, and accurate description that we possibly can.

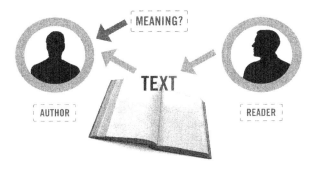

TRADITIONAL STAGE

Over the past century a great, two-stage shift has taken place in how people read and interpret literature. Until recently, people around the world and throughout history commonly identified the meaning of a literary work with what the author intended to communicate through a written text. But during the last hundred years, literary critics and teachers of literature began arguing that once a piece of literature has been written, it takes on a life of its own, independent of what the original author may have had in mind. It becomes a cultural artifact, subject to the changing tides of cultural perspectives and opinions. Therefore the reader who wants to understand its meaning should focus on the *text* itself, not the author.[2]

The second stage was to shift the location of meaning from the text to the *reader*. As a high schooler, I remember an assignment given in my sophomore level World Literature class. We were to read William Golding's

FIRST SHIFT

Lord of the Flies[3] and then write an essay in which we explained what it meant. By this time in the semester, the teacher had told us many times already that the important part of reading any book was to find a meaning in it *for you*. It occurred to me that, as long as I spelled my words correctly, my sentences contained no major grammatical flaws, and I was able to avoid flat out self-contradictions, then I could invent just about anything I wanted to say about what it meant to me, and I would earn an "A."

Feeling a little perverse and mischievous, that's exactly what I did, concocting an elaborately absurd interpretation of symbolism, an interpretation of that book probably never seen before or since. (And yes, I did get my "A" on the assignment and for the course.) Yet I must confess that, while part of me laughed at what I was able to get away with, another part felt twinges of guilt. Even then, I sensed I was doing something very irresponsible and foolish. In fact, though I wouldn't have understood it in exactly these terms at that time, I felt like I had been a traitor to the text.

The situation today is remarkably the same, with perhaps one difference. I'm not sure that young literature students would still feel the twinges of guilt that I did. Perhaps the most common approach, even when studying the Bible, is to start with the assumption of "What's in it *for me*?" Actually, so far this is not a real problem. Of course I ought to read the Bible with the expectation that it is saying something relevant to my own personal life. The crossover point into relativism occurs with the assumptions that (1) what it means to me will be different from what it means to you and (2) having different opinions doesn't really matter. In other words, the expectation is that the meaning of any text of the Bible depends entirely on the reader.[4] Not only has what the author intended been sidelined, now even the limits of what the text seems to permit have been eliminated. The individual reader's self-reflection is the only significant factor remaining.[5]

SECOND SHIFT

MEANING?

TEXT

AUTHOR

READER

It is certainly possible to study the Bible in either of the latter two ways. In fact, the last way *does* happen, very frequently in fact. But the point is, as long as we're reading the Bible in order to exploit it for our own purposes, whether consciously or not, we're not really *following* it; we're not submitting ourselves to it; we're not allowing it to assert any authority over our lives. Quite the opposite, we remain authorities over it. The question we need to ask ourselves is, "Is this the proper goal of reading the Bible for someone who wants to *follow* God's Word?"

For those who are serious about following Scripture, the Bible doesn't have "your" or "my" meaning. Instead, the Bible presents a message that the author has intended to communicate to his readers.

There are actually many ways to illustrate how authors, rather than readers, are the ones who are responsible for their texts (whether spoken or written). This is, and must be, the case in order for a society to function.

- A person who has just spoken is offended when listeners attribute to his or her message meanings and goals that were not *intended*. "That's not what I meant!" is a straightforward claim that speakers have greater rights than listeners over their own words. Likewise, a written text is also the result of a human action, meaningfully produced by an author to communicate something.

- In court cases examining someone who has caused the death of another person, it is crucial to determine the level of intention. If there was no intention whatsoever and the unfortunate tragedy was unforeseen, then there are no charges filed—it was simply an accident. The more the person was aware of potential danger and harm, the more severe are the consequences, from legal insanity to involuntary manslaughter through first-degree murder. If it is possible to judge the intentions underlying one human action (a criminal case), then in principle it is also possible to judge the intentions of another human action, namely, a written text such as the Bible. Authors write texts for a purpose and with specific intentions, in order to communicate and accomplish certain goals. Readers, using the text as "evidence," can also infer those purposes and intentions just as well as court jurors.

- Copyright law protects authors' rights to ownership of what is their property, that is, their texts. The use of their texts by somebody else without permission constitutes an infringement (theft) of what is legally theirs.

- Students who copy the texts belonging to other people are rightly charged with plagiarizing (cheating).

- Authors of texts that publicly state things about others that are not true can be held legally responsible for libel.

- We frequently use words with very negative connotations to describe various ways people misuse someone else's words: "out of context," "misquoted," "prooftexting," "misrepresenting," or "plagiarizing."

- A person speaking, while under oath, anything that turns out to be false may be prosecuted for perjury (lying) and obstruction of justice. But once again, it depends on what the court decides about his or her *intention*. If the person unintentionally says what is false due to ignorance or misunderstanding, he or she is not considered evil or legally liable, but simply wrong. But that person may be charged if it was his or her *intent* to deceive.

- A signature on a contract or a bank check is a personal authorization which is legally binding.

I could offer more examples, but I hope by now the point is becoming very clear. It is authors (and not their readers) who are the morally and legally responsible agents for the texts they produce and the meanings and purposes they intend. And this is no less the case when we're talking about the Bible.

At the most basic level, interpreters of the Bible attempt to clarify either (1) the author's meaning or (2) someone else's meaning. In light of the illustrations and examples above, it seems reasonable to aim at understanding the author's intent rather than look for the desired meanings that someone else may be trying to import into the passage, even (especially) when that other person is myself!

Let me put it very simply: a Bible reader who is more concerned with his or her own "meaning" in a passage is a very selfish person, one who does not respect what belongs to another person. If I, as a reader, cannot or will not allow myself to adopt another person's perspective, I am acting immaturely. In terms of developmental psychology, I remain at an "egocentric stage."[6] In other words, the inability or refusal to give a fair hearing to another person's voice is evidence of the inadequate socialization of the reader. On the other hand, the ability to step into someone else's shoes in order to see the world from a new and different angle is a mark of both intellectual and social maturity. Learning to de-center myself is a healthy step beyond egocentrism—it's not "all about me" after all. In more biblical terms, it allows for our minds to be "transformed" and "renewed" (Romans 12:2) by someone who is outside of and greater than ourselves. Seen this way, understanding the Bible requires a willing attitude of cooperation perhaps more than it does mental agility.

> LET ME PUT IT
> # VERY SIMPLY:
> A BIBLE READER WHO IS MORE CONCERNED WITH HIS OR HER OWN "MEANING" IN A PASSAGE IS A VERY SELFISH PERSON . . .

If we can agree that our goal for reading the Bible involves re-centering our attention back on the intention of the author, then I would like to offer the following proposals for understanding the Bible. Taken together, these represent a package deal that can help readers move closer to identifying what the biblical authors are communicating to us as God's message.[7]

1. It is possible for finite humans to understand the meaning of Scripture.

The Bible is God's revelation to us, which means that God is revealing (i.e., communicating) truth to us. There are some persons, especially in our current postmodern context, who despair of being able to find any fixed truth whatsoever.[8] But Isaiah 55:11 states, "my word . . . goes out from my mouth: it will not return to me empty, but will accomplish what I desire and achieve the purpose for which I sent it."

The Bible can and does accomplish its revelatory goals. It proves itself "useful for teaching, rebuking, correcting and training in righteousness, so that the man of God may be thoroughly equipped for every good work" (2 Timothy 3:16-17).

It was given in order for us to learn about God and his ways, as Psalm 119 (the longest chapter of the Bible) so eloquently expresses. All these biblical claims presuppose that the Bible can be understood, and that our lives will be transformed as we increasingly understand it better.

2. Our understanding can increase, yet it will never be exhaustive.

The Bible is sufficiently clear: God can hold all people accountable for whether or not they have followed it. Two opposing dangers in biblical interpretation are (1) that we can't really know any text's meaning for sure (see the point above), and (2) that I can fully know God's own perspective, and consequently *my* understanding of any particular passage is the same thing as God's. A more moderate approach that I'm arguing for here is that (a) the essential teachings of the Bible are clear enough for the simplest of readers to understand (the theological term for this is *perspicuity*), (b) significant growth in understanding Scripture requires time, effort, careful study, and a willingness to be led by the Holy Spirit, and (c) that complete understanding will never be achieved in this lifetime but awaits the future.

Level of Readers's Understanding

SUFFICIENT	COMPREHENSIVE	EXHAUSTIVE
all readers (now)	some readers (now)	no readers (now)
Essential teachings of the Bible are adequately clear	A reader's understanding can gradually improve with skill, study, and willingness	A future hope in eternity

3. There is normally only one correct meaning to any given passage of Scripture.

Though it is always possible for readers to "see" many different interpretations to a given text, authors don't usually intend to convey multiple messages simultaneously in the texts that they write. Granted, biblical authors do occasionally use word plays or double entendres, but these are exceptions to the rule, not the norm. And even when this is the case, it is the author, not the reader, who *intends* this word play.[9]

4. The correct meaning is what the author intended to communicate.

Every believer has both the right and the responsibility to read and thoughtfully contemplate Scripture, but that does not mean that all interpretations are equally valid. Readers have the freedom to disagree with one another about the true meaning of a biblical passage. The history of biblical interpretation through the centuries reflects the wide variety of perspectives that different readers have brought to the Bible. But the point is that we disagree about what the *author* meant. If the author were to join our debate, he would settle it once and for all: "Yes, that's what I meant," or "No, you missed my point." So our goal in seeking to understand a biblical passage, then, is to identify accurately the author's message and goals that he intends to communicate to his readers as presented in the text.

5. Various interpretations are simply hypotheses which attempt to account for what the author has said, and how and why he has said it in that way.

We would all probably be better off by putting aside viewing interpretations as either "right" or "wrong." Instead, it's better to operate in terms of probable validity: given all the facts within the text, how well does our interpretation square with what the author is saying in the passage? The more textual details that our hypothesis explains, the greater the likelihood that we are actually tracking with the author's own thought processes. It becomes a matter of trying on different solutions for size, and seeing which one works best, not to suit our preferences, but in actually providing the most comprehensive and convincing explanation.

Let's say the following circle represents all the details discovered through a very close reading of a biblical text.

Next, we have three possible interpretations for explaining the text. The first explains some of the text, but still does not account for a large portion.

INTERPRETATION #1

A second interpretation does explain more of the text, but also has to depend on certain assumptions or information that is not found in the text.

INTERPRETATION #2

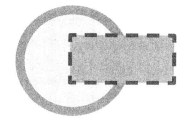

A third interpretation explains more than either of the previous two, yet does not require going outside of the text for clues to make the hypothesis "work."

INTERPRETATION #3

The third interpretation of the details of the text has the greatest likelihood of being the closest to what the author actually had in mind. By sticking close to the text, we increase the probability that we are respecting the author's intentions that are communicated in the text. The probability of our interpretation being correct rests on two factors: (1) how carefully we have seen the entire text, noticing the details of the entire context, and (2) how well our interpretation explains and integrates all that we have seen.

Like the murder mystery detective, we are sifting and sorting the clues into a clear re-telling of the story which bears the "beyond reasonable doubt" stamp. The following comments on creative thinking apply to interpretation equally well.

Creative thinking is a process of becoming sensitive to problems, deficiencies, gaps in knowledge, missing elements, disharmonies, and so on. It is identifying the difficulty; searching for solutions, making guesses or formulating hypotheses about the deficiencies, testing and retesting these hypotheses, and finally communicating the results.[10]

6. Though every passage has just one meaning (the author's), it has many applications.

The way that the Bible's truth relates to individual lives is specific and unique. (I'll say more on this in chapter seven). The Holy Spirit can and does use the Scripture in our lives in very personal ways, even though it remains the same timeless truth meant for everyone. It is the *relevance* that is special and unique and varies with each individual reader.

On the other hand, the textual meaning that God has inspired is designed for everyone to understand, and so it doesn't change. This is reflected in scriptural statements such as "the word of the Lord stands forever" (1 Peter 1:25).[11] It doesn't matter who is reading the text, or whether or not the reader has respected the intentions of the author; the truth revealed through the text is stable and enduring, fixed by the mind of the author.[12]

IT DOESN'T MATTER WHO IS READING THE TEXT, OR WHETHER OR NOT THE READER HAS RESPECTED THE INTENTIONS OF THE AUTHOR; THE TRUTH REVEALED THROUGH THE TEXT IS STABLE AND ENDURING, FIXED BY THE MIND OF THE AUTHOR.

It is valuable here to draw a necessary distinction between what truths the author intends to communicate through the text versus the significance of those truths in the lives of his readers. The truth claims that the author has presented in the text are not dependent on or relative to individual readers, but how those truths affect people's lives will be different from one reader to the next. The human author, while knowing with God the truth claims of the text, obviously cannot know all the effects that the text will have in the lives of particular readers down through the centuries.

Likewise, it is helpful to realize that what the text asserts about being true is not identical with what it refers to. For example, in Philippians 4:2, Paul urges Euodia and Syntyche to agree with each other. While he is directly *referring* to these two individuals, a greater truth is being presented in this wider context. In chapter two, Paul has already urged all the Philippian believers (and presumably, all the anticipated readers of this epistle) to adopt the attitude of Christ, an attitude of self-sacrifice, putting the interests of others above our own. This Christ-like attitude is necessary for unity between one another. And this sameness of attitude cannot coexist with ongoing personal disagreement. This is not meant to be a mere theoretical or "positional" unity. This unity is worthless without practical agreement, in tangible ways, between actual people who harbor disagreement between one another.

His advice for Euodia and Syntyche is not just for them as individuals but is a signal to all readers that this greater truth has practical implications for real human relationships. So while he *refers* to these two, they are representative: he intends this message more broadly for all believers who disagree. This important insight, that the truth being endorsed by the author (the *meaning*) can be distinguished from the specific people and events that that truth refers to (the *reference*), will be a valuable key when we move to the third and fourth steps, sharing and responding.[13]

Human authors thus know the truth claims they present (the meaning), while all the implications of that truth—all who are affected by it, and how they are affected—is known to God alone.

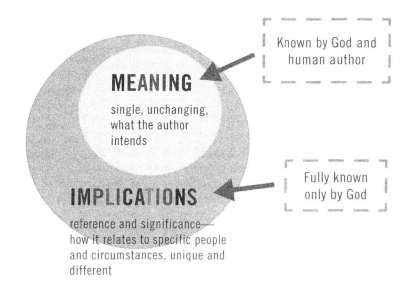

MEANING
single, unchanging, what the author intends

Known by God and human author

IMPLICATIONS
reference and significance—how it relates to specific people and circumstances, unique and different

Fully known only by God

7. Every passage of Scripture needs to be understood in light of its literary type and genre.

Many reading errors can be avoided if we simply remember that the Bible comes to us packaged in a kind of literary "wrapping" (see chapter two). What I look for as I read thus varies from one literary category to the next. For example, some of the narratives of the Hebrew Bible describe polygamy (marriage to two or more wives). But it doesn't *teach* or *endorse* polygamy. It describes the way things were, not what should have been. In fact, I would point out that every single time that polygamy does occur in narratives, it turns out disastrously for the characters involved. Narratives do teach truths, but they do so differently than poetry or discourse—by "showing" rather than "telling."

8. Scriptural passages are best understood when read in light of their context.

Have you ever had someone take your words and use them in a completely different way, misrepresenting what you said? We call that being "misquoted" or taken "out of context," and we are rightly convinced that we are being treated unfairly. When we're reading the Bible, we constantly run the risk of doing that very thing—to God! And that is a very serious business.

To misrepresent what God says is tantamount to using God's name to endorse our error, which violates one of the Ten Commandments by misusing God's name (see Exodus 20:7). It is also bearing false witness, violating another of the Ten Commandments (Exodus 20:16). Not only that, but if we misrepresent God himself, using Scripture to say things about God that are not fully accurate, we are "building" a false image of him, an "idol" made not of stone or wood but of words, which is just as dangerous. And that is breaking another of the Ten Commandments, which forbids people to make idols of God (see Exodus 20:4-6). That is why knowing how to understand and use God's Word correctly is so important.

How do we know the point that a particular biblical text is communicating? We read it in light of the text around it—its context. The context is the words, sentences, paragraphs, chapters, and sections of the text that surround a given passage. No passage of Scripture was intended to be read in isolation. Words do not mean anything until they are put into sentences. And sentences link together into paragraphs. And paragraphs communicate thoughts by the way they relate to the neighboring paragraphs. The best manner of understanding a passage is always the one that fits the entire flow of thought within the "big picture" of the entire paragraph, section, and book. Stated negatively, nearly every misinterpretation of the Bible betrays a failure to respect the larger context. Stated positively, sensitivity to context is the single most decisive factor in understanding the intended meaning of any passage.

> SENSITIVITY TO CONTEXT IS THE SINGLE MOST DECISIVE FACTOR IN UNDERSTANDING THE INTENDED MEANING OF ANY PASSAGE.

The authors of Scripture each wrote with specific purposes in mind and used literary strategies to accomplish these purposes. Looking for these larger structures of thought enables us to understand how each part properly functions within the larger whole. Individual verses of the Bible are threads woven into a rope, which are then woven into a net. The usefulness of each individual thread lies in the interconnectedness of a larger whole; a pile of threads by themselves may not be helpful for catching a fish, but when correctly connected into a net they can be very effective. For that reason, we should not approach individual verses as self-contained units.[14] Every verse fits within the logical sequence of an entire passage, and must be understood in light of the whole.

Furthermore, each passage of Scripture is illuminated by other passages. So our understanding of any particular passage should be compared with other Scriptures. Because the Bible has a coherent unity and wholeness that underlies all the wide variety of literary styles and themes, it has a kind of built-in self-correcting mechanism to help attentive and cooperative readers from going too far astray. Theologians from the past described this dimension with the expression "Scripture interprets itself."[15] What this means is that if my interpretation of any particular passage leads into direct conflict with the clear teaching of another passage, then I need to revise my original hypothesis.

One other aspect of reading the Bible in context is tracing how biblical authors may be drawing or building upon other Scriptures. This "backgrounding" (scholars refer to this phenomenon as *intertextuality* or sometimes *intratextuality*) grows as the storyline of the Bible emerges and expands from one book to the next. For example, those who are most experienced in understanding the Bible are adept at seeing that laws given to ancient Israel are set within the larger framework of the surrounding narrative which shapes how we should view them.[16] In the same way, they also read the psalms, proverbs, prophecies, epistles, and apocalyptic literature of the Bible against the backdrop of the circumstances of the time, comparing each text to the texts leading into them.

9. Following the Bible means that we emphasize what the text emphasizes, not building main points from the details.

This statement has two aspects. First, when interpreting Scripture, our primary concern is the meaning of the overall passage. Second, our interpretation of the details occurs within the context of the entire passage. This doesn't diminish the importance of details in Scripture, but it recognizes that details are the building blocks the author is using to construct a message. That overall message is the main point of the passage, and understanding that main point is our primary objective.

10. We need to evaluate our personal experience in light of Scripture, not the other way around.

The Bible is perfect and unchanging, designed to penetrate to our inmost being (Hebrews 4:12-13), a standard to use for measuring all other truth claims. As real and vivid as our personal experiences may be to us, the same cannot be said for them. In fact, there are many statements and stories in the Bible that caution readers that what seems right "in their own eyes" cannot be used as a reliable guide to what is right in God's perspective.[17] Because of this, it is best to avoid saying things like, "Here's what this verse means to me." Statements like this actually reveal more about the person making them than about the message and purposes that the Holy Spirit intended to be shared with all Scripture readers. Instead, we should ask ourselves, "How does the Bible's own message, inspired by God, relate to my life?"

WE SHOULD ASK OURSELVES, "HOW DOES THE BIBLE'S OWN MESSAGE, INSPIRED BY GOD, RELATE TO MY LIFE?"

11. We should check out our understanding of God's Word with other believers.

A wise Bible reader will offer his or her perception of what the text is saying to fellow believers for their evaluation. This could include both those we know as well as what others have written about the same passage we're studying. We're not asking others to do our own work by interpreting for us, but to help us assess the work we have already done. It is also wise to check with a number of believers, not just one or two people— especially if we know that they are inclined to agree with us. Getting a variety of feedback—from young and old, men and women, from differing church backgrounds, theological viewpoints, and walks of life—can add some fresh perspectives that we may not have considered. This is one of the reasons why God has placed us within a community of other believers, the "body of Christ" (see Romans 12:4-8).[18]

12. Every passage of Scripture has meaning and relevance for the believer.

Some passages have more direct application while others have more indirect application, but ALL Scripture is profitable for Christian growth. While it is not uncommon to encounter believers who minimize or even dismiss the importance of some sections of the Bible, especially the "Old Testament" in general and the "Law" in particular, even those passages which present the old covenant as something that has been replaced (for example, the book of Hebrews) reflect a high view of the authority of those Scriptures.[19] The entire Bible is intended for our benefit, and we shortchange ourselves if we begin with the assumption that any part of it isn't really significant (a point to be developed further in the next two chapters).

In chapter two, I presented the idea that all forms of communication take place at three levels:

- Each author or speaker is relating some content: the ideas, events, people, situation, etc. that the person is talking about. The content is the subject matter and what the author is saying about that particular topic.

- The next level is the purpose for the communication. The act of communicating is inevitably goal oriented, intended to fulfill some function. Even casual conversation accomplishes certain things, such as acknowledging another's presence, conveying an attitude of friendliness toward the other person, sharing something of mutual interest that strengthens the relationship, coordinating thoughts and opinions, etc.

- The third level is the anticipated response that is appropriate to what has just been communicated. It may be nothing more than an acknowledgement that the listener has heard: a brief smile, a nod, or "uh, huh." It may be a request for affirmation, such as, "Does that make any sense?"

Over the last several hundred years in particular, the tendency among those who read and study the Bible (at least in western culture) has been to focus on the first of these, often neglecting the second two. Enlightenment thinking placed priority on human rationality, so interpretive attention was focused on the subject matter. Many Bible commentaries produced during this time frame go to great lengths to explain the content of a biblical book yet devote only a couple of pages to the purpose of the book as a whole (rarely looking at the purpose of particular sentences, paragraphs, or sections of the book). And the anticipated response is not addressed at all, leaving such "practical" matters for devotional books, preachers, or the Holy Spirit.

However, I maintain that understanding the Bible involves looking for the author's intentions at all three of these levels. The ideal listener does not passively grasp the concepts of the other person's comments, but co-operates further by recognizing the person's purposes and "replying" with the right kinds of responses, both verbal and otherwise.

Perhaps you may be thinking that all of this sounds complicated and too difficult for normal people with real lives. Actually, while it may be a new way of approaching things, it's simpler than it seems right now. In fact, your brain is already very well trained in deciding the purposes and appropriate responses from things that people in your own life say and do.

Let me give a common example. You see someone lifting his or her hand. What does this gesture actually mean? The way that you understand the hand raiser's purpose and the response expected from someone else depends on the *context* in which this act of communication takes place.

Context	Intended Purpose	Expected Response
Seeing a friend	Greeting	Wave back
Downtown street or airport	Hail a taxicab	Taxicab stops to give a ride
Worship service	Express worship	None
Classroom	Permission to speak or ask question	Teacher grants permission
Voting during a business meeting	Casting a vote	Vote acknowledged and counted
Restaurant	Gain the attention of waiter	Waiter approaches and takes the request
Player at a football game	Congratulate OR Celebrate	Give high-five OR cheer, clap
Traffic control	Make cars stop	Cars stop
Courtroom	Swearing in	Pledging to tell truth or fulfill responsibilities
Auction	Place a bid	Acknowledgment of bid by auctioneer
Merging or changing lanes in heavy traffic	Express appreciation	Waving back or nod

When and how did you learn to recognize all those functions of hand raising? When it's laid out like this in a chart, it actually looks pretty complicated, but in reality you learned all these just by seeing it done. So it is with Bible reading—once you start watching for the different communication purposes, it will become easier and easier for you to identify them.

Let me offer a biblical example, based on a single verse (though sensitive to its wider context). Joel 2:13 says: "Rend your heart and not your garments." How do we understand this sentence using this three-layered approach?

Content—Obviously, a figure of speech is used here—a literal tearing of cardiac muscles is certainly not the point of what is being communicated. In context, this line is paralleled with "Return to the LORD your God," where the term for "return"[20] is frequently translated as "repent." Thus the topic is the importance of repenting/turning from sin, especially in the face of the terrifying, impending judgment when the day of the LORD arrives. The figure represents a repentance that is sincere and reflects a total change of character (accompanied by weeping, fasting, and mourning over past sins—v.12), not merely going through the motions of changing superficial behaviors or "looking" sorry.

Purpose—The purpose for this statement is to *urge* a change of thinking and action on the part of the readers. It also has elements of both *persuading*—positively, "for he is gracious and compassionate, slow to anger and abounding in love, and he relents from sending calamity" (verse 12, and continuing through verse 32), and *warning*—negatively, in view of the threatened judgment (verses 1-11).

Response—Readers cannot simply acknowledge that the text is saying that we should change by wholeheartedly returning to a faithful commitment to God. Mentally saying, "Yes, that would be a good thing," is not the same as obeying this passage. Readers must also respond accordingly by first turning away from any idol of the heart that vies for our attention and, second, rejecting hope for the "good life" independently of God. It may involve giving up or giving over a snowboard, a car, an unhealthy relationship, or a high-paying job that compromises moral integrity. We have only completed the communicative action if we have responded in a way consistent with the intended response envisioned by the author.

As you can probably guess, this third level of communication, the level of response, overlaps with the fourth step of the four-step method promoted in this book: seeing, understanding, sharing, and *responding*. I will have more to say about this in chapter seven. My reason for bringing up this three-level approach to language again here is to emphasize that the step of *understanding* needs to address more than just the ideas of the text (the first level of content). This is one of the weaknesses in traditional interpretation over the last two hundred years. We also need to go further by identifying what purpose(s) the text is intended to serve.

In the following list, I have compiled a number of potential purposes that may motivate people who are communicating to others. I've also tried to arrange these into several larger categories to make it easier for you to see how they relate to each other.

Perhaps there are more functions that could be added to this list, but it should give you a very good idea of what things to look for when trying to understand an author's intent within a text. You will have a better grasp of the passage itself by asking very important questions like, "What is the author trying to accomplish by telling me this?" and, "Why has the author chosen to communicate to his readers in this way?"

Initiating and closing conversation: Closure, dismiss, drawing attention, greet, introduce, welcome

Responding sympathetically: Acknowledge, affirm, agree, answer, apologize, comfort, concede, congratulate, consent, permit, thank

Responding unfavorably: Accuse, complain, correct, critique, dissent, lament, obstruct, rebuke, satirize, scold, threaten

Informing: Advise, announce, assert, coerce, command, defend, describe, explain, evaluate, illustrate, inform, instruct, summarize

Performing (*the very act of saying it makes it happen*): Bless, boast, curse, inquire, request, honor, invite, judge, legislate, mock, name, pardon, praise, predict, promise, pronounce, ratify, swear, tease, validate, wish

Misleading: deceive, evade, obstruct

Stimulating: Amuse, arouse, challenge, decree, entertain, express emotion, impress, motivate, persuade, remind, suggest, tempt, urge, warn

---

Ultimately, understanding the Bible is an aspect of following it. It is not a matter of bringing my own meaning to the text, nor of readers merely shrugging at one another and saying, "Well, you've got your interpretation, I think I'll keep mine."

As Kevin Vanhoozer rightly points out, the attitude we need to adopt as Bible readers is not a matter of standing over the text ("overstanding" it), as if we can or should have the final word on its meaning. Instead, respect for the intention of the author should be our interpretive goal.[21] We need to assume the posture of standing under the text ("understanding" it), looking to what the author is asserting within the text we are reading.[22]

Let me return to my analogy of the mystery novel that I brought up in the previous chapter. The first step of seeing corresponds to a detective poring over all the details surrounding the crime, leaving no stone unturned while searching for any and all possible clues. The second step of understanding involves sorting through all these clues in order to rebuild the "second narrative," seeing relationships, discerning the significance of the details, and drawing conclusions. The most convincing interpretations of the information the author has communicated in the text will be, quite simply, those that do the best job of actually explaining what is in the text. Giving the most comprehensive and coherent explanation to what

ULTIMATELY,
UNDERSTANDING THE BIBLE IS AN ASPECT OF FOLLOWING IT.

the author has given to us is thus a way of honoring, of following, and of understanding the life-changing message of the Bible.

CHAPTER SIX

Communing with Truth
Sharing

If you've been around the Christian subculture for very long, you've seen it too. I first started noticing it in high school, from time to time, at church or at youth retreats or camps. I saw it a lot more as "Christian" television and radio stations began popping up all over, along with the thousands of books and articles published each year, and building to a crescendo with the Internet.

Arguably, people are using the Bible today as much as they ever have. The problem is *how* they use it. The way that the Bible is used is often confusing, surprising, or even alarming. Sometimes when a person uses a verse, my response is merely a silent, "That doesn't sound quite right." From there, the categories range from "Wait a minute," to "That's not what is says," to "Give me a break," to "That's outrageous!"

Consider the following scenarios:

- A woman explains to her therapist that God had guided her to divorce her husband and marry the man with whom she was having an affair, through a verse God had laid on her heart: "Put on the new man" (Ephesians 4:24).[1]

- A student decides from Jonah 4:6 that "if you just sit there, God will immediately know your need and provide for it." No, it was not intended as a joke.

- Scholars conclude that God the Father planning and carrying out the death of his own son Jesus constitutes "divine child abuse."[2]

- Someone argues that a theory developed by psychologist Carl Jung, that there is a female within every man, and a male within every woman, "always seemed exceptionally scriptural to me," basing this on Genesis 5:2: "*Male and female* he created them."[3]

- An Internet author states that it is an "absolute requirement" for home schooling families to own and use an answering machine for their home telephone. He further states that in this case, there is a *command* from the Lord to do so, found in two passages: "Call if you will, but who will answer you?" (Job 5:1) and, "Then they will call to me, but I will not answer" (Proverbs 1:28).[4]

- A preacher who is doing a sermon series on "The United States in Biblical Prophecy" "explains" that modern day traffic jams, the use of headlights, and speeding drivers are predicted in Nahum 2:4: "The chariots storm through the streets, rushing back and forth through the squares. They look like flaming torches; they dart about like lightning."

I have many more examples that I could offer, and you may also have your own "favorite" list of terrible misuses of the Bible. I've been building a case throughout this book that the proper meaning is the message that the author is communicating. Mathematician, theologian, and philosopher Blaise Pascal sharpens the same point: "He who will give the meaning of Scripture, and does not take it from Scripture, is the enemy of Scripture." Bible scholars have long recognized a difference between proper *exegesis*—drawing out the inherent meaning of the text—and improper *eisegesis*—importing one's own meaning into the text. Good readers of Scripture, those who want to learn from it, resist the temptation merely to use the text for their own empowerment and purposes.[5] In the last chapter, in the discussion of *understanding*, I presented a number of ideas that emphasized both why and how to follow the author's intent. This chapter takes it to the next level.

The third step of the four-step approach for following Scripture is *sharing*. Sharing asks the question, "What truths is it teaching?"

In my quest to learn how to best study the Bible, taking classes and reading many books on the topic, I have frequently encountered a three-step method: observation, interpretation, and application.[6] These three steps overlap to a certain degree with three of the steps that I am proposing here: seeing (observation), understanding (interpretation), and responding (application)—though, hopefully, I have added dimensions to these steps not usually seen in these older works.

However, these steps overlook or undervalue the third element in my four-step approach, the one that is the central idea of this chapter: sharing. I am convinced that this is the missing link of Bible study, a key ingredient without which we end up having many problems.

The problem arises when we try to go from a biblical passage directly into application to our own lives. For example, should we obey the following biblical passages today or not?

- "Leave your country, your people and your father's household and go to the land I will show you." (Genesis 12:1)

- "Therefore go and make disciples of all nations." (Matthew 28:19).

- "Do not plow with an ox and a donkey yoked together." (Deuteronomy 22:10)

- "It is better not to eat meat or drink wine or do anything else that will cause your brother to fall." (Romans 14:21)

- "Snatch others from the fire and save them." (Jude 23)

- "Blow the trumpet in Zion, declare a holy fast, call a sacred assembly." (Joel 2:15)

- "For a man may do his work with wisdom, knowledge and skill, and then he must leave all he owns to someone who has not worked for it." (Ecclesiastes 2:21)

- "Anyone who blasphemes the name of the LORD must be put to death." (Leviticus 24:16)

- "Love the LORD your God with all your heart and with all you soul and with all your strength." (Deuteronomy 6:5)

- "Are you unmarried? Do not look for a wife." (1 Corinthians 7:27)

- "Husbands, love your wives, just as Christ loved the church." (Ephesians 5:25)

- "On the Sabbath day, make an offering of two lambs a year old without defect." (Numbers 28:9)

- "And if your eye causes you to sin, gouge it out and throw it away." (Matthew 18:9)

- "A new command I give you: love one another." (John 13:34)

Some of these passages should be obeyed at face value today. Some are figures of speech that we need to follow, not literally, but figuratively. Some were given to specific people at a specific time and so we believe that we are exempt. All of these have been lifted out of their context, and so there are bigger ideas and principles at stake that are valid.

If the process were as simple as observation → interpretation → application, we would still lack a tool for deciding whether biblical commands like these are to be obeyed, altered, or set aside. That is why an intermediate step like *sharing* is so important.

The prime concern here is identifying what truth(s) the biblical author is sharing with his readers for their own benefit. The author has communicated to his readers, by means of the written text, ideas which serve a deliberate purpose. I use the term *sharing* to describe the truths that the author has offered to readers through the text. Sharing involves mutuality between author and reader. The author presents the ideas that he claims to be true and seeks to convince his readers that they need both to accept these ideas as real and to embrace them personally as life changing. The reader meets these ideas, or *shares* them, by recognizing and adopting the message as it was intended. The following illustration, already introduced in an earlier chapter, reflects my concept of *sharing*.

For genuine sharing to take place, it is essential for readers to respect the purpose and function of the message in the manner that the author had in mind. To echo the phrase I heard one of my professors often repeat, "Keep your finger in the text." This was his way of insisting that our claims about the biblical passages were in fact found right in the passage, rather than in our own imaginations.

Some of the commands given in the list above were intended by the author, or by a character in the narrative, for a certain person or situation. For example, the first one is a direct commission given by God to Abram (Genesis 12:2). When we read this passage in context, we recognize that it is not a command being given directly to readers by the author of Genesis, but a description of what God said to Abram at that time. In a sense, we are overhearing a conversation between two characters (God and Abram).

But every part of the Bible, more broadly speaking, is given for our instruction and benefit. Here I think it is crucial for us to draw a distinction between whom a biblical command is given *to*, and whom it is designed *for*. God may speak a command to one person, yet a biblical author intentionally incorporated this command and its context into a text meant for a different audience. For example, Deuteronomy 6:1 says, "These are the commands, decrees and laws the LORD your God directed me to teach you to observe in the land that you are crossing the Jordan to possess." In what follows in the book of Deuteronomy, we read the commands given *to* Moses that were intended *for* all the people.

Now if you are ready to recognize and accept that God can speak *to* one person, yet intend the message to be *for* the benefit of another group of people, then you are ready to take the next logical step.

The Bible as a whole was not intended merely for the benefit of the original audiences. It is God's message (revelation) to all of humanity, to those "who have the ears to hear" by receiving and responding appropriately to the things it presents. Several biblical passages inform us that the original audience was *not* the same as the intended audience—it was intended much more broadly.

- "For everything that was written in the past was written to teach us, so that through endurance and the encouragement of the Scriptures we might have hope" (Romans 15:4). Here Paul (after quoting from Psalms) implies that previous Scriptures were written for the benefit of Gentile believers centuries later.

- "It was revealed to [the earlier prophets] that they were not serving themselves but you, when they spoke of the things that have now been told you by those who have preached the gospel to you by the Holy Spirit sent from heaven" (1 Peter 1:12). Peter recognizes that prophets who wrote of the Messiah were aware that their prophecies were intended to serve future generations of readers.

Christians (and even nonbelievers) turn to the Bible precisely because it is timeless in the truth that it tells. "When believers approach Scripture, they generally seek guidance or revelation. They want the Scripture to speak to their present lives, not just be a document from the past."[7] Viewing the Bible as God's Word to mankind expands its intended readership beyond the first audience and first readers.[8]

So now we can reflect this with another illustration.

GOD — TO — MOSES — FOR — ISRAELITES — FOR — LATER READERS

This point is of crucial importance: things that are written in the Bible are valuable and instructive for a bigger target of readers than the initial audience, who all too frequently misunderstood the message in the first place. More simply put, the ideal reader that the author has in mind is anyone who is willing to read cooperatively with the author's intentions. In fact, even critical scholars are rediscovering this fact: the Bible is not simply a collection of ancient, religious, literary pieces. It is *Scripture*, meant to be read by people of faith, and therefore possessing qualities that are not limited to distant localized places or long ago time periods.[9]

The next logical step, then, is to rethink the nature and purpose of the letters of Paul and others. It has been customary for the last century or so for Bible interpreters to emphasize that Paul's epistles were "occasional," that is, triggered by special problems that were unique to the first century and the individuals to whom he was writing. But some people are recognizing the significance of the presence of these letters in the Bible (the "canon"), which lifts them beyond being so restricted. The truths found in them are meant to cross the boundaries of space and time. The purposes, principles, and points that echo through Paul's writings are designed to be transferable, at least indirectly, to a wider audience of intended readers. Ben Witherington puts it this way: "[T]he assumption that Paul's thought arises out of, and only in response to, particular situations in his congregations, I would suggest . . . is essentially incorrect."[10] Instead, it is better to view these situations as case studies. When Paul addresses the problems of Corinth, for example, he is presenting sample problems. By writing *for* a larger circle of readers, he is demonstrating how to deal with church problems. All his potential readers can benefit from the advice he offers.

Suppose you would like to prepare for a vocation as a licensed, professional counselor. At your graduate level of training, you enroll in a class specializing in group therapy. Now suppose that your professor provides five individuals with clinical disorders who have volunteered to participate as her "guinea pigs" (compensated by receiving their counseling free of charge). They attend their group session, which is observed by your entire class, on a weekly basis as your professor models several modes of group therapy. You and your classmates all observe how she conducts the weekly session, leading her counselees into greater self-understanding and psycho-emotional health.

The question can now be raised: who is benefiting from these group counseling sessions? Is it the counselees, or is it you and your classmates? And the answer, of course, is *both*. The counselees gain insight into themselves and their own, special and idiosyncratic problems from one another and from their counselor. At the same time, you and your classmates learn about how to direct these sessions productively. The whole purpose of your observing these sessions is not merely to learn how to deal with these particular five individuals (should you ever encounter one of them in a future counseling setting), but to derive general ideas that are applicable to a wide range of future counselees. While they are learning from their counselor, you are learning from your professor.

This is how best to approach the so-called "occasional" nature of biblical books. While many situations that are unique to an ancient setting are discussed, we are meant to encounter enduring, universal Truths that are equally valid, though not identically applicable. I don't own any oxen that

GOD **TO** PAUL **FOR** CORINTHIANS **FOR** LATER READERS

SHARED TRUTH

may injure a neighbor with its horns, but I do own several dogs. And while in my church there are no individuals named Apollos and Cephas, if there are quarrelsome, hero-worshipping, rival group(ie)s within my church, they should work toward reconciling, regardless of their names.

The constant factor in the diagram above——from God to Paul to the Corinthians to later readers——is theological Truth. This Truth-with-a-capital-T can be shared between all the parties because it is the same regardless of the audience. As we saw in the scriptural examples above, not all the details and particulars are meant to be copied by subsequent readers. Nevertheless, there is Truth communicated, and that is what this chapter is about: *sharing* of Truth between God as the ultimate author, the human author, the initial audience, and the entirety of all the anticipated future audiences.

One way to think of these Truths that can be shared between cultures and times is to think of bridging a gap that exists between the ancient and modern worlds. This is a fairly common way of describing what we are seeking to accomplish in this third step.[11]

BRIDGING THE GAP

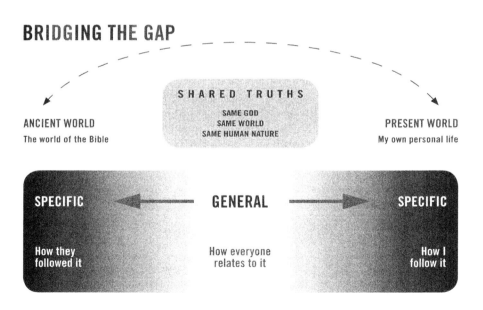

In every given passage of Scripture, there is timeless Truth that the author intends to communicate. As God's Word, the Bible is not merely a record of the way that God *did* communicate to people in the past. It *is* God's communication to us—dynamic, powerful, living, and life changing (Hebrews 4:12) for present day readers just as much as it was in earlier generations. It communicates Truth to all people of all times everywhere. This means that its theological Truth is both *eternal* and *universal.*

Paul offers us a clear and intriguing example of this step of *sharing* in his discussion on giving in 1 Corinthians 9. In this context, Paul is explaining the rights that he deserves as an apostle, which include receiving payment from them for his labors that benefited them. Yet surprisingly, he has chosen not to exercise the right to financial compensation, because it is his desire to give the Good News to them as freely as God's grace was shown to him. He also wants to prevent any accusation of being in ministry just for the money. Ironically, however, the Corinthians have misunderstood Paul on this point. Since the other apostles do accept payment, his refusal to do so is something they interpret as evidence that he is not a legitimate apostle of equal rank to the others. Against this backdrop Paul is forced into defending his rights, while at the same time choosing not to exercise them so that he can offer the gospel free of charge—an implicit object lesson in how God's grace is offered to humanity without "payment" of human works.

In defending his right to receive payment, Paul argues his case by using several examples, followed by a quotation from Deuteronomy. These are his examples: soldiers don't serve in the military for free but get paid, vineyard owners eat from the grapes they grow, and those who herd flocks drink the milk produced. He then drives his point home by demonstrating that the Scriptures say the same thing: "Do not muzzle an ox while it is treading out the grain" (1 Corinthians 9:9, citing Deuteronomy 25:4). There seems to be huge leap of logic here. How can Paul say that paying ministers of the gospel is what Moses is talking about in the requirement that animals should be allowed to eat on the job? At first glance, it appears that Paul is quoting Moses out of context rather badly.

But he explains in the next few verses. He poses two questions, "Does God say this just for the sake of oxen?" (implied answer: "No!"), and, "Surely he says this for us, doesn't he?" (implied answer: "Of course!"). He insists, "Yes, this *was* written for us, because when the plowman plows and the thresher threshes, they ought to do so in the hope of sharing in the harvest." If an animal can eat from the harvested seed while doing the farm work, how much more deserving is a human when doing the same job of farm work. But he really brings it home when he says, "If *we* have sown spiritual seed among you, is it too much if *we* reap a material harvest from you?" Here he uses a metaphor that he uses elsewhere: sharing the gospel with others is like farm work (planting seeds), and assisting in their conversion is also like farm work (harvesting the crops). There is a common thread of theological Truth that underlies all three of these particular examples.

Oxen should be fed from the harvest for their farm work ⟶ Human farm workers should be fed from the harvest for their farm work ⟶ Ministers of the gospel should be fed from the "harvest" (converts) for their (spiritual) farm work

SHARED TRUTH:

THOSE WHO BENEFIT FROM THE WORK OF OTHERS SHOULD PROVIDE FOR THOSE WORKERS.

This one statement of shared Truth can now be applied to a wide variety of situations, including those not specifically addressed either by Moses or Paul in their immediate contexts.

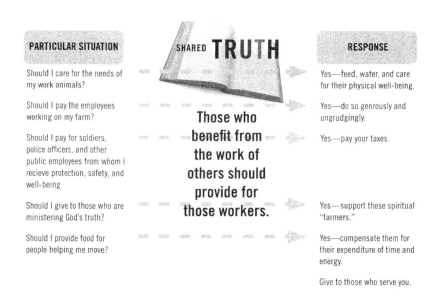

PARTICULAR SITUATION	SHARED **TRUTH**	RESPONSE
Should I care for the needs of my work animals?		Yes—feed, water, and care for their physical well-being.
Should I pay the employees working on my farm?	Those who	Yes—do so genrously and ungrudgingly.
Should I pay for soldiers, police officers, and other public employees from whom I recieve protection, safety, and well-being	benefit from the work of others should provide for	Yes—pay your taxes.
Should I give to those who are ministering God's truth?	those workers.	Yes—support these spiritual "farmers."
Should I provide food for people helping me move?		Yes—compensate them for their expenditure of time and energy.

Give to those who serve you.

The one thing glaringly absent in Paul's argument in 1 Corinthians 9 is that he never explicitly states this one, shared Truth in a simple and straightforward proposition. Instead, he demonstrates that it is implicit in his argument, and, in fact, was also implicit in the law that was given to Moses. Jesus does precisely the same thing in the Sermon on the Mount (Matthew 5), when he draws out the implications of Moses' laws, extending and applying them in ways far beyond the literalistic and minimalistic interpretations of the Pharisees.

The challenge and blessing of the third step of *sharing* is to identify, just as Paul did in the example above, the timeless, shared Truths that are being commended to us by the biblical authors in the texts that they have written.

A number of biblical interpreters refer to these eternal and universal Truths within the Bible with the term *principles*. And I myself have employed this term, though always somewhat uneasily (increasingly so recently). I stand in agreement with those who use this word in stressing the importance of seeking and clearly identifying the universal teachings of a passage. But the term *principle* is in some ways too limiting for what I wish to bring out in this third step of following the Bible. Instead of *principle*, I prefer the term *sharing*.

Approaching the Bible with a goal of deriving and assigning principles faces particular challenges and creates unfortunate tendencies. Here are the key problems with the practice of arriving at principles as I see them most often presented.

- It ultimately converts everything in the Bible into propositional statements. This reflects a truth-bias that Western culture has inherited from Aristotle onward. That all truths need to be expressed in propositions is a limitation that we may be imposing on the Bible (and ourselves) unnecessarily. Propositions may even present an obstacle to the truth when Christians interact with non-western thinkers (an increasing percentage even in the western world).

- It tends to steamroll over the literary diversity found within the Bible. Everything from symbolic and figurative language to parables, poems, and proverbs is reduced to factual statements.[12] The different literary styles of the Bible are not merely ornamental in order to keep our interest. They are fundamentally different perspectives for viewing the world.

- The Scriptures are predominantly a complex, extended story, telling readers what God is like by retelling his dynamic interactions with people rather than listing static, abstract statements of his properties and attributes.

- Principles also tend to overlook the emotional and spiritual effects that biblical authors intend for their readers, and instead stress, almost exclusively, the ideas (cognitive aspects) found in the text. In other words, principles are more for the head than the heart.

- Imaginative language, like so much of the literature of the Bible, is intended to evoke further thought and reflection by the readers. Once this language is distilled down into a propositional statement, however, the tendency is to think that it has been exhausted, we are done, and we should move on to something else. When this is the case, we have wrung the life out of the passage.[13]

- Principles also tend toward being action oriented—very frequently (though not necessarily) bringing out those things that we ought to *do* much more than how our emotions, imaginations, and attitudes are also being addressed.

In recommending to you the term and concept of *sharing* rather than *principles*, I hope to minimize or eliminate most of these tendencies. Following the Bible is a whole-person task that is bigger than things to know and do.

I have come up with some guidelines to keep in mind as you seek to identify and express the theological Truths in the Bible. These should prove to be useful as you develop your skills in following and sharing with others biblical Truth.

1. Shared Truth is *eternal*: It is not time-bound, locked into the ancient past.

Text	Poorly stated shared Truth	Better stated shared Truth
"If you do not believe that I AM, you will indeed die in your sins." (John 8:24)	"When Jesus was on earth, the Jews needed to believe in him." *Problem: This is a description of something which happened long ago, not a timeless statement.*	"Anyone who believes in Jesus does not die in sin. We should therefore actively respond to him by believing his claim to be God, and trusting in his solution to our sin problem."

2. Shared Truth is *universal*: It applies to a broad audience—to everyone.

Text	Poorly stated shared Truth	Better stated shared Truth
"You are still worldly. For since there is jealousy and quarreling among you, are you not worldly? . . . When one says, 'I follow Paul,' and another, 'I follow Apollos,' are you not mere men?" (1 Corinthians 3:3-4)	The Corinthian church had a problem with hero-worship. *Problem: This speaks only about one particular church (and also again describes only a past event).*	Division in the church indicates worldliness. We should be grieved by it and take measures (prayer, listening, and dialogue with one another, etc.) to eliminate divisiveness in churches.

3. The shared Truth should be drawn from careful attention to the first two steps of Bible study, *seeing* and *understanding*. It is not uncommon for people to "moralize" or spiritualize from the Bible. The difference between merely moralizing or spiritualizing and identifying shared Truth has to do with respecting the intentions of the author as presented in the written context of the Bible. In the story of Abraham's offering of Isaac, Genesis 22:3 reads, "Early the next morning Abraham got up and saddled his donkey." Someone might draw a moral from this verse: "It's best to get an early start when you start out on a trip." Yet the purpose of the text is not to instruct people in trip planning. The larger context is emphasizing the resolute faith of Abraham in God through this excruciating trial, the defining moment of his life. Biblical authors usually highlight their central idea through various techniques. (These are discussed in upcoming chapters). We should develop an eye for seeing and valuing what is important to the author. Reading the context closely and carefully while looking for what the author has highlighted can eliminate these misrepresentations of the text.

4. The shared Truth should reflect the same intended content that the author had in mind. In other words, it should be the same main point

as the entire passage. In the last chapter, we discussed the three level nature of communication. Texts communicate the authors' intended content (ideas), purpose (function), and response. The shared Truth that we're looking for should be the same main idea rather than "offshoots."

Text	Poorly stated shared Truth	Better stated shared Truth
"Love your neighbor as yourself." (Matthew 22:39)	In order to love other people, we must first accept and love ourselves. *Problem: It is not enough that a statement is true, or that it doesn't contradict the Bible, or that you can "find" it in a verse. The shared Truth must be either clearly stated or unquestionably implied as the same point the author is trying to make in the passage.*	We should love other people unselfishly.

5.   The shared Truth should reflect the same communication purpose that the author had in mind. For example, the shared Truth of a passage intended to offer thanks to God should therefore also express thanks to him; a passage intended to warn should have its shared Truth expressed as a warning, and so on.

Text	Poorly stated shared Truth	Better stated shared Truth
"You are my hiding place; you will protect me from trouble and surround me with songs of deliverance." (Psalm 32:7)	When we are in trouble, we should listen to Christian music. *Problem: This passage affirms confident, joyful hope in God and expresses thanks to him—it is not a command or urging readers to do something like listen to music.*	During times when we are specially overcome with our own sin (see context), we may be assured of God's protection and deliverance. It is therefore appropriate to express our thanks to him for his forgiveness.

Most of the shared Truths we encounter in the Bible fall into two very broad categories. There are those which are action oriented, intending the readers to obey through their behaviors. Then there are shared Truths that are intended to teach us so as to influence our attitudes, affections, feelings, and perspectives.

	Text	Shared Truth
Behavioral	"Let no debt remain outstanding, except the continuing debt to love one another, for he who loves his fellowman has fulfilled the law." (Romans 13:8)	We ought to express love to others, which is the "bottom line" behind all ethical laws (see context).
Teaching	"For I am convinced that neither death nor life, neither angels nor demons, neither the present nor the future, nor any powers, neither height nor depth, nor anything else in all creation, will be able to separate us from the love of God that is in Christ Jesus our Lord." (Romans 8:38-39)	Nothing can thwart God's love for those who are saved through faith in Jesus.

Again, if we are determined to *follow* the Bible, we need to ensure that the shared Truth we see in the passage preserves its intended purposes. If we use a passage for rebuking that is intended to bring comfort, then we are not following Scripture nor respecting its author.

6. Shared Truths that are developed across larger sections of text are generally more important than those drawn from short passages. The reasoning behind this is fairly simple: a Truth expressed in only a few words does not occupy the author's attention or emphasis the way that a Truth developed throughout a whole book does. Paul's exhortation, "Do everything without complaining or arguing" (Philippians 2:14) is a timeless, behavior-oriented Truth intended for all readers. But it merits less than a single complete sentence of Paul's attention in a book that lays repeated stress on adopting a Christ-like servant's attitude that promotes unity. As the old adage goes, "The main thing is that the main thing remains the main thing." As we seek to follow the text, we want to ensure that main ideas and purposes are given the emphasis that the authors have placed on them.

These guidelines are essential in order for us to be cooperative readers and faithful followers. The following guidelines fall more into the category of suggestions. They are not essential as we pursue timeless Truth in the Bible. The way that Truths are worded and expressed can have a bearing on how effectively people respond to them.

- Avoid using the second person ("you"), either stated or implied, when expressing the shared Truth. "You should avoid hypocrisy" is more abrasive and accusatory than "we should avoid hypocrisy." "You" carries a connotation of finger-pointing.

Text	Poorly stated shared Truth	Better stated shared Truth
"Each man should give what he has decided in his heart to give, not reluctantly or under compulsion, for God loves a cheerful giver." (2 Corinthians 9:7)	You should give willingly. *Problem: Implicit accusations that the people addressed are guilty of not doing this; could possibly sound mercenary.*	We should give willingly.

- Attempt to formulate the Truth as simply and clearly as possible. This includes staying away from complicated sentences and language, and using figures of speech only when they are very clear.

Poorly stated shared Truth	Better stated shared Truth
"God's eye is upon us through the storms of life."	"God cares for us during difficult times."
"Christian life is like a fresh spring shower across a parched and barren wasteland."	"Following God's Word enables us to enjoy life more fully."
"Because our almighty God is in absolute, sovereign control over his entire created order from galaxies to gluons, he possesses infinite omniscience of all things throughout the space and time continuum, including the minutest details of the lives of each and every person throughout history."	"God knows every detail of our lives."

There is no automatic formula for identifying the timeless, shared Truths in the text of Scripture. However, if you follow the guidelines given in this chapter, you will be on the right track. Let me review these briefly. (1) The shared Truth is eternal rather than only relevant to the age of antiquity. (2) The shared Truth is intended for a universal audience. (3) Careful attention to the previous steps of *seeing* and *understanding* will enable you to identify what the author most clearly intends to communicate. (4) The topic of the shared Truth will be the same as the author's content—the main idea being presented. (5) The shared Truth aims for the same purpose that the author had in mind. (6) Shared Truths taken from large sections of text, including entire books and beyond, have greater priority of emphasis over "smaller" Truths. Following these guidelines can remove much of the guesswork in identifying the Truths from the Bible that we are meant to follow.

Once we have reached conclusions regarding the Truths presented, it is possible to test further. A shared Truth is more likely to be valid and scripturally-endorsed if any of the conditions below apply.

- Is this Truth taught both before and after Christ's first coming?
  Point: If it was true in ancient Israel before Christ *and* also in the early church after Christ, then it is probably true for all time.
  Example: "The righteous will live by his faith" (Habakkuk. 2:4) occurs not only in Habakkuk, but also in Romans 1:17; Galatians 3:11; and Hebrews 10:38. It is very likely, then, that this is appropriate for all people of all times.

- Is the *reason* for a specific command given in the passage?
  Point: While sometimes a specific command was intended for a limited time and place, the reason behind the command applies to everyone.
  Example: "Therefore, if what I eat causes my brother to fall into sin, I will never eat meat again, so that I will not cause him to fall" (1 Corinthians 8:13). Here the issue isn't about what kinds of food to eat; the issue is avoiding activities that may cause others to sin.

- Does this statement inform readers about God?
  Point: Since God does not change, any statement about him made in the past is still true today.
  Example: "the LORD, the compassionate and gracious God, slow to anger, abounding in love and faithfulness" (Exodus 34:6, quoted elsewhere many times).

- Does it present a general reality about the character of human beings?
  Point: All people have certain things in common: (1) we are made in the image of God, (2) we are sin-contaminated, and (3) we have similar experiences (hope, frustration, shame, outrage,

discouragement, etc.). Therefore, general statements about humanity which reflect these common points are always true. *Example:* "He who conceals his sins does not prosper, but whoever confesses and renounces them finds mercy" (Proverbs 28:13). Shared Truth: "We should confess rather than conceal our sins."

- Is it a statement about the relationship of God and man?
  Point: There are Truths that describe the relationship between God and human beings generally.
  Examples: "God judges evil," "God forgives those who repent," etc.

- If the text is a narrative, does the author pass judgment in the text on what is happening in the story?
  Point: If the narrator says that what a person did is good, then that person is an example to us. If the narrator says that what a person did was wrong or if it is something that is clearly forbidden elsewhere in Scriptures, then that person is a negative example to us. If the author offers no evaluation within the text, then it is best to reserve judgment. That behavior might still be wrong, or perhaps right, or perhaps it makes no difference——look for a clearer passage (see chapter seven).
  Example: "After Yahweh had said these things to Job, he said to Eliphaz the Temanite, 'I am angry with you and your two friends, because *you have not spoken of me what is right, as my servant Job has'*" (Job 42:7). Job is a positive example; Eliphaz and his two friends are negative examples.

Let me conclude with one final thought. *Every* biblical passage is teaching eternal Truth intended for all mankind——this is the shareable element of the Scriptures. The issue is not whether some passages are intended to be relevant to a broader reading audience while others are not. Rather, we are looking at how the timeless Truth is being presented in the text. It is precisely the timeless and universal properties of shared Truth that make it relevant for everyone. As Simone Weil puts it, "To be always relevant, you have to say things which are eternal."[14]

CHAPTER SEVEN

Taking It Personally

Responding

The late Neil Postman was sometimes funny, sometimes irreverent, sometimes alarming, usually edgy, but he was always provocative. Like the "tactless" boy in Hans Christian Andersen's *The Emperor's New Clothes*[1] who blurted out the naked truth exposing the king and the foolish towns-people, Postman had a knack for seeing the obvious but unnoticed. He made public announcements in ways that embarrassed and sometimes infuriated his audiences. The widely published critic, writer, teacher, and communication theorist was a professor of communication at New York University. He "told on" the establishment on a variety of topics, including public education, democracy, childhood, and technology.

In one of his most powerful exposés, he took on television. He included a chapter on network news called, "Now . . . This,"[2] a very common catch-phrase that you hear almost exclusively on television news. He points out that this is a verbal bridge, a way of saying "and," except that it's a kind of anti-conjunction. Instead of joining two ideas together, it is a verbal sepa-rator. Two things presented back-to-back, which have nothing to do with one another——like a natural disaster in Bangladesh and the frontrunners for the upcoming Oscars, or a commercial for whiter teeth——are "linked" by the phrase, uttered so earnestly, "and now . . . this."

Postman is not merely engaging in grammatical nit-picking, however. He's sees a much larger issue at stake that relates to how humans com-municate knowledge itself through the means of television. The phrase, "Now . . . this,"

> indicate[s] that what one has just heard or seen has no relevance to what one is about to hear or see, or possibly to anything one is ever likely to hear or see. . . . [W]e are presented not only with fragmented

news but news without context, without consequences, without value, and therefore without essential seriousness; that is to say, news as pure entertainment.[3]

With over half a century of watching television news——"serious" television——in our collective social consciousness, we are clearly a culture accustomed to seeing information with no expectation whatsoever of doing anything about it. "Now . . . this," implies urgency and immediacy, but also complete change of topic, and the anchorperson's impassiveness is a cue to watchers that they, too, should remain removed, unemotional and unaffected by this information.

WE ARE CLEARLY
A CULTURE ACCUSTOMED TO SEEING INFORMATION WITH NO EXPECTATION WHATSOEVER OF DOING ANYTHING ABOUT IT.

Following this lead, we frequently are unresponsive and non-committal about what we "know," in part because we are so overwhelmed by a daily tidal wave of information that we couldn't possibly keep up with dwelling on its consequences for our lives. Rather than possessing knowledge that spurs us into action, for much of what we watch and hear we are simply passive observers——once described by education theorist John Dewey as practicing "the spectator theory of knowledge."[4] In the place of wisdom, we have developed a craving for sound bites, factoids, one liner politics, infomercials, edutainment, docudramas, and game show trivia. In contrast to Nietzsche's claim, knowledge is not power; it's the servant of entertainment, amusement, and marketing.

Actually, my point here is not to tell you to kill your television. Television is here to stay and is a dimension of our culture that cannot be ignored. But it has intensified two problems for our Bible reading. The first is the expectation that we shouldn't have to work very long before receiving a psycho-spiritual ("devotional") payoff. We'd like our blessings to come quickly and easily, without having to read too much or think too hard. But this is surely an unreasonable demand for one who genuinely wishes to follow the Bible, a point I've tried to stress in earlier chapters.

The second challenge, and the one I want to stress here, is that we have disconnected what we know from what we do. I'm sure we are not the first or only culture to do so. Both the prophets and Jesus severely rebuked those who "heard" the Truth, but who neither received it nor followed it. The Bible both explains and demonstrates that understanding and responding are inseparable. Those who claim to "know" the word of God but who are unmoved

THE BIBLE BOTH
EXPLAINS AND DEMONSTRATES THAT UNDERSTANDING AND RESPONDING ARE INSEPARABLE.

and either refuse or neglect to follow its Truth are deluded: they "do not know the Scriptures or the power of God" (Matthew 22:29). But perhaps our culture is even more prone to this disconnect between Truth and its consequences because it is such a common practice in our information overload everyday lifestyle.

The final step of the four-step method is *responding*. Responding asks the question, "So what?" It probes the implications of the Truth for my own life, personally and specifically.

Earlier, I presented the three levels of meaning that authors communicate: the *content* (the topic and ideas), the *purpose* (reason for writing), and the anticipated *response*. If we do not cooperate with the author's intention here by responding in a way that is appropriate to what the author had in mind, then the act of communication itself has failed. *Following* the Bible necessarily means doing something about what we read.

Suppose a young man comes running into a college classroom yelling, "Fire! Fire!" Each of the students in the room now needs to evaluate his intentions for performing this particular communicative action.

(1) The students recognize that the young man has just done something significant; he is trying to communicate a message.

(2) The students will probably also conclude that the young man meant to do this; this isn't something that happened "accidentally."

(3) The students assume that the young man must have a purpose for behaving in this way, especially if he has interrupted a class session to do so.

(4) Now the students must draw clues from this context, at all three levels of communication, to find out what the speaker intends:

Content—The students must interpret what the topic of discussion is—it has something to do with "fire"—and what the young man is trying to say about it. Is he talking about shooting someone? Terminating someone from his/her job position? Is he claiming that something is burning somewhere? Given the circumstances (that is, the context), the last of these possibilities seems much more likely than the first two.

Function—Now, each student mentally proposes a hypothesis to explain why the young man has interrupted the class to communicate this message. Their brains surge through a barrage of questions and answers, much faster than they even realize.

- Is this a prearranged teaching method which the teacher planned in order to make a point in today's lesson?

- Is this a skit intended to advertise an upcoming campus event, being performed with (or without) the instructor's permission?

- Is this a prank being pulled by a mischievous student (with a bad sense of propriety)?

- Is this a student demonstration intended to dramatize a perceived injustice somewhere in the world?

- Is this a warning of imminent danger to those sitting in the classroom?

The students may seek other "contextual" clues to help them decide on the questions above:

- What kind of facial expression and body language does the young man have?

- How is the professor responding to this interruption— surprise, anger, alarm, bemusement, etc.?

- Do the students recognize the young man as a teaching assistant for the professor?

- Has this young man performed other skits to advertise campus events?

- Does this young man have a reputation as a campus prankster?

- Is the young man wearing a campus security officer uniform or a local Fire Department uniform which would authorize him for making this announcement?

- Can they detect a whiff of smoke?

- How are the other classmates responding?

The students will then infer what they believe is most likely the intended purpose of the young man. If they sense that the contextual clues indicate seriousness, urgency, and alarm from somebody that they do not suspect is merely acting, then they will presumably take this message as a warning.

Response—Let's say that the students (and the professor) collectively have concluded that the young man is warning them about a fire which is burning in the nearby vicinity, imminently endangering their safety. Next they will have to determine an appropriate response to his message.

The following are included in reasonable, appropriate responses that are "acceptable" in the young man's intentions for telling the students this message:

- Fleeing from the building as quickly as possible.
- Rushing to the aid of a physically-challenged fellow student to assist his/her immediate departure.
- Running to the nearest telephone and dialing 9-1-1 to report a fire to the civil authorities.
- Finding the nearest fire extinguisher to help put out the fire if possible.
- Counting the number of people in the room to ensure that everyone is accounted for after exiting.

Other responses would be deemed less appropriate—questionable, but at least somewhat sensible:

- Grabbing a camera and taking pictures for use in the student newspaper or yearbook.
- Making a list of classroom equipment (with make and model numbers) likely to be damaged or destroyed if the fire should come into the classroom, so that any insurance claims would be as accurate as possible.

And other responses would be deemed inappropriate:

- Asking if anyone has marshmallows or wieners that could be roasted.
- Singing "This Little Light of Mine" or "Fire and Rain."
- Doing a rain dance.
- Writing a poem, newly inspired by the circumstances, about how breaking up with a girlfriend is like a fire in a school building.
- Fixing one's hair and makeup in order to look good in the event that a television crew shows up.

(5) The communication of the message "Fire! Fire!" will be successful if the meaning understood by the students in the classroom "agrees with" what the young man intended to accomplish through performing this act of communication. If the students have comprehended the content of message, the purpose behind it, and consequently responded in a manner

that fits with the young man's expectation, then genuine communication has taken place.

When broken down in this way, the whole procedure seems enormously complex. And actually it is. The remarkable thing about the human brain is that it can process this kind of information with speed and agility that is quite astonishing. If this situation were to occur in real life, the students would make up their minds in a matter of mere seconds.

Following the message of the Bible as I'm presenting it can also seem very complex, especially initially. However, I'm simply laying out something that our minds are adept at doing in order to emphasize a point. The Truth claims of the Bible have not been followed until or unless we *respond* in ways that are in keeping with the authors' intentions. We cannot truly claim to have encountered the Truth if we remain unchanged and unaffected. Furthermore, the changes and responses need to fit with the message and the purpose that the author had in mind in communicating to us.

Becoming the ideal reader of the Bible means that the reader desires to follow everything that the biblical author intends. The ideal reader carefully *sees* all that the author has communicated without importing his or her own ideas onto it (step one). The ideal reader identifies the author's message and *understands* how the author has presented his thoughts (step two). The ideal reader then determines from the text what Truths the author has offered that are intended to be *shared* among all readers throughout time (step three). Finally, the ideal reader demonstrates his or her willingness to comply with the author by responding in ways that are fitting with the author's expectations.

WE FOLLOW THE BIBLE WHEN WE RECOGNIZE THE VOICE OF GOD IN IT, CALLING US TO A NEW WAY OF ENVISIONING REALITY, AND LIVING ACCORDING TO THIS FRESHLY IMAGINED PERSPECTIVE.

In the previous illustration, the students' possible actions fit in a few categories. (1) Most of us would easily agree that some are appropriate, (2) others are perhaps surprising but comprehensible, and (3) some don't fit the situation at all. The ideal reader of the Bible may be characterized as a person who consistently strives to respond in the ways that are appropriate to the Truth as intended by the author. The Bible has achieved the goal of transforming us when we prove that we are willing participants to its Truth claims. It is not enough for us to read the Bible, or to study it. We follow the Bible when we recognize the voice of God in it, calling us to a new way of envisioning reality, and living according to this freshly imagined perspective.

The final step of *responding* is frequently referred to as "application." Earlier, I mentioned a weakness in using this term. While the Bible certainly does call for me to change my behaviors, application (as well as the term "obedience") tends to focus entirely on the outward actions to the point where the inward character is overlooked. As important as my actions are, the inward character is also of great concern. I've chosen the term *responding* to emphasize the heart and the head as well as the hands.

In Moses' farewell speech in Deuteronomy 30, again and again he intertwines obedience to God's commands with loving the Lord with all the heart. Loving God does involve obedient action, but also our affections, emotions, our attitudes, values, and our attention. It sounds a bit odd and inapt to say we should apply the verse, "Love the LORD your God," because of the connotation of doing things. *Responding* seems to be a more inclusive, holistic term that more appropriately involves our hearts, minds, and souls.

See how both outward behaviors and inward attitudes (thinking, values, perspectives, affections, and character) are combined in Paul's advice in Colossians chapter three. Thinking, feeling, and doing are interwoven, such that responding in the ways that Paul intends involves the whole person.

Colossians 3	Outward behaviors	Inward attitudes
"Set your hearts on things above . . . set your minds on things above" (v.1-2)		✓
"Rid yourselves of . . . anger, rage, malice, slander, and filthy language" (v.8)	✓	✓
"Do not lie to each other" (v.9)	✓	
"Clothe yourselves with compassion, kindness, humility, gentleness and patience" (v.12)	✓	✓
"Let the peace of Christ rule in your hearts" (v.15)		✓
"Be thankful" (v.15)	✓	✓
"Whatever you do, whether in word or deed, do it all in the name of the Lord Jesus" (v.17)	✓	✓
"Fathers, do not embitter your children" (v.21)	✓	
"Slaves, obey your earthly masters . . . with sincerity of heart and reverence for the Lord" (v.22)	✓	✓

Paul is urging his readers in each of these verses, engaging us and prompting us to live a new quality of life in light of the reconciliation we have with God through the work of Christ (see the wider context). We become ideal readers by affirming and practicing the Truths he presents in this context. To follow the Bible, we live out these Truths in practical, specific ways that include both actions and attitudes.

Imagination plays a vital role in this step. As God created humanity in his own image, one facet of our own god-likeness is that we have the capacity to reflect his own creativity. God is the Creator, forming everything that exists out of nothing (*ex nihilo*) by the power of his spoken word. None of us has the capacity to copy him in this; the First Law of Thermodynamics says we can't make something out of nothing. But we can put two things together in relationship in new and original ways. And that, in the simplest terms possible, is the essence of all forms of art. Art is the creating of new metaphors: the heat of battle is like this ballet; the aching anguish of lost love is like the sound of this music; the "feminine mystique" is like the inscrutable facial expression of this painting; the frivolity of spring is like the lines of this poem; the symmetry of marital love is seen in the fluid harmony of movement of this figure skating pair. Words, pictures, sounds, and movements are symbols, comparing one reality to another in unique, insightful ways.[5]

From the simplicity of Charles Schultz's line, "Happiness is a warm puppy," to the self-exalting, arrogant architecture of the Tower of Babel, to the "attitude" of a hip-hop hit, to the morbid heaviness of Steinbeck's *Of Mice and Men*, art is a way of imaging life. It creates a parallel, a comparison between things, that both draws upon and triggers new ways of seeing and being in the world.[6] Imagining the world in a different way lies at the heart of imaging it through artistic work.

In the courses that I teach on Bible study, I have given assignments that required the students to list specific application suggestions for themselves on the basis of the shared Truths they have discovered in the text. In observing their tendencies, I have been struck by two things: nearly all of their suggestions have to do with outward actions rather than attitudes, and they lack this element of imagination. What frequently happens is that, regardless of the shared Truth (from "Christ is the head of his body, the church" to "God promises never to leave his people" to "we should show compassion to society's outcasts"), the students suggest they "apply" the Truth to themselves by (1) reading the Bible more—e.g., memorizing some verses that state this Truth clearly or studying other passages that also deal with this subject, (2) praying more—somehow making this Truth a topic of conversation with God, and (3) writing about this Truth in their journal. But there must be more to *following* the Bible than this. When Habakkuk tells us that "the righteous shall live by his faith" (2:4), we have not fully cooperated with his intentions by memorizing the verse, doing a word study on "faith," praying a prayer of thanksgiving for salvation, and writing an entry about it in our journals. Though we might complete this checklist, our lives could remain unaffected by this potentially revolutionary Truth. Rather, the author intends to involve the reader's whole self in responding to this Truth by learning to trust God's wisdom, timing, will, and goodness for countless areas of our lives that may cause us anxiety: finances, work situations, family relationships, ministry responsibilities, etc.

THE WORLD ITSELF
CAN BE RE-CREATED IN OUR MINDS, NOT AS THE FRIVOLOUS FICTIONS OF WISHFUL THINKING, BUT BY MY FULLY EMBRACING THE FACT THAT GOD'S OWN VERSION OF REALITY, SEEN WITH EYES OF FAITH WHILE I READ THE SCRIPTURES, IS MORE ACCURATE, MORE TRUTHFUL, AND MORE SOUL SATISFYING THAN ANY RIVAL VERSION, INCLUDING (ESPECIALLY) THOSE IN WHICH I AM AT THE CENTER OF MY UNIVERSE OF REALITY.

Following the Bible is not about reforming our behaviors by strict rule keeping. Rather, it is an invitation to our imagination, offering to us whole new ways of seeing and being in the world in the ways that God describes it. God does not liberate us in Christ by giving us more and different laws, but by enabling us to look at literally everything from a different perspective, with a new reference point for reality. Instead of depending upon our eyesight to provide us with reliable information on the way things really are, we are offered hope by depending on faith-empowered imagination to conceive of things from a God's-eye view. The world itself can be re-created in our minds, not as the frivolous fictions of wishful thinking, but by my fully embracing the fact that God's own version of reality, seen with eyes of faith while I read the Scriptures, is more accurate, more truthful, and more soul satisfying than any rival version, including (especially) those in which I am at the center of my universe of reality.

Reading the Bible with the goal of creatively re-imagining the world, in ways that agree with God's own perspective, is light years removed from approaches to application that center on duties and obligations. Living life itself can be viewed as an artistic expression of "obedient" imaginations. If I am willing to buy into a whole new way of perceiving Truth and reality, then certain actions will make perfect sense, they will logically follow from having my mind reprogrammed. And this is precisely Paul's point in Romans 12 when, after sharing eleven chapters of mind-boggling, old-paradigm-smashing Truths, he then urges his readers to live "logically"

(Greek *logiken*, verse one) in keeping with these newly-seen realities. Freed from the constraints of old world thinking, our minds are transformed by these liberating Truths (verse two), and we are free to live according to a divine logic that is other worldly.

Our lives can then be lived as walking, breathing, animate works of art—"for we are God's workmanship [*poiema*, from which we get the English word "poetry"], created in Christ Jesus to do good works" (Ephesians 2:10). As we imagine the world really being as the Bible describes it, we artistically "render" the world around us, thinking, imagining, feeling, and acting in ways that cooperate, that fit with, the values of this invisible but very real kingdom of God. Francis Schaeffer fully understood this perspective:

> No work of art is more important than the Christian's own life, and every Christian is called upon to be an artist in this sense. He may have no gift of writing, no gift of composing or singing, but each man has the gift of creativity in terms of the way he lives his life. In this sense, the Christian life is to be an art work. The Christian life is to be a thing of truth and also a thing of beauty in the midst of a lost and despairing world.[7]

Responding to the Bible is a matter, then, of awakening our imaginations to living as if we are natives of a different world of thinking. And far from beating ourselves and others up for failure to perform according to legalistic rules, our Bible reading should be characterized by adopting the customs and "habits of the heart" that are the (super)natural result of sensibly cooperating with reality—what Paul calls "[living] a life worthy of the calling you have received" (Ephesians 4:1). It is a tragic mistake to pound the story of grace into a mere sourcebook for ethical rules.[8]

There is one other sense in which imagination plays an operative role in responding to the Bible. Adam and Eve were created "in God's own image." In other words, they were visible representations of God on earth. That image was marred through human sinfulness, leaving a flawed representation of God. But when Jesus became human, he was the perfect image of God on earth. In Colossians 1, Paul asserts that Christ is "the image of the invisible God" and that "God was pleased to have all his fullness dwell in him" (verses 15 and 19). With Jesus as our example, and with the Holy Spirit living within us, then, we are designed to be the physical presence of God on earth.

IT IS THROUGH

RESPONDING

THAT WE TRANSLATE OUR THEOLOGY INTO PERSONAL AUTOBIOGRAPHY

Following the Bible, then, is a form of re-imaging Jesus in today's world. As we imagine how Jesus would live in our present age, we image him in our lives. As Mary Warnock points out, "the production of images is the work, *par excellence*, of the imagination."[9] Our lives, inevitably, will either reflect the image of God, or distortions of him, that is, false images (idols of our own imagination). The way that we live is the best and final measure of the effectiveness of our Bible reading. God has revealed himself to us through the Bible that we might become like Jesus. To put it another way, it is through responding that we translate our theology into personal autobiography.

There is a familiar saying that goes, "For every complex problem, there is a solution that is simple, neat, and wrong."[10] The point is that complex problems are complex precisely because simplistic answers are inadequate. In the last chapter, I presented the problem of trying to import a specific biblical command or action directly over to today. That solution would be simple, not very neat, and very wrong. We would all need to move to Israel, refrain from eating shrimp salad, every fiftieth year we would reclaim for ourselves any property we have sold, and we would need to kiss everyone we wish to greet. The more complex yet appropriate way of dealing with issues like this is first to identify the shared Truth intended by the author to be universally relevant and profitable for all readers.

A friend of mine was preparing to take her driver's education course and wanted to be well prepared in advance in order to avoid any embarrassing mishaps. She studied and mentally rehearsed all the steps and procedures until everything felt just right. She prepared for changing lanes: indicate intention through using the turn signal, check the mirror, look over the shoulder to check the "blind spot," and gently steer into the lane. When the time came for her to actually perform this driving maneuver in moving from the slow lane into the passing lane, she performed each of the tasks in exactly the right order: she signaled, checked her mirrors, carefully looked over her *right* shoulder for traffic, and steered into the lane. Fortunately, no car was in the left lane because she never thought to look over her *left* shoulder first—after all, the manual hadn't specified *which* shoulder!

Though she had copied all the specified tasks just as they were written, she hadn't stopped to think *why* the driver would look over her shoulder. The thought hadn't occurred to her until she was enlightened by her driving instructor. Responding to the Bible is more complex than simply copying behaviors that are talked about—or ignoring them if we don't like the sound of them. It involves understanding why people did what they did, and asking what shared Truth underlies the actions.

I suggest that we ask the following questions to ensure that our response to the Bible is appropriate to what the author intended.

Identifying

- What is the shared Truth?
  The reader's response relates the universal Truth that is relevant for all people to the circumstances of his or her own life. This Truth is *what* the reader is responding to (the first level of communication discussed earlier).

- What is the author's purpose in communicating this Truth?
  Does this shared Truth appear in a context that was designed to affirm, to critique, to explain, to urge, to promise, etc.? The purpose determines *how* the reader is to respond (the second level of communication discussed earlier).

- Who needs to hear this message the most?
  The text may give clues as to what kind of people are being addressed most directly——e.g., the outwardly religious yet inwardly rebellious (Isaiah 1), those suffering catastrophic loss (Lamentations), those who are saved and fully adopted into God's "family" (Ephesians), those who have not understood that the essence of the gospel is diametrically opposed to self-righteousness (Galatians).

Imagining

- If the author's purpose is going to be fulfilled in my life, what will it look like?
  If this Truth was intended to foster hope, then the appropriate *response* is hopeful living, which will affect the reader's outlook as well as how he may handle a specific situation. If the text is meant to elicit thanks from the reader because of God's work on behalf of his people, then thanking God is the appropriate response.

- What implications does this truth have for my life?
  - How would I think differently if I was convinced that this Truth is really true, i.e., is reality?
  - How would I feel differently?
  - How would I behave differently?

- Does the text give me any clues for what is an (in)appropriate response?
  Often the context will either indicate commands or describe the responses of characters. Whether we are meant to follow this pattern identically or to adapt it in a different but comparable and suitable way can be discerned from the context (see flow chart below).

- If the author were present, would he approve of my attitudes, feelings, and actions in response to this Truth?
  We only genuinely know the Truth the author has shared when we have recognized its implications for our own lives, have adopted this new perspective on reality for ourselves, and live accordingly to it. Imaginatively, we would want the author (or the Hebrews 12 "cloud of witnesses") to nod enthusiastically and say, "Yes— that's exactly the way I meant for your life to be changed!"

Another way to approach the problem of whether or not we should adopt actions in the Bible is by using the following flow chart. It may help you to analyze whether a particular behavior that is presented in the Bible (whether commanded or merely described) should be adopted "as is." It involves answering a series of questions (all but the first question are yes or no), and then following the lines depending on your answers.

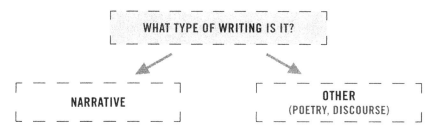

If it is a narrative, does the author interpret or pass judgment on that action in the text itself?

If the answer is "yes," does the author approve (e.g., "so the LORD gave them rest on every side") or disapprove (e.g., "and the anger of the LORD burned against him"). In either case, the next question is, "Is the author approving of general traits (e.g., obedience to a direct command, faith) or a specific action (e.g., sacrificing a son)?" If the answer is "no" (the author is not passing judgment or interpreting), is the same action given as a command elsewhere in the Bible? The rest of the narrative side of this flow chart looks like this:

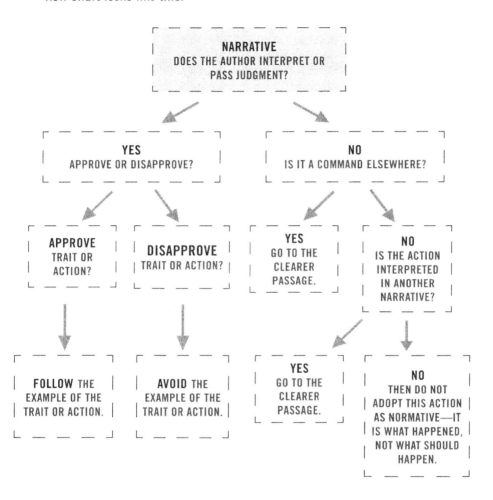

Let me offer two biblical examples to illustrate the process illustrated this chart. Daniel refused a direct edict from King Darius which forbid prayer to anyone but the king for thirty days (Daniel 6). *Is Daniel 6 a narrative?* Yes. *Does the author interpret or pass judgment?* In the story, violation of this edict required that the dissident be thrown into a den of lions. The king, bound by his own law, does so, yet announces his desire for Daniel's God to protect him. Darius remains sleepless all night. At first light, he discovers, to his great joy, that God has indeed protected Daniel. The king blesses and prospers Daniel, and issues an edict that all his people revere Daniel's God. So, yes, Daniel's actions are approved within the narrative.

Trait or action? Daniel was not protected for the act of disobeying the king. The text identifies for us the positive trait for which he was rewarded: "no wound was found on him, because *he had trusted in his God*" (6:23). The shared Truth in this story is that God delivers those who trust in him. According to the flow chart, then, we should *follow the example of the trait.* Our own *response* to this story might involve (1) reflecting on the circumstances of our own lives for those ways and areas where we are neglecting or failing to trust God, and adopting a new perspective on how we should view and act within our own situation, and (2) following Darius' example, we should revere God in thankful worship for rescuing those who trust in him.

In Judges 6, Gideon was commissioned by (the angel of) the LORD to lead Israel out of subjugation to Midian. Gideon first protests, then asks for a sign, and then another sign——both involving laying out a sheepskin ("fleece"). Is this passage teaching us to devise tests for God when seeking to discern his will for our lives? Let's look through the flow chart again. *Is Judges 6 a narrative?* Yes. *Does the author interpret or pass judgment?* No——there is no indication whether Gideon's action was right or wrong, although God does perform the requested signs. *Is this action ever given as a command in a passage elsewhere?* No, it is not. In fact, the opposite is commanded: "Do not test the LORD your God" (Deuteronomy 6:16).[11] *Is the action interpreted in another narrative?* No, this action is not repeated in any other Bible story.

What is the result from the flow chart? *Do* not *adopt this action as normative——it is what happened, not what should happen.* Just because something did take place within a biblical narrative does not mean that it was supposed to happen that way in order to serve as an example to all generations of readers of the biblical story. It has accurately described past events for us, not prescribed actions that we must take. The author's intent is not to convince us to imitate that particular course of action, but to learn from it some other shared Truth to which we should respond.

Now let's return to the first question on the flow chart again, but trace it out for non-narrative literature.

WHAT TYPE OF WRITING IS IT?

NARRATIVE

OTHER
(POETRY, DISCOURSE)

The next question to ask is, "Is the author or speaker in the text addressing a limited audience, (i.e., only an individual or a particular group of people)?"

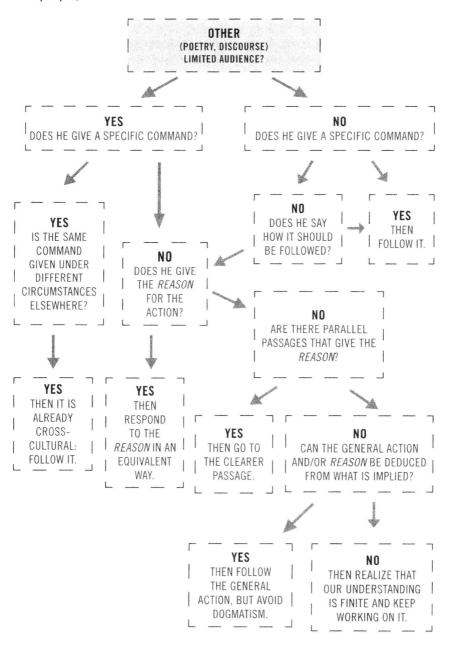

Let me again offer two biblical examples. Leviticus 7:26 states, "You must not eat the blood of any bird or animal." Beginning with the very top of the flow chart, *is this passage narrative or other?* It is a discourse. *Is this discourse addressed to a limited audience?* The answer is yes—these commands are specially intended for the Israelites, who have recently been drawn into a covenant relationship with God at Mount Sinai. *Does he give a specific command?* Yes—eating of blood is forbidden. *Is the same command given under different circumstances elsewhere?* Yes—in Genesis 9:4, God gives this command to Noah, from whom all humanity will descend: "You must not eat meat that has its lifeblood still in it."

In Acts 15, James addresses a council held in Jerusalem regarding whether or not Gentiles would be allowed equal participation in the newly formed church. After hearing testimonies from Peter, Barnabas, and Paul, all of whom speak in favor of Gentile inclusion, James offers the clinching argument, quoting from Amos 9, that it was in fact God's plan all along that all mankind should be included in the remnant that are called by God's name. He then continues, "We should write to them, telling them to abstain from food polluted by idols, from sexual immorality, from the meat of strangled animals and *from blood*" (verse 20). This command was given to humanity before the covenant at Sinai, within the covenant at Sinai, and after the covenant at Sinai and the formation of the church. Following the flow chart, then, *this command is already cross-cultural: follow it!*

In Leviticus 19:19, Moses tells the people, "Do not wear clothing woven of two kinds of material." *Is this passage narrative or another literary type?* Once again, it is discourse. *Does he address a limited audience?* Yes, it is still the Israelites under the covenant at Sinai, as in the example above. *Does he give a specific command?* Yes, it is a prohibition against blending fabrics for clothing. *Is the same command given under different circumstances elsewhere?* No. Although the command does have a parallel in Deuteronomy 22:11, the circumstances are the same: the Israelites, living in the wilderness under the requirements of the covenant at Sinai. *Does he give the* reason *for the action?* No, there is not a clear statement in this context that indicates the reason. *Are there parallel passages that give the* reason? No, the Deuteronomy context does not provide a clear statement of the reason either. *Can the general action and/or reason be deduced from what is implied?* Yes—in both contexts there are a number of covenant-specific regulations about blurring distinctions and separations, which is a reflection of the nature of holiness.

Holiness (being specially designated for covenant relationship with God) is the prominent shared Truth throughout the book of Leviticus. According to the flow chart, then, *follow the general action, but avoid dogmatism.* What might that look like for me today? I may choose to *respond* by adopting a mindset that even how I dress should be yielded to the higher priority of holiness. Thinking imaginatively, is there any way that my dress might reflect positively or negatively upon my calling to be holy? Yes, if God's holiness is granted me by virtue of Christ's sacrifice for me, then I may deliberately choose to dress in a way that will not draw attention to myself. I would rather dress in a way that would embody Christ, so that others who see me won't be distracted by my clothes in any way but will be more apt to see Christ within me. I'll neither overdress nor underdress, but instead seek to avoid attracting attention to my outward appearance, preferring others to see Jesus' character in me.

Hopefully, this flow chart can be a useful tool as you sort through various passages yourself. But please remember, it is only a tool to help you to think, not the final answer; it's the "simple solution" to our complex problem.

——— ——— ——— ——— ——— ——— ——— ——— ——— ——— ——— ———

Below are further perspectives regarding this final step of *responding*. They are intended as helps and insights rather than set rules.

- Responding is a matter of making Truth real, visible, and practical. It demonstrates the significance, relevance, and intended effects of the shared Truth that we encounter in the Bible.[12] We show that we truly understand the Bible only when we recognize its relevance to our personal life in new and different situations.

- While the Bible's message can be comprehended by the unsaved, the proper spiritual response that it calls for comes only through the Holy Spirit's work. The steps, strategies, and techniques for Bible study advocated in this book are in no way intended to replace the Holy Spirit's role in clarifying ("illuminating") the same Truth that he originally inspired in the Scriptures.

- The content, the purpose, and the response that the author intended are the criteria that readers should use to identify its shared Truth and how we are to respond to it. Some shared Truths are more informational in nature (e.g., God forgives those who genuinely repent), and therefore the way that we respond starts with adopting this new way of thinking and perceiving. Other shared Truths are intended to call us into action, and will therefore have a more directly behavioral response (e.g., we should not complain or argue).

- While shared Truth is universal to all people throughout history, responding is intensely personal and individual. How the Truth will be lived out is a unique interplay of the work of the Holy Spirit, the creative imagination of the reader, and the special circumstances of the reader's life.

- Some of our responses will be circumstantial: "Whenever I find myself hearing others gossip, I will either leave or confront the gossipers." Other responses will be pro-active: "I will make a point of praying for my boss on my way to work each weekday—that his misery would cause him to look for answers to his spiritual needs."

HOW THE TRUTH
WILL BE LIVED OUT IS A UNIQUE INTERPLAY OF THE WORK OF THE HOLY SPIRIT, THE CREATIVE IMAGINATION OF THE READER, AND THE SPECIAL CIRCUMSTANCES OF THE READER'S LIFE.

- It is often helpful to consider responses that are specific, measurable, and limited. "I will try to be more generous with my money in the future" sounds like a good intention rather than a resolve to action. Committing to monthly financial support of a set amount of money for a specific time period may instill a new habit and a new perspective—allowing a character trait to "get off the ground" through repeated actions. Several warnings are in order here, however. It is very easy for this to deteriorate into pharisaism, which is multiplying self-imposed rules upon ourselves. The dangers include becoming proud in our rule keeping, deluding ourselves into believing that we are righteous by what we do, comparing ourselves to others, or condemning ourselves when our self-discipline fails us. Nevertheless, despite these risks, imagining living out the shared Truth may very well involve some very concrete and practical responses.

- Responding starts with recognizing that we need to change. If our Bible reading ever leaves us feeling smug or self-satisfied, then we have certainly missed the point altogether. God's Truth changes lives, inwardly and outwardly. Until we sense a need and desire for change, we will lack the motivation for significant response.

- Ignoring or refusing to follow the Holy Spirit's direction in our lives on the basis of shared Truth will drive us from fellowship with God, crippling our ability even to see the Truth. According to Paul's terminology (Romans 1), there is a direct relationship between hard hearts and darkened minds.

- We should recognize that biblical authors intend some responses to be universal—they are commands for all to follow, and anyone who does not do so is sinning. Other responses are Spirit-guided convictions: if I neglect or refuse to follow the Spirit's leading in this area, then *I* am sinning, even if it is not sin for anyone else. Other responses are personal preferences, things which I may choose to do out of love for God rather than out of a sense of obligation. In these cases, if I choose not to perform this action in a certain situation, then it is not sin, and I should not feel guilty.

- There are many typical problem areas common to most people. As we imagine artistically portraying the Truth through the living drama of our lives, these are issues that we might consider: addictive habits, anxiety, attitudes toward others, boredom, conflicts in relationships, controlling emotions, crippling memories, depression, difficult circumstances, discouragement, financial issues, health, integrity, priorities, self-control, self-perception, self-preoccupation, serving others, struggles for power, trust, use of time, and unresolved guilt.

I have had the privilege of teaching God's Word to many people who were highly motivated about their spiritual lives. Yet I've come to agree with this axiom: people are not really interested in learning about the Bible; they're interested in learning about *themselves* from the Bible.[13] The Truth of the Bible is powerful, yet it is so often presented in ways that are stifling, accusatory, and deadening. I assume that you have reached this far in the book because you are serious about experiencing the power of God's Word in your own everyday life. The four-step process to which I'm urging you—*seeing, understanding, sharing,* and *responding*—only succeeds when all four steps are taken. Truth that has not yet been related to our lives in dramatic and practical ways is Truth that has not really been learned at all.

CHAPTER EIGHT

The Plot Thickens
Narrative

Our family had just arrived at a local Christian bookstore. My wife was looking for a particular book, and I was watching our two children, then ages four and six. I made my way to the children's section, selected a very interesting looking storybook, and took the children over to a kids' play area. Three or four other young children, unattended, were already there, watching a large screen television playing a video. I took my children into a corner and began to read aloud to them. As was my custom, I read dramatically, making faces and giving characters different voices, and entering into the story world. Out of the corner of my eye, I noticed that the other children had quit watching television and were attentively listening. Within a few pages, they were right up alongside my own children. Halfway through the thirty-page story, other children had appeared, seemingly out of nowhere. By the time the story was over, there were about fifteen children all circled around, together with three or four parents.

What is it about stories that people find so attractive? A good story, told well, is almost irresistible. Nearly everyone knows what it is like to stay up at night, much later than we should have, because we were caught up in a story that we just couldn't put down.

Recent research suggests that our brains are actually hardwired for narratives. Neurobiologist Mark Turner argues that, "*Story* is a basic principle of mind. Most of our experience, our knowledge, and our thinking is organized as stories."[1] He goes on to say that narrative structure is essential not only for effective communication but also for thinking itself. Children everywhere plead, "Tell [read] me a story!" This request isn't due to some biological craving for amusement, nor is it simply a demand for the undivided attention of an adult. Instead, it arises out of a genuine human need to make sense of life, something that is actually communicated best through storytelling. Through stories, we learn how to see patterns, how to understand people and the way that nature and things work; we discover the consequences of people's behaviors; we distinguish right from wrong; and we grasp the important things in life. Stories do not merely tell us about life; stories are the essential means for us to experience life. "We all live out narratives in our lives and we understand our own lives in terms of narratives,"[2] thinking, dreaming, planning, and imagining by rehearsing and playing out mental stories.[3]

It makes perfect sense, then, that the Bible is one great story—a meta-narrative, or perhaps mega-narrative. It begins like a story and ends like a story. We discover our self-identity by viewing ourselves within the story itself—not merely as observers but as active participants and actors within this great drama. We learn where we came from, how we should live, and what our final destiny will be, all in light of the biblical narrative, a great love story. Like ancient sailors steering their way through open oceans by the position of the stars, all of our points of orientation (origin, ethics, identity, and destiny) are found within the context of this mega-narrative.

WE LEARN WHERE WE CAME FROM, HOW WE SHOULD LIVE, AND WHAT OUR FINAL DESTINY WILL BE, ALL IN LIGHT OF THE BIBLICAL NARRATIVE, A GREAT LOVE STORY.

The Bible does not tell stories that illustrate something true apart from the story. The Bible tells a story that is *the* story, the story of which our human life is a part. It is not that stories are part of human life, but that human life is part of a story.[4]

Christians may be defined as those who share a common story, a community of people whose unity flows from the shared narrative we tell about ourselves. We are interdependent characters playing our roles in the same drama, scripted out for us in the Bible.

— — — — — — — — — — — — — — — — — —

The starting point in reading biblical narratives is to realize that the biblical authors have an important purpose: to show us a "God's-eye-view" of life. God wants people of all ages and all places to understand his plan. So the biblical authors had a holy agenda, a goal for writing: to change our thinking and behavior. In narratives, they have chosen the strategy of storytelling as the most effective way to influence us. Thus, while the stories are *about* other people, places, and times, they are really *for* us. Biblical characters serve as object lessons, illustrating patterns for how God operates in the world. "For everything that was written in the past was written to teach us, so that through endurance and the encouragement of the Scriptures we might have hope" (Romans 15:4).

Bible stories are not intended to be objective reports about past events. The authors have carefully and deliberately chosen what to say, and what to leave out. They also select *when* and *how* they tell us particular pieces of information. In doing so, the narrator can manipulate our perspective, surprise us, confuse us, enlighten us, keep us in suspense, make us feel superior in understanding to the characters in the story, influence our emotional reactions, and more.

CHRISTIANS MAY BE DEFINED AS THOSE WHO SHARE A COMMON STORY, A COMMUNITY OF PEOPLE WHOSE UNITY FLOWS FROM THE SHARED NARRATIVE WE TELL ABOUT OURSELVES.

As a result, the stories of the Bible are not primarily to teach us the *history* of past events, but eternal, universal Truths about reality.[5] Just as sharing our testimonies not only tells people about ourselves but about God and how we understand the world around us, so Bible stories are designed to (re)shape the way we view all of reality.[6] Or perhaps another way of saying this is that the world of the Bible presents an alternative story to the other, rival stories of reality.[7] It invites us to choose this world of grace, where a loving God takes the initiative in saving us, instead of people seeking their ultimate well being on their own terms.

Our task as Bible story readers is ultimately to ask, "What response or effect does the author have in mind for me in choosing to tell me this story, and in choosing to tell it in exactly this way?"

There are three elements that distinguish a narrative from other forms of communication. Every narrative has a setting, the environment in which the action takes place. It also includes characters, who are the participants in the actions. And it develops a plot, a series of events that are linked together. Whenever we are reading a biblical narrative, we should look for how these elements are presented by the author.

Setting

The setting is the "where" and "when" of a story, the surrounding "stage" where the action of the story takes place. In biblical narrative, the author influences the way we respond to the story by the way he describes the "narrative world." Careful attention to *what* the author chooses to tell us about the setting of the story, and *the way* he describes it, can give us clues to the overall impact and meaning of the text as a whole. Always assume that every detail about the setting is important. Setting is comprised of two elements: *place* and *time*.

In the Bible, *places* are not only real locations, but also contain meaning. Frequently the geographical location and/or physical circumstances themselves convey a stereotypical atmosphere, and therefore influence the meaning of the action. Today in America, Las Vegas is associated with gambling, New York with big time entertainment, Florida as a place for retirees, Hollywood with movie star glitz, and Washington, D.C. with power politics. These settings have all gained a character because of unique patterns that are frequently seen there.

ALWAYS ASSUME
THAT EVERY DETAIL ABOUT THE SETTING IS IMPORTANT.

Biblical settings likewise are stigmatized because typical things come to be associated with them. For instance, the Bible consistently portrays the sea as a threat, a dangerous place to be (there are several sea storm stories in the Bible). The wilderness is both a difficult place to survive and a place where people must learn to trust in God to provide for their needs. When settings are consistently connected with certain events, they are called "type-scenes."[8]

Numerous places in the Bible should create for us consistent literary and theological associations. These places include:

Jerusalem / Zion	the Temple	North
Samaria	Bethel	East
Babel / Babylon	Egypt	Galilee
Jericho	Nineveh / Assyria	Edom
Moab	Sinai / Horeb	the Jordan River
"the land"	Sodom and Gomorrah	garden / pasture

There are many other significant places in the Bible. In order to discover these, check out all place names in a particular narrative in a Bible concordance to see if similar events typically take place there.

Setting also includes the *time* the story takes place. Just as with place, time can also convey a "mood" (e.g., winter, night, the Sabbath, dawn, sheep shearing time, the Passover, etc.). What big-picture events are going on at the same time? A famine? A harvest? If an episode is introduced with a time reference to a king, is this king an Israelite (a good sign) or a foreign king (a bad sign, indicating that Israel was under foreign power); and if the king is Israelite, is he a good king or an evil one?

The time that it takes for a reader to read the text (called "narrative time") is not the same as the amount of time required for those events to have actually happened in real life. The author may choose to tell us the events or give us information that is in a different sequence than the way it actually happened. In Bible stories, literary and theological reasons usually govern the author's decisions regarding the order of presentation. The following are different ways that the author may use time in storytelling:

- *Chronological succession*: This is a straightforward sequence of events: "First, *a* happened, then *b*, next *c*, and finally the result was *d*."

- *Foreshadowing*: Foreshadowing occurs when the author gives the reader a "sneak preview" into what will happen in the future. This is a technique frequently used by John: e.g., "The Jews replied, 'It has taken forty-six years to build this temple, and you are going to raise it in three days?' But the temple he had spoken of was his body. *After he was raised from the dead, his disciples recalled what he had said. Then they believed the Scripture and the words that Jesus had spoken*" (John 2:20-22).

  Foreshadowing can be done in several ways:

  a. Prophetic prediction: rebuilding of Jericho at the expense of the death of the builder's sons (see Joshua 6:26 and 1 Kings 16:34).

  b. Direct comment by narrator: "(He meant Judas, the son of Simon Iscariot, who, though one of the Twelve, was later to betray him.)" (John 6:71).

  c. Predictive or portentous statement made by one of the characters in the story: "Just as Moses lifted up the snake in the desert, so the Son of Man must be lifted up" (John 3:14).

  d. Analogy: when we encounter a story that is similar to a previous story, we sense what is about to happen; we take the previous occurrence as the norm for what is unfolding in the current context. For example, when, because of famine, Isaac goes to a foreign king along with his wife, you suspect he will try to lie about and give away his wife just as his father Abraham did (twice!).

- *Flashback*: Flashback occurs when the storyline is interrupted to provide us with details that occurred previously, but which are only just now important to understanding what is happening in the story: "(His disciples had gone into the town to buy food)," which explains why Jesus was alone with the Samaritan woman at the well (John 4:8).

- *Freeze*: Freeze occurs when, in the middle of presenting the actions and events of a story, the author interrupts the action in order to give us some other kind of information. In other words, the action stalls and waits for something else to happen. Freezing the action creates *suspense*, and thereby draws us into the story, as well as heightens the dramatic impact of the climax. This can be done by lengthening the sentences, becoming redundant, inserting a prayer or a poem, digressing, providing description or explanation, etc.

  Freezing the action may be necessary for the author to provide us with *description* of either some aspect of a character within the story ("Now Esau was a hairy man") or of something in the setting ("meanwhile the storm was worsening").

- *Explanation* occurs when the author provides additional information that is necessary for readers to understand or recognize the significance of what is happening: "Finally the other disciple, who had reached the tomb first, also went inside. He saw and believed. (*They still did not understand from Scripture that Jesus had to rise from the dead.*)" (John 20:8-9).

- *Gapping*: Authors sometimes leave gaps in the plot to entice us to become involved in the story as we guess at what was intentionally omitted. Thus they tease us into coming up with theories and interpretations as we read along. There are several effects of gapping. First, it makes for more interesting reading as we become more active participants in the reading process. Second, if our interpretive guesses turn out right, we feel somewhat superior as being a clever and enlightened reader— and we feel a special kinship with the author. Third, the author may surprise us with something unexpected, and we feel a sudden flash of insight as we "get it." Finally, if I discover that my initial interpretive guess was wrong, then I am especially vulnerable to the author's poin; usually we are guilty of the same sins, weaknesses, and problems as the characters in the story.[9]

Though biblical authors will sometimes withhold clues that would help us figure things out more quickly and easily, a literary tactic that creates suspense, it is always clear that God is never uncertain about the future——as sovereign Lord, he knows about and controls all outcomes.

Occasionally, the setting may even function as an opposing force to the characters when it challenges their survival. We see this is in stories recounting storms at sea, hunger and thirst in the wilderness, extreme heat, etc.

Characters

Stories develop by the interaction of characters and plot. Characters are the *who* of the story, while the plot tells us what the "who's" are doing. Biblical authors shape the way we view characters using a number of ways. *Characterization* is the term used to describe how the author creatively shapes the way we perceive each person in the story. Even when the biblical record is historically factual, the authors always shape the characters by what they choose to tell us about them.[10]

The characters make the story come alive. Authors may reveal them to us by name (if the name has a meaning, it is often indicative of character), status (king, widow, rich, old), profession (shepherd, prophet, tax collector, prostitute), nationality (Philistine, Samaritan) or tribe (Levite, Benjaminite), physical traits (beautiful, lame, ruddy, leper, long-haired),[11] and personality traits (wise, foolish, meek, cunning, righteous).

What these characters have to say——about God, about themselves, and about others——says a lot about them. What other characters say about them also helps us understand them better. And what the narrator of the story says is reliable. But what *God* says about them is what it is——he has the most accurate opinion! Here are some of the ways that our impressions about characters are shaped, some more direct than others.

- *Narrative Comment* (direct) occurs when the storyteller actually passes a judgment on the character. For example, "His name was Nabal and his wife's name was Abigail. *She was an intelligent and beautiful woman, but her husband, a Calebite, was surly and mean in his dealings"* (1 Samuel 25:3). These kinds of statements are *not* frequent in the Bible.

- *Comments of other characters* (direct) occur when another, reliable character within the story passes judgment upon someone: "When Jesus saw Nathanael approaching, he said of him, '*Here is a true Israelite, in whom there is nothing false*'" (John 1:47).

- *Speech* (indirect): Here the storyteller lets the characters speak for themselves and leaves it up to the reader to evaluate whether their comments reflect positively or negatively upon them.

- *Thoughts* (indirect): In this case, the storyteller gets in the character's head, telling us what the character is thinking or feeling inside. Again the reader is left to determine whether that character is good or bad: "Absalom never said a word to Amnon, either good or bad; *he hated Amnon because he had disgraced his sister Tamar*" (2 Samuel 13:22).

- *Self-description* (indirect): Sometimes the storyteller allows characters to describe themselves and lets the reader draw his or her own conclusion. Self-description cannot be taken at face value, however, for a boastful person is characterized best by listening to his boasting: "[King Nebuchadnezzar] said, 'Is not this the great Babylon I have built as the royal residence, *by my mighty power and for the glory of my majesty?*'" (Daniel 4:30). Also an evil person may lie or be self-deceived.

- *Action* (indirect): Biblical narrators usually let their characters' actions do the talking—our opinion of them is shaped by their action, which we must interpret (e.g., Moses breaking the tablets [Exodus 32:19] and Jesus frequently withdrawing to pray alone).

- *Abilities* (indirect): Readers draw clues about characters from their abilities: Apollos' ability to teach about Jesus with great fervor and accuracy (Acts 18:24-28); "There were seven hundred chosen men who were left-handed, each of whom could sling a stone at a hair and not miss" (Judges 20:16).

- *Location*: Where a person chooses to be often tells us about him or her: John the Baptist living in the wilderness; Naomi living in Moab (Ruth); Esther and Mordecai living in Susa, i.e., Persia.

- *Contrasts*: A character is often seen in juxtaposition with another to highlight certain traits: Esau is seen as a primitive, impulsive, and ignorant outdoorsman compared to Jacob who is a shrewd, calculating, manipulating "mama's-boy." Besides contrasting a character with another character, sometimes an author contrasts a character with what that character was like previously (e.g., Saul/Paul), or with what you expect of that character (e.g., a Samaritan who was a good neighbor to a Jew).

There are four factors that are very helpful to consider when studying character: *depth, dynamic, roles,* and *identification.*

Depth

It is common when studying narrative literature to distinguish characters as either *flat* or *round. Flat* characters have only one or two features or traits, and serve as a kind of background to the main characters. They're like the wicked stepmother in Cinderella: all you really know about her is that she's mean and wicked (like Goliath in 1 Samuel 17). If they're bad, we don't see good traits. Sometimes, a whole group serves as a flat character (e.g., the crowd at Jesus' trial, the grumbling Israelites in the wilderness). By contrast, *round* characters are complicated, having a multifaceted personality, emotional variations, doing both good and evil, and possessing sometimes conflicting traits, like Abraham, Naomi, David, Peter—and the rest of us![12]

Dynamic

Another way to understand characters is to note whether they are *static* (unchanging and predictable) or *developing* (undergoing change, either for better or for worse). Unlike the static ones (for example, Eli's wicked sons in 1 Samuel 2:12-4:11), developing characters are different at the end of the story from what they were at the beginning (like Jesus' disciples).

The Truth of the Bible forces a response from people, so the stories of the Bible describe people whose lives are changed. That means that most of the characters within the Bible who are very well developed are not static but changing, for good or bad. A consistent theme throughout the Bible is the weak, poor, and humble becoming strong, rich, and powerful, and vice versa. Compared to God, even the most powerful human personalities and nations are insignificant: the exalted are humbled. On the other hand, even the lowliest person is of infinite value to God: the humble are exalted. As a result, many Bible stories present before-and-after pictures of their main characters. Reversal of circumstances is a frequent motif. As Conrad Hyers suggests, in the Bible, "[G]iants are felled, and underlings are victorious. Tyrants are defeated and slaves liberated. Beautiful people are splattered with mud and Cinderellas fitted with glass slippers. Despite our love of greatness, the Bible does not offer the kind of heroic literature that emphasizes and eulogizes human greatness. The Bible, in fact, has very little to say about human greatness. . . . Like comedy, the biblical impulse is to find foolishness in wisdom and wisdom in foolishness."[13]

God is not at all impressed with human importance, and is especially opposed to human self-importance and those suffering from a superiority complex.

Roles

It is also possible to categorize characters like this:

Protagonist	The central character of a story is called the *protagonist*. Of course, "in the final analysis, God is the hero of all biblical narratives."[14] But the protagonist is the one on whom the narrator has specially focused in the telling of a particular story—the one the narrator is following with the "spotlight."
Antagonist	A character opposing the protagonist is called an *antagonist*. This does not have to do with goodness (i.e., an "antagonistic" attitude) but with role—e.g., the story can focus on an evil person (the protagonist) who is being opposed by (the all-good) God (the antagonist).
Foil	A *foil* is a character who serves as a contrast to another character—e.g., the young men who ate the royal food of Nebuchadnezzar serve as foils to Daniel, Hananiah, Mishael, and Azariah, who ate vegetables and water (Daniel 1).
Satiric Portrait	A *satiric portrait* is a character who is held up for ridicule by the author—e.g., Ahab the king (a supposedly powerful person) is completely dominated and overshadowed by both Elijah the prophet and his own wife Jezebel (1 Kings 16-22).
Entourage	The *entourage* consists of those who accompany either the protagonist or antagonist. David's mighty men (2 Samuel 23:8-39) were his entourage.
Stereotype	A *stereotype* is a flat figure that fits into a category, like a proud king, a self-righteous Pharisee, an outcast leper, or a brave warrior.
Agent	An *agent* is one who lacks any distinguishing traits but performs an action necessary to the plot.

Identification

The final aspect to consider with a character is how much we identify with him or her, and if so, whether positively or negatively. In other words, I may see myself in a particular character's sins (Thomas' lack of faith) or good traits (David's passion for worship). Some characters tend to arouse strong feelings of liking or disliking, while with others we sense little or no connection.

Thus with identification, I see a continuum, which looks like this:

Strong	Weak	Strong
liking		disliking

One reason why the Bible speaks so powerfully to us is that even the heroes are shown with all their flaws. Unlike personages in other religious writings, they are shown as real people, believably "normal," with whom we can identify more easily. "Biblical stories present patriarchs, matriarchs, and disciples not as perfectly faithful and ethical persons whom we could not hope to emulate but, rather, as persons who are often immoral, unfaithful, and thickheaded. Therefore, in spite of our own failings, we, too, can hope to be disciples."[15]

Putting it all together, these are the things to look for in considering biblical characters.

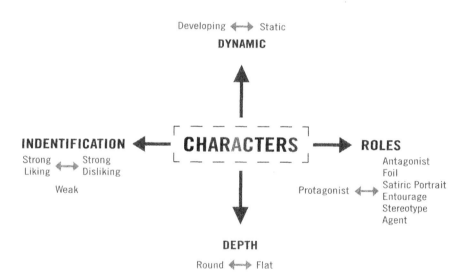

Getting to know a character in a Bible story requires us to continually adjust our opinion of that person,[16] just as we continually update our opinion of the real people we encounter in our own everyday lives. It involves interpretive leaps and tentative conclusions that we hold until some new element forces us to alter our opinion. In studying characters, then, we are doing the same thing that we do in studying plot or setting: the more attention we pay to detail, the more we see in the text and the better we are able to explain what is happening in the text. The more we see what is *not*

there (and is supposed to be), the more accurate our understanding of the meaning of the entire story will be.[17]

Plot

Biblical narratives teach us Truth by telling us stories. In a story, things happen, and the way that these things happen makes up the plot of that story. Because Bible stories are Scripture, they cannot be read merely for entertainment; they communicate Truth about reality. We can actually learn *more* about our lives from reading Bible stories than from our own experiences. This is due to two reasons.

First, when we read a Bible story, we know that every event that is described will be significant. The narratives of the Bible are told in an extremely economical way: every detail is important; there is no embellishment. In real life, we have great difficulty determining what things are most important, that is, what our priorities should be and which events in our life will actually affect us and others the most in the long run.

Second, when we read a Bible story, we know that all of the events will relate to one another. The Bible pre-screens and filters human experience, sifting out the important from the other "stuff." A key aspect of plot is that it always presumes that events have cause-and-effect relationships: one action necessarily leads to the next, and each incident also has a dramatic effect upon us, the readers.[18]

A KEY ASPECT OF PLOT IS THAT IT ALWAYS PRESUMES THAT EVENTS HAVE CAUSE-AND-EFFECT RELATIONSHIPS: ONE ACTION NECESSARILY LEADS TO THE NEXT, AND EACH INCIDENT ALSO HAS A DRAMATIC EFFECT UPON US, THE READERS

We need to recognize that in Bible stories, the narrators have very carefully selected and arranged every detail— giving us precisely the right amount of information, in precisely the right order, and at just the right time to cause us to view Truth the way they wish us to view it. Alan Culpepper comments that "The plot interprets events by placing them in a sequence, a context, a narrative world, which defines their meaning. The events are then secondary to the story or message which gives them meaning."[19]

Plot Movement

The plot is the story line—the thing that keeps things moving. The typical story revolves around a *conflict* of some kind, and progresses through these six stages.

- *Opening*: the setting is described and one or more of the characters introduced, but usually no action has begun.

- *Conflict*: the protagonist encounters a problem or takes on some kind of task. There are various kinds of *opponents* that a character might face in conflict: *God* (through sin or through testing), *other human characters* within the story, *spiritual beings, nature or physical hardships, oneself* (inner struggling with conflicting beliefs, emotions, or behaviors).[20]

- *Intensity*: more complications arise, making the task even more difficult—from bad to worse.

- *Climax*: "do or die," "make it or break it," the turning point (crux) of the story.

- *Resolution*: the task is completed (or ended in failure), and the loose ends are tied off (denouement).

- *Ending*: there may be comments by the narrator that evaluate the action, or indication that the protagonist has gained knowledge; often others benefit from his or her success.

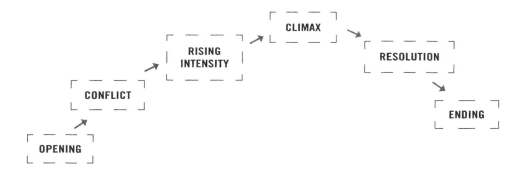

The plot, then, is a chain of interconnected events, deliberately arranged to influence the reader with meaningful Truth, arousing the reader's interest or emotions, and giving meaning to the events.[21] Authors draw us into the story by causing us to identify with what is happening to the characters in the plot, either by having us root for a particular character, or sympathize with the character through misfortune, or by having us boo another character. The point is that the author causes us to root, sympathize, or boo through a careful narrative strategy that guides the telling of the story. As interpreters, we need to identify which of these responses the author is eliciting from us, how he does it, and what we should do in light of the story.

Plot Type

It is customary in literature classes to distinguish between two types of plot: tragedy and comedy. Traditionally, *tragedy* takes characters that are noble or superior in quality to other human beings, throws overwhelming problems at them, and shows how they maintain their dignity and integrity to the bitter end, finally being utterly defeated, yet heroically refusing to compromise their virtuous character. If this is to be the definition of tragedy, then there are no clear examples of tragedy in the entire Bible.[22]

In the same way, *comedy* in literature generally portrays a main character that is more ordinary than heroic, but who ultimately overcomes all obstacles to emerge triumphant. (Comedy is not necessarily funny, the way we usually use the word).

THERE ARE NO HUMAN HEROES IN AN ULTIMATE SENSE. GOD ALONE IS CHAMPION AND ADVOCATE FOR THE HUMAN RACE, THE SOURCE OF EVERY GOOD THING.

However, when dealing with biblical literature, these definitions aren't helpful at all, mostly because they are both so human-centered——they focus almost exclusively on the deeds of people rather than on the role of God. Tragedy typically idealizes the human spirit, presenting characters as noble, principled, and good. In the Bible, while humans are granted special dignity as bearers of the image of God, the emphasis remains that no human being is essentially righteous; no one is deserving of God's blessing based upon his or her own personal character, but only because of the grace of God. In other words, there are no human heroes in an ultimate sense. God alone is champion and advocate for the human race, the source of every good thing.

Yet, it is possible, and still appropriate, to continue to use the terms *tragedy* and *comedy* for discussing biblical plots, but only if we redefine the categories. Simply put, *tragedy* refers to plots in which the main character (the protagonist) sets out to accomplish some objective, but ultimately fails to achieve that objective, or any other comparably good objective. Sometimes, the tragic figure will merely fail, other times he or she may die in the attempt. For example, Samson's life ends tragically, for although he kills many Philistines as their temple collapses, he dies in the process. Other examples of *tragedy* by this definition include Moses' failure to enter the promised land, the failure of the tribes of Israel to conquer the inhabitants of Canaan during the period of the judges, the failure of Nehemiah to effect any lasting spiritual reform among his contemporaries, and the failure of the kingly Davidic heirs to uphold Torah (see 1-2 Chronicles).

On the other hand, *comedy* occurs when the protagonist's initial objective is met or exceeded in the end. Further, unlike most other comedies in literature, the success is not due to the human character's strength, skill, cunning, or luck, but to the grace of God, who either empowers the protagonist or intervenes to rescue him or her.

Analyzing a plot for a biblical story involves answering each of the following related questions:

- Who is the protagonist in the story?
- What is his or her calling, desire, or objective?
- Are the objectives realized (or exceeded) in the narrative?

If these objectives or desires are met, then the story can be seen as a *comedy*. *Comedy* typically starts by identifying who the protagonist is. Often the protagonist will gather a "motley crew" of associates (the protagonist's entourage): for example, Moses and the Israelites, Jesus and his disciples. Then the story will reveal the protagonist's goals or desires, followed by the arrival of obstacles or enemies that threaten to thwart the hero's goals. Eventually, due to the intervention of God's grace, the protagonist prevails and succeeds, despite his or her own sinfulness. Frequently, the protagonist has learned the lesson of grace and extends it to the enemies who opposed him or her. The story then climaxes in a victory celebration. Most Bible stories do not contain every one of these elements, but enough of these elements are present to recognize the pattern.

Introduction	Moses	David
Calling, desires, or objectives	Special commission to lead Hebrew slaves out of Egypt, prophet, priest	Anointed to succeed Saul as king of Israel
Unlikely entourage	Aaron, Joshua Jethro, Miriam, Zipporah Israelites	Jonathan Philistines (!) His band of mighty men
Obstacles	Pharaoh, Egyptian troops, Red Sea, destitution of wilderness, disobedience and grumbling of Israelites	Saul is still ruling, and repeatedly tries to kill him; Philistine enemies; repeated crises within his family
God's grace	Deliverance from Egypt, receiving direct revelation from God, miraculous empowerment, daily provision of manna, covenant relationship with God	Repeatedly protects David from Goliath, Saul, other enemies; establishes eternal covenant of blessing with David's offspring
Protagonist prevails	Successfully leads people out of Egypt, there has never been anyone else like him	Becomes king, the measure of all succeeding kings, receives forgiveness for sins
Sinful failure	Lack of faith by striking the rock	Adultery with Bathsheba, murder of Uriah
Extends grace	Intercedes for his people who deserve punishment	Spares Saul, shows kindness to Saul's household
Victory celebration	Moses' song by the sea	Joyful bringing of the ark and tabernacle to David's city

The conclusion of the story is the key factor to study carefully when reading a story—how it ends is all-important. [23] What changes have taken place in the telling of the story? How has the main character changed in his or her behavior? Thinking? Morals? What has he or she learned? How has God been revealed through the events? How have the secondary characters changed? How have the opponents changed? How have the circumstances changed? Does the story conclude on a good note or a bad note? Is there a clear sense of ending, or is it open-ended and unresolved?[24] If the story stops before a satisfactory resolution, we are left with a hanging ending (like the ending of Genesis or Deuteronomy). This lack of closure tends to frustrate us, but also keeps us reading into the next book. If this is the case, why has the storyteller *not* told us the rest of the story?

Here, then, are elements to observe as we read for the plot.

TYPE
TRAGEDY (OBJECTIVE MISSED)
COMEDY (OBJECTIVE REACHED)
HANGING (UNRESOLVED)

OPPONENT
GOD
(AN)OTHER PERSON(S)
SPIRITS
NATURE/CIRCUMSTANCES
SELF

PLOT CONFLICT

MOVEMENT
OPENING
CONFLICT
INTENSITY
CLIMAX
RESOLUTION
EVALUATION

Style (or Technique)

The clearest and best argument for the fact that God did not simply dictate the Bible to human authors is that there is so much literary variety from one book to the next. Even in comparing the narrative parts of the Bible, there is significant diversity, not just in different events being told, but also in how these stories are told. There are a number of variables that can be compared, each of which may have significant bearing upon the Truths that are intended by the author. These techniques are used strategically to highlight main ideas and draw out their significance.

While each of these techniques perhaps deserves much more extensive treatment, here is a brief introduction to each.

Allusion

Some biblical stories refer back to other, earlier passages of the Bible. This can be done in several ways. The most obvious of these is a *direct quotation*. For example, in his lengthy prayer, Nehemiah says to God, "You are a forgiving God, gracious and compassionate, slow to anger and abounding in love" (Nehemiah 9:17). Here he is quoting from Exodus 34:6, when Moses is dialoguing with the Lord. When this happens, it invites further comparison between the two passages. In this case, both Moses and Nehemiah serve as intercessors, praying for and on behalf of the sinful people they represent. Both Moses and Nehemiah have served directly under a foreign king in his court, during a time when the Israelites have been out of the land under that king's rule. Moses has just led the people out of their Egyptian captivity, while Nehemiah lives during the time when the Jews are also returning to the land after being in captivity. And in both situations, God's gracious character provides the grounds on which they can hope for forgiveness and grace and blessing as they enter into the land.

Frequently the events of one story sound very familiar, because they are similar to the events of an earlier story. In these *parallel plots*, again we can profitably consider the significance of these similarities as well as differences. Upon hearing from the Magi that the promised king of the Jews has been recently born, and then consulting with the Jewish religious leaders to discover that Messiah's birth would be in Bethlehem, Herod orders all babies under the age of two to be killed (Matthew 2). This is not the first time that a foreign king has ordered the killing of Israelite male infants. Pharaoh did the same thing, though for different reasons, during the time of Moses' birth (Exodus 1-2). In each situation, God miraculously preserves the special babies Jesus and Moses. In Moses' case, he is spared from Egypt's threat; in Jesus' case, he is spared by going to Egypt. In both cases, they will eventually come out of Egypt. What is the significance of this parallel? Matthew uniquely presents Jesus as a new Moses—like Moses, but better than him. Both are deliverers of God's people, prophets, priests, and the spokesmen of a covenant between God and his people. They also explain God's commands on a mount, spend forty days and nights in the wilderness without food or water, and have a radiant face. While Hebrews draws out at great length a comparison and contrast between the old and new covenants, Matthew accomplishes this in narrative form through parallel plots between the two figures.

Biblical stories may also refer to one another through *type scenes*, where similar things happen at the same venue (see Setting above), and through *stereotypical characters*, where characters fit predictable roles (see Characters above). Frequently, there are shared *motifs* and *vocabulary* (like light and darkness and the spoken word in Genesis 1 and John 1) that also invite linking two or more passages together. Some biblical authors make profuse use of allusion, as seen in John's Gospel.

Forms

The author can also choose from a wide variety of literary forms. These may include stylistic features such as a prologue, commission, birth announcement, genealogy, as well as the baseline form of history. (For a complete listing of these forms, see the Appendix.)

Gapping and Suspense

Authors sometimes leave *gaps* in the plot on purpose, to entice us to become involved in the story. A gap is a missing piece of information or an unanswered question raised by the text, deliberately withheld but necessary to making sense of the story. Readers take the bait by getting caught up into a guessing game as they speculate about what was deliberately withheld. In this way, authors tease readers into coming up with theories and interpretations while they read. There are several effects of gapping. First, it makes for more interesting reading as we become more active participants in the reading process. Second, when authors initially hold back important details, it generates *suspense*, another interest-producing narrative element. Third, if our interpretive guesses turn out to be right (often by a flashback or explanation in the narrative), we feel pretty clever (and maybe a little smug), and we sense that we're on the same wavelength with the author. Fourth, the author may surprise us with something unexpected, and we feel a sudden flash of insight as we "get it" (see Setting above).

Humor

Many readers of the Bible fail to see anything funny about the Bible at all, because of the seriousness of their reverence for God and God's Word. Assuming God to be omni-serious, then, they assume that the Bible is entirely humorless. In their opinion, God is infinitely somber, and we should follow his example (at least when reading the Bible).

Consequently, they cannot see what they are not looking for. For example, Alfred North Whitehead once commented that "the total absence of humour from the Bible is one of the most singular things in all of literature."[25] For those with eyes to see, however, humor is present in the Bible in many forms: wit, joke, satire, irony, sarcasm, caricature, parody, and wordplay. There are several main reasons for the presence of humor in biblical narrative.

The Bible ends on a happy note, with the bad guys duly punished and the good guys (i.e., those who put their faith in God) living happily ever after. Though there are dark hours along the way, the Bible is essentially an optimistic, upbeat comedy. It is "good news" which brings joy, and with it, laughter.

The most essential sin of humanity is pride, and one of the most effective ways of exposing pride is to ridicule and poke fun at those who are self-important. Thus God himself uses sarcasm, ridicule, and scorn in dealing with human arrogance and presumptuousness: "The One enthroned in heaven laughs; the LORD scoffs at them" (Psalm 2:4).[26]

Humor and laughter are a natural, spontaneous response to joyful, serendipitous surprises. For example, in the exuberance of the birth of a baby boy to a formerly-childless couple, the parents name him "Isaac" (*laughter*). Humor is also a healthy coping mechanism in dealing with the hardships of life.

Humor is an effective way for speakers or writers to charm an audience into accepting their point of view. People's defenses are lowered when they find themselves laughing, and the biblical writers take advantage of this rhetorical strategy frequently to win over their audience, that is, readers, to their point of view.

Irony

Another common feature of biblical narrative is the use of *irony*. Irony is a literary technique used by speakers and authors to communicate something different from what they actually say.[27] Irony occurs whenever:

- . . . there is a discrepancy between what is actually said and what is meant. For example, Paul asks the Corinthians to "forgive" him for not requiring them to pay him for his ministry (2 Corinthians 12:13).

- . . . what occurs is the opposite of what you expect—like when the new "kid," instead of the head-and-shoulders-taller-than-anyone-else king, takes on the warrior giant Goliath, and wins (1 Samuel 17).

- . . . certain characters know more than the others but don't let on. For example, when Jesus tells the Samaritan woman to come back with her husband, she says, "I have no husband." Jesus replies, "You are right when you say you have no husband. The fact is, you have had five husbands, and the man you now have is not your husband" (John 4:16-18). Here Jesus knew the answer even before he asked the question, and asked the question not to gain new understanding but to force the Samaritan woman to deal with her issues.

- . . . you as the reader know more than the characters. (This situation is called *dramatic irony*). The premiere case of this in the Bible is the book of Job. The reader knows about the discussion between God and Satan and why Job experiences his suffering, but Job never does get clued in.

- . . . circumstances bring about a reversal: important people are humbled, lowly people are honored. For example, the prisoners Joseph, Daniel, and Mordecai are given privileges, while the ruling king in each case (Pharaoh, Nebuchadnezzar and Belshazzar, and Artaxerxes) is perplexed and foolish without them.

- . . . a character's words carry far more meaning or truth than they realize—e.g., Caiaphas saying that "it is better for you that one man die for the people than that the whole nation perish" (John 11:50).

Irony can be a powerful tool in writing because it makes us readers feel smarter than the characters. When that happens, the author can more easily win us over to his way of thinking. Irony also tends to make us chuckle, and when we're laughing, we're also more likely to agree with the author. In fact, we might wind up laughing at the stupidity of some of our own faults when the characters remind us of ourselves.

Narrator's Point of View

The author's point of view involves the implied storyteller. An anonymous work gives no clue as to who the author actually is (e.g., Ruth, 1 and 2 Kings, Esther). An implied author is involved where the text either implicitly[28] or explicitly identifies its author.[29] The Bible sometimes relates stories in the first person (I/me, we/us),[30] but most often in the third person (he/him, she/her, they/them).

The goal of an author is to convince his readers of a way of thinking and responding to God that is different from what they currently practice but which they now know to be correct.

Some authors "intrude" into the text more frequently by explaining things and drawing conclusions. Instead of letting you draw your own conclusions about the characters, he assists and influences your opinion by providing his own interpretations and explanations. But the more he does this, the more "preachy" his tone becomes. From the standpoint of literary strategy, there is a trade-off here:

Narrative Interference	Narrative Non-interference
Less likely to be misunderstood	A more powerful message
More control over the reader	More dramatic and emotional
A clearer message	More reader interest and involvement
Less ambiguity	(filling in gaps, maintaining suspense, etc.)
Less realistic	

There is a high degree of narrative interference in John's gospel. He explains details of geography (1:28) and chronology (3:24), gives translations (1:37, 42; 6:1), interprets cryptic sayings from a retrospective position (2:21-22; 6:64, 71), explains customs (4:9) and provides insights which have bearing upon the action (4:44).

Whether or not the narrator intrudes into the storyline, readers will always view the events and characters only through the viewpoint that the author chooses for them. In biblical narrative we must assume that our author is a reliable source for two reasons. First, it is *God's* Word, and God does not lie, mislead, or deceive. Secondly, the human authors of Scripture possess what is called "narrative omniscience." Narrative omniscience refers to the narrator's ability to know things that no mere observer could, such as unspoken thoughts of the characters, events happening simultaneously elsewhere, and knowledge of God's perspective and attitude.[31]

Pace

Pace is the term used to refer to how quickly new action occurs within the story. For example, when a storyteller recites the actual words of a speech or prayer, the pace slows, because we read only several times faster than the time required to listen to the spoken words. By contrast, see how quickly things happen in this passage:

> Once again the Israelites did evil in the eyes of the LORD, and because they did this evil the LORD gave Eglon king of Moab power over Israel. Getting the Ammonites and Amalekites to join him, Eglon came and attacked Israel, and they took possession of the City of Palms [Jericho]. The Israelites were subject to Eglon king of Moab for eighteen years (Judges 3:12-14).

Here perhaps twenty or more years take place in the course of a mere three verses of text.

Repetition

In all three major types of biblical literature (narrative, poetry, discourse), *repetition* is perhaps the most common literary device for emphasizing and drawing attention. A *repeated motif* is a repeated pattern or image. For example, one pattern of events repeated again and again in the book of Judges is the following:

- Israel sins against God.
- God allows the Israelites' enemies to oppress them.
- Israel cries to God for help.
- God sends a judge to rescue Israel.
- The land has peace.
- Israel sins again.
- . . . and so on, and so on.

Examples of repeated *images* are:

- The godly legacy of King David (1 and 2 Kings): he is the measuring stick by which all succeeding kings are evaluated.
- Help for disadvantaged people in the Gospel of Luke.
- Repeated symbols of a snake, dove, and lion.
- Certain numbers such as three, five, seven, twelve, forty, and a thousand.

Sentence Types

Different kinds of information are given according to the kinds of sentences that the storytellers choose. Attention may be given to description of the physical geography, circumstances of the time period, or the characters in the story. Action is carried along by the storyline. In explanation, the author breaks into the action to add his own comments (see Narrator's Point of View above). Narrators may also include dialogue between the characters in the story. Each biblical author establishes a storytelling climate through his own unique blend of these sentence elements.

Conclusion on Narrative

If you're feeling a little overwhelmed at how complex reading a Bible story has just become, let me offer some words of encouragement and reassurance. First of all, stories (including Bible stories) are a fun kind of literature for most people to read, and becoming aware of more features to look for can enhance your experience of enjoyment. Like going to a ball game where you know the players personally, or listening to music after taking a music appreciation class, familiarity can heighten our pleasure and sense of connectedness.

Second, because it is God's revelation, he wants us to understand his Truth. Once we begin understanding how these stories work to communicate his messages, and begin reading them in light of their larger context, the task becomes increasingly easier.

Third, in this chapter I have pointed out for you many different things to look at and look for. There is new enough material here for advanced and experienced Bible readers to try out, so you can discover new insights and perspectives, opening new dimensions of the text for investigation that you may not have yet considered.

Finally, I can boil down these pages much more simply for those who are just getting their feet wet in Bible study. A Bible story usually works—it changes us—by causing us to identify with one of the characters that is experiencing a hardship. We end up thinking to ourselves, "I'm a lot like that." Noticing what happens to the *characters* is crucial to reading Bible stories. Has the author portrayed them as *positive or negative examples* for us? If the story turns out well for that character, then we should do the same things as they did to succeed (showing mercy, having faith in God, etc.), and avoid anything that hindered their progress. If they failed, then we should avoid the same things that led to the failure.

In the simplest terms possible, here is a basic layout of how a story works in shaping us.

"Once upon a time . . .	→ Setting: time
in a land far away . . .	→ Setting: place
a person . . .	→ Character
had a problem . . .	→ Plot conflict
which got really bad . . .	→ Plot intensity
until finally . . .	→ Plot climax
it got better or . . . ended unhappily."	→ Plot resolution
The moral of the story	→ Evaluation / shared truth

However, the "moral of the story" often will have much more to do with what we learn of God than in identifying with a particular character. In other words, the characters are meant to be an example for us to avoid or imitate, but ultimately we are meant to encounter God in a fresh and new way. Observing how he deals with the characters gives us valuable insight into what he is like, as well as understanding others in our own world better.

Here are a few very brief examples. Abraham did many things in his life, both good and bad, but overall his life ends as a success. The chief thing that he did right was to "believe in the Lord" (see Genesis 15:6, quoted in Romans 4:3, 22; Galatians 3:6; James 2:23). Thus a shared Truth from this passage is, "We should believe that God will keep his promises." But Abraham also did a number of things which hindered his success along the way, like bringing Lot with him, having a child through a servant girl, and trying to give his wife away to save his own skin. So another shared Truth is, "We cannot fulfill God's promises by doing things our way."

Saul's life does not end happily; he is a failure. What did he do to cause his own failure? He "rejected the word of the Lord" (1 Samuel 15:26). So a Truth statement here would be, "We cannot please God when we are disobeying him."

Sometimes biblical authors will make a statement—a Truth claim— that challenges us by forcing us either to accept or reject it as Truth. There are inevitable consequences to our decision either way. For example, Mark begins his gospel with, "The beginning of the gospel about Jesus Christ, the Son of God" (1:1). He hasn't proved it, and actually he never even tries to in this gospel account. If you "buy it," then the logic of the story, once understood, will have dramatic consequences for your life. If you don't, then little of what follows will even make much sense. We readers must decide at the very outset to believe or disbelieve, and our decision will have a far-reaching impact on our lives.

One final word is appropriate here. If, as I have argued throughout this book, our goal in Bible reading is not to create meaning for ourselves but to *follow* what the author is sharing with us, then looking at the features discussed in this chapter is simply a schematic approach to noticing things. The first step of Bible study is *seeing*, and knowing what things to look for will help you to *see* more clearly. In a popular book, the authors put it this way:

> Our problem is most of us live our lives like a movie we've arrived at twenty minutes late. The action is well under way and we haven't a clue what's happening. Who are these people? Who are the good guys and who are the bad guys? Why are they doing that? What's going on?

We sense that something really important, perhaps even glorious, is taking place, and yet it all seems so *random*.

Learning to read biblical narratives is like "catching up" to a movie after arriving late. It is ultimately becoming aware of the context which gives all of these actions their meaning.[32]

CHAPTER NINE

A Well-turned Phrase
Poetry

A sailor was assigned to active sea duty aboard an aircraft carrier. He really was not the military sort in the first place. He was talented musically and artistically, but these are not very valuable qualities for naval duty. Furthermore, during times of stress he found that his brain would freeze up on him, making it almost impossible for him to talk. Ironically, when this happened, he could still sing. One day, he was working on deck during a visit from a top-ranking admiral. To his shock, he witnessed the admiral, who was strolling along the edge of the deck, slip and fall overboard. The sailor immediately ran to tell his captain what had just happened. But, because he was so flustered, the words just wouldn't come up. Desperate, he sang out his message to the captain.

Should auld acquaintance be forgot, and never brought to mind?
The admiral's fallen overboard; he's half a mile behind.

I heard this old joke when I was kid. But it raises an interesting question for me. What is it about this story that makes it a joke? There's nothing funny about a person falling overboard (although the fact that the admiral was a high ranking officer seems important to the story). The humor stems from the fact that singing just seems so out of place for delivering this kind of message. Information that is really important isn't supposed to be communicated in poetry. Instead, it should be given clearly, in as few words as possible. In fact, the reason this joke is funny at all (I'll let you be the judge) is exactly the same reason why singing telegrams are always, well, ridiculous. News messages, from telegrams to urgent reports of floating brass, should be given *normally*, that is, in a no-frills way of talking rather than song.

It raises for me another intriguing question. One-third of the entire Bible is written in poetry. Why would God choose to communicate religious Truth—information about very important things—in poetry rather than in straightforward discourse? What is the value of poetry—what is it good for?

Poetry is a form of writing where normal language is changed in order to intensify its impact. Poetry is "a kind of language that says *more* and says it *more intensely* than does ordinary language."[1] It is probably easier for us to recognize poetry than to define it. *Encyclopedia Britannica* defines poetry as "literature that evokes a concentrated imaginative awareness of experience or a specific emotional response through language chosen and arranged for its meaning, sound, and rhythm."[2] It's difficult to distinguish poetry by formal features like rhyme or meter or line structure because there isn't any one unique element that all poetry has in common. Like the encyclopedia definition, it's better to focus on the use and function of poetry: it stimulates imagination and emotion to a higher degree than other forms of writing.

Why would God choose to use imaginative, emotional language to describe reality instead of a theological treatise, with its greater clarity and precision of expression? In communicating to us in poetry, God is addressing us intimately and evocatively in ways that should touch us and move us. Well over half of the quoted speech of the LORD in the Hebrew Bible is poetry, which implicitly tells us something about how he wishes to relate to us. In the Bible, we find Truth expressed in ways that appeal to the entire person. God's communication to humanity, the Scriptures, is both word-based and image-based, able to connect with all kinds of thinkers and responders.

WORD	Logical	Imaginative	**IMAGE**
Discourse	Linear	Global	Biblical Imagery
Commandments	Analytical	Synthetic	Figures of Speech
Prophecy	Verbal	Pictorial	Poetry
Biblical sermons	Left-brained	Right-brained	Stories
	Christ: "and the Word was God" (John 1:1)	Christ: "the image of the invisible God" (Colossians 1:15)	Parables

Poetry is a significant facet of this total-package revelation and has a special role to play as a method of human communication. In comparison with other literature, poetry is normally more concentrated and terse; it says a lot in a few words. As a result, it makes for slower reading as we allow the thoughts to simmer and we ponder over its appeal. Poetry also traffics in specific, concrete word-pictures rather than abstract ideas. It seems awkward to talk about the "argument" of a poem—poems don't argue points. Instead they create mental images and experiences, offering to us new windows of perception.

Poetry beckons the reader's emotions and senses, encouraging us to feel as well as understand. For these reasons, poetry is also memorable: it leaves a more lasting impact upon us than prose does. A well-turned phrase, a new world created through words (consider Genesis 1) in which we're welcome to linger and browse, a startling metaphor, words that tease, tantalize, and suggest, all invite us mentally to inhale slowly and deeply—and we're not likely to quickly forget the experience.

Notice the effect of the wording of the following passage. Taken from Deborah's song of victory in Judges 5, it describes how Jael killed the enemy Canaanite captain after he burst into her tent seeking rest and refuge. The story relates how, after he quenched his thirst with the milk she offered and then fell asleep in the tent, she drove a tent peg through his skull. The narrative account shocks us with its sordidness. But the poetic retelling interprets the blow in extra slow motion, allowing us to see the point differently.

> She **struck** Sisera,
> she **crushed** his head,
> she **shattered**
> and **pierced** his temple.
> At her feet he **sank**,
> he **fell**;
> there he **lay**.
> At her feet he **sank**,
> he **fell**;
> where he **sank**,
> there he **fell** —
> **dead**.
>
> (Judges 5:26-27)

The succession of redundant verbs would bog down a narrative. But here in poetry, the words themselves have a pounding effect, and the verbal choreography describing his final demise creates a dramatically slow death spiral.

The effects of poetry on us have been characterized well by Thomas G. Long: "Poetry works to disrupt the customary ways in which we use language. Poetry stretches the ordinary uses of words, and places them into unfamiliar relationships with each other, thereby cutting fresh paths across the well-worn grooves of everyday language."[3]

— —

Where do we find poetry within the Bible? Of course, poetry is used for the genre of *psalms*. It is also used extensively in *Wisdom Literature*. Poetry is a favorite way for the *prophets* to express themselves, and nearly all of God's quoted speech in the prophetic genre is poetic. Poetry is found embedded within each of the other genres: in *apocalyptic* literature (Revelation 15:3-4), in the *Gospels* (Luke 1:46—55), and even in the *Epistles* (2 Timothy 2:11—13). It is also found in the middle of *stories* (Exodus 15:1—18). Poetry is also used in conjunction with many different literary forms: aphorisms, blessings, curses, doxologies, hymns, laments, oracles, praises, proverbs, riddles, thanksgivings, woes, and others. (See Appendix.)

> **WHENEVER YOU** SEE POETRY EMBEDDED WITHIN A LARGER NARRATIVE, PAY SPECIAL ATTENTION—SOMETHING VERY SIGNIFICANT IS BEING SAID.

Here is an important tip: whenever you see poetry embedded within a larger narrative, pay special attention—something very significant is being said. In the mid-twentieth century, a number of highly successful musical stage plays and movies were written: *The Sound of Music*, *Music Man*, *Fiddler on the Roof*, *Westside Story*, *Seven Brides for Seven Brothers*, to name several. Typically these were humorous, romantic comedies in which the storyline drama was frequently delayed by singing. However, these songs were far from being interruptions into the story. The lyrics were often a crucial component to understanding the story, because they identified and clarified the characters' thoughts and feelings; they continually interpreted the action for their audiences. Without these songs, the story would be much less interesting, perhaps even impossible for the audience to follow. So it is with poetic interludes in biblical narratives. Jacob's blessing (Genesis 49), Moses' victory song (Exodus 15), Balaam's oracles (Number 23-24), Deborah's song (Judges 5), Hannah's song (1 Samuel 2), and David's song (2 Samuel 22) are *not* extraneous embellishment to the story intended for the pleasure of artsy people. These are special, interpretive announcements, highlighted for our attention by the fact that the authors have broken the mold (the literary type) to announce these messages.

— —

In English, there isn't any single element that distinguishes poetry from other kinds of literature. But nearly all of us are introduced to poetry that is simple, has a clear rhythm (meter), and rhymes. Children's poetry—from nursery rhymes to Dr. Seuss to jump rope verses to humorous limericks—all share these in common.

What about poetry in the Bible? How can a reader tell the difference between poetry as opposed to narrative or discourse?

Parallelism

By far the most important thing to look for in biblical poetry is *parallelism*. Parallelism is the "rhyming" of ideas and forms instead of sounds. The phrases and concepts in the first line relate to the phrases and concepts in the next. The great thing about this is that, unlike words, rhymes and meter, it survives translation from the original languages of Hebrew and Greek into English much more easily. The following is an example of parallelism:

the grave	cannot	praise you	
death	cannot	sing your praise	(Isaiah 38:18)

In Psalm 148:7-13, the author uses parallelism in a clear way to offer a poetic description of the world around us. I have used vertical lines and spacing to help identify the parallel elements.

Praise the LORD from the earth,

you great sea creatures
and all ocean depths,

lightning	and hail,
snow	and clouds,

stormy winds   that do his bidding,

you mountains	and all hills,
fruit trees	and all cedars,
wild animals	and all cattle,
small creatures	and flying birds,

kings of the earth	and all nations,
you princes	and all rulers on earth,
young men	and maidens,
old men	and children.

Let them praise the name of the Lord,

| for his name alone | is exalted; |
| his splendor | is above the earth and the heavens. |

Actually, there are several main kinds of parallelism. It can be helpful to recognize these, as long as we resist getting rigid. Some of these categories are occasionally tough to distinguish, and there is some overlap.

In *synonymous parallelism*, the second line repeats the same idea as the first, only in different words:

| Defend | the cause | of the weak | and fatherless; |
| maintain | the rights | of the poor | and oppressed. |

(Psalm 82:3)

| Yahweh is my light and my salvation | whom | shall I fear? |
| Yahweh is the stronghold of my life | of whom | shall I be afraid? |

(Psalm 27:1)

| I will sing | to Yahweh | all my life |
| I will sing praise | to my God | as long as I live. |

(Psalm 104:33)

In *synthetic parallelism*, the idea of the second line builds on the first:[4]

Vindicate me, O Yahweh,
For I have led a blameless life   (Psalm 26:1)

You broaden the path beneath me
so that my ankles do not turn.   (Psalm 18:36)

Especially with these first two categories of synonymous and synthetic, we need to resist either/or pigeon-holing. Instead we should think along a continuum:

Virtually identical   Completely different[5]

In *antithetic parallelism*, the second line contrasts the idea of the first line. The words *but* or *yet* are clues to look for in this kind of parallelism:

I	hate and abhor	falsehood
BUT I	love	your law

(Psalm 119:163)

	The prospect	of the righteous	is joy
BUT	the hopes	of the wicked	come to nothing

(Proverbs 10:28)

Yahweh	tears down	the proud man's	house
BUT he	keeps	the widow's	boundaries intact

(Proverbs 15:25)

In *comparative parallelism*, the second line makes a comparison with the first, using "as" or "like":

AS water	reflects	a face,
so a man's heart	reflects	the man.

(Proverbs 27:19)

Inverted parallelism is parallelism with a twist: the similar parts in the second line are in reverse order from the first.

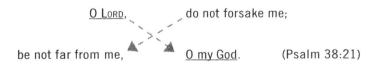

O Lord,   do not forsake me;

be not far from me,   O my God.   (Psalm 38:21)

It is even possible, and fairly common, to have *simultaneous* ("multi-tasking") *parallelism* going on at the same time:

A With bitterness   archers attacked him;

A they shot at him   with hostility.

B But his bow   remained steady

B his strong arms   stayed limber.   (Genesis 49:23–24)

         A and A are synonymous (and inverted)

         AA and BB are antithetic

         B and B are synonymous

Chiastic parallelism occurs whenever parallel lines are in a mirrored or patterned order. A very simple pattern (really just an enlarged synonymous parallelism) looks like this:

A   Unless Yahweh builds the house

   B   its builders labor in vain

A   Unless Yahweh watches over the city

   B   the watchmen stand guard in vain   (Psalm 127:1)

There are a number of possible variations:

```
A           A           A
  B           B           B
    C           C           C
  B           A           B
A           B           C
          C       A
```

A *May the peoples*   PRAISE YOU, *O GOD;*

     may all the peoples   PRAISE YOU.

         B May <u>the nations</u> be glad and sing for joy,

            C for you rule the peoples justly

         B and guide <u>the nations</u> of the earth.

A *May the peoples*   PRAISE YOU, *O GOD;*

     may all the peoples PRAISE YOU.   (Psalm 67:3-5)

One other wrinkle in the use of parallelism in biblical poetry is the use of *ellipsis*, a frequently used device where the second line will omit an implied element from the first line.

May the LORD	cut off	all flattering lips	
and ---	---	every boasting tongue	(Psalm 12:3)

Here you naturally understand the implied subject (LORD) and verb "will cut off" from the first line and import it to the second line. This omission is called an *ellipsis*. Most often, when one or two elements are missing, they are compensated for by an added, different element in the second line.

to bind	their kings	with fetters	---	
---	their nobles	with shackles	**of iron**	(Psalm 149:8)

For you	O God	tested us	---	
you	---	refined us	**like silver**	(Psalm 66:10)

These added words serve to balance out the length of the two lines, and are sometimes referred to as "ballast." When this happens, the corresponding elements are simply lengthened to compensate for the missing element.

Sometimes words from the first line are repeated verbatim with a different emphasis added in the second (or more) line(s)——this is frequently referred to as *"stair step" parallelism*.

Ascribe to Yahweh	O mighty ones	
ascribe to Yahweh	**glory and strength**	
ascribe to Yahweh	**the glory due his name**	
worship Yahweh	**in the splendor of his holiness**[6]	(Psalm 29:1-2)

Other Poetic Techniques

- In inclusio (or "bookends"), the opening line or phrase is repeated at the end of a unit.

Praise Yahweh, O my soul . . .
>   Praise Yahweh, O my soul.   (Psalm 103)

Give thanks to the LORD, for he is good;
>   his love endures forever . . .
Give thanks to the LORD, for he is good;
>   his love endures forever.   (Psalm 118:1, 29)

- An acrostic is an "alphabet" poem in which the first verse begins with the first letter of the Hebrew alphabet, the second verse with the second letter, and so on. Most Bibles list this out very clearly in Psalm 119, but there are other poetic passages that use this technique as well: Psalm 9-10; 25; 34; 37; 111; 112; 145; Proverbs 31:10-31; Lamentations 1, 2, 3, 4; Nahum 1:2-10.

- Because biblical poetry operates by paralleling the lines, certain words become commonly-linked, that is, they are pairs which frequently appear in parallel lines of poetry. Some of these stock word-pairs include: foes/enemies; the LORD/God; nations/peoples; kings/rulers (or princes); thousand/ten thousand; poor/oppressed; justice/righteousness; heavens/earth; silver/gold; sin/transgression; wickedness/evil; way/path; wilderness/desert; plan/purpose; sing/rejoice; instruct/teach; eyes/ears; love (or truth)/faithfulness; etc.

  Some of these appear together to indicate totality. The pair "day" and "night" means "all the time" (so does "[when I] sleep" and "wake"); "heaven and earth" means "everywhere" (as does "near" and "far"); "young" and "old" means all people; etc. This technique is actually a figure of speech called *merism*.[7]

- "Interruptions": Biblical poets use patterns of words to create symmetry, balance, and artistic appeal. How tidy is the structure of the poem? Is it consistent? If the parallelism or form is interrupted or erratic, the author may be trying to emphasize something or come across as troubled. Frequently in biblical poetry, an established pattern will break form. Be especially alert when this happens, because the odd element is being emphasized. I like to think of these as literary speed-bumps—they force us to slow down our normal reading and pay special attention to what is being said. The patterns which may be broken include:

→ Parallelism: if a psalm with an established pattern of two-line pairs has a three-line unit (e.g., Psalm 148:13-14).

→ Chiasm: in a chiastic arrangement, whenever there is a central element that is not paralleled, this pivot is being highlighted.

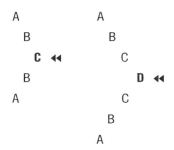

→ Acrostic: sometimes an acrostic (alphabet) pattern. Unfortunately, these do not come through in translation, but good commentaries should note these. (e.g., Psalms 9-10; Lamentations 3 [cp. 1-2], 5 [cp. 1-4]; Nahum 1:9 [cp. 1-8]).

Pattern	Interruption
Psalm 9:1-10:1 and 10:14-18	10:2-13
Lamentations 1-4	Lamentations 5
Nahum 1:1-8	Nahum 1:9

→ Form: The forms of the psalms (praise, lament, thanksgiving, hymn) are standard outlines which govern their structure. These may also be altered for emphasis (For what to expect in each of these forms, see the Appendix).

Where to Focus

Like most poetry, biblical poetry wants to elicit an emotional response from the reader, such as shock, empathy, fear, hope, or worship. When reading it, then, we should identify its emotional direction. What mood or tone is established, and what response is this poetic passage seeking to evoke?

It's important to determine the structure of the poem. If it is a psalm, then there are several forms that can provide an outline for the text: hymn, lament, praise, or thanksgiving. Other structural items to watch out for are the parallelisms, chiasm, inclusio, refrain, change of images, or boundary markers such as "says the Lᴏʀᴅ" or "Selah" (for more on these and other forms, see the Appendix).

Because poetry also deals with drawing comparisons and analogies, we need to stay attuned to the images and figures of speech. The concepts presented in poetry are most often found precisely in these images. Common biblical figures of speech found in poetry include metaphors, similes (comparisons using the terms "like" or "as"), hyperboles (deliberate exaggeration), anthropomorphism (describing God with human characteristics), and personification (giving living qualities to nonliving things). You will also encounter recurring themes, such as the suffering of the innocent (Job), the emptiness of idols (Isaiah 40–66), the day of the Lᴏʀᴅ (Joel and Zephaniah). There are also repeated *motifs*, such as darkness (Job 3:1-10) and the cup of God's wrath (Isaiah 51:17-23).

CHAPTER TEN

Here's the Point

Discourse

As I mentioned in chapter two, discourse is a type of literature that makes its point by presenting a logical sequence of thought. Biblical discourse requires a different set of methods and skills to follow when compared to narrative or poetry. Narratives communicate Truths through telling stories; characters and events dominate the flow of the text. Poetry communicates Truths through figures, images, emotional language, and parallelism. Discourse, however, communicates its Truths through presenting ideas that are logically related. Instead of events (narrative) or images (poetry), discourse is ideas that happen on center stage. In a sense, you could say that discourse is more up front about its topic than the other two literary types, because it clearly states its point directly in the text, whereas in the other two types the points are illustrated.

Because of this reason, discourse is considered by many to be the easiest to understand. In many of the churches where I have attended regularly, discourse passages were preached much more frequently than either of the other two literary types, and the preaching especially favored the epistle genre.[1] On the one hand, this is ironic, because discourse is the least common of the three major types of biblical literature (see chapter two). On the other hand, it underscores the importance of discourse, because the Truths shared in it are both more compressed and presented more plainly.

The most common places to find discourse in the Bible are in the legal commandments, in prophecy, in the Epistles, and in the extended speeches by characters within stories. However discourse also appears within other genres as well (i.e., apocalyptic, gospel, and wisdom).

How Discourses Are Structured

In the speech or English composition classes that most of us took in high school and college, we were taught a standard, three-part structure for presenting our ideas. In the introduction, the topic is identified, often with something that either arouses our curiosity or creates in us a desire to know what is being said. The body develops this topic in various ways: defining it, defending it, clarifying it, illustrating it, and persuading us. In the conclusion, the discussion may be summarized, and its relevance to the audience is emphasized. These same elements are frequently present in biblical discourses and can be a helpful starting point as we read.

A discourse can be divided into units of thought—that is, it is separated into paragraphs. Each paragraph develops a single aspect of an idea or argument. And the main idea of each paragraph follows logically from the ones before. Although the ancient Hebrew and Greek manuscripts of the Bible don't have paragraph indentations, most current translations have done a good job of indicating where these paragraph changes occur. To follow the flow of an entire discourse, then, we must identify the main thought and purpose of each individual paragraph, then "build up" to the overall argument

How Arguments Are Built

Since discourse operates through presenting well-developed, logical argumentation, a key factor in properly interpreting the flow of thought is to identify the relationship of ideas within the text. The author is trying to convince us of his point of view, and may use many forms of persuasion and rational arguments to do so. The author's main point (the proposition) will be supported and defended in various ways. You will find the following argumentative strategies in biblical discourse.

- Sometimes authors build an argument from a general, shared Truth to a specific case or application.

  Shared Truth: Followers of Jesus should think like ("have the same mind as") Christ, which involves putting others above ourselves. If we are all thinking like him, then we will also be thinking like one another (being "like-minded"; Philippians 2). Particular situations where like-mindedness is not occurring is evidence that the parties have not adopted the mind of Christ.

Specific case: "Therefore, Euodia and Syntyche, you need to have the same mind, in the Lord" (Philippians 4:2).

- Another form of argument reasons from specific cases to a general, shared Truth which may or may not be explicitly stated.

  Specific cases:

  > Death does not separate us from the love of God
  > Life does not separate us from the love of God
  > Angels do not separate us from the love of God
  > Demons do not separate us from the love of God
  > The present does not separate us from the love of God
  > The future does not separate us from the love of God . . .

  Shared Truth:

  > Nothing in all creation can separate us from the love of God (Romans 8:38-39).

- Sometimes the argument is based upon a comparison: since we know A is true, and that A is like B in some important way, then B must also be true.

  (A) Sin entered the world through one man, Adam. All sinners are "in" Adam.

  (A=B) Christ is like Adam in that both are the "father" of an entire race (Jesus being the father of all those who are saved).

  (B) Salvation entered the world through one man, Christ. All those who are saved are "in Christ" (Romans 5:12-19).

- The argument can also be based on a contrast: A is truth, and B is also truth. A general, shared Truth can be derived by looking at them both together.

  (A) The one who speaks in a tongue edifies only one person (himself or herself).

  (B) The one who prophesies edifies more people: the whole church.

  Shared Truth: The one who prophesies is greater, i.e., builds up more people, than one who speaks in tongues (1 Corinthians 14:4-5).

- The author may ground his appeal to us in a quotation from a mutually recognized, reliable authority, such as the following:

  Previous Scriptures: "As it is written . . . ," "This was to fulfill what was spoken . . . ," "I am saying nothing beyond what the prophets and Moses said would happen" (Acts 26:22). The prophets very frequently refer to the first five books of the Bible, and sometimes to one another. Matthew through Revelation contain hundreds of direct quotations and literally thousands of allusions to previous Scripture.

Jesus: "To the married I give this command (not I, but the Lord) . . ."[2] (1 Corinthians 7:10; cf. 11:23).

Other "experts" (i.e., pagan philosophers): "For in him we live and move and have our being" (Acts 17:28 [twice]; see also 1 Corinthians 15:32; Titus 1:12).

Folk wisdom: "Surely you will quote this proverb to me, 'Physician, heal yourself!'" (Luke 4:23); "Everything is permissible" (1 Corinthians 10:23).

The point for us is to recognize *how* the author has crafted his argument and built his case within the text, and *why* he used those particular forms of argument.

Other Discourse Techniques

Within biblical discourse, there is a rich diversity of creativity that the various authors display in communicating their messages. Frequently they appeal to us in captivating ways, through diverse techniques. These include the following:

- Some authors will tell a thought-provoking story which illustrates their ideas. Jesus frequently told memorable parables in his discourses. The biblical writers also use this literary tactic, sometimes including very detailed and developed stories (e.g., Ezekiel 16). They may also recount previous history, interpreting the significance of what happened earlier (e.g., Romans 4).

- Sometimes the discourse will incorporate a short poem (e.g., Romans 11:33-36; 1 Timothy 3:16). When this is the case, just as when poetry is placed within narrative, there is special emphasis on its content. It merits our special attention.

- Very often there are graphic, striking images, metaphors, and other figures of speech which cause us to see his point in an entirely new way. For example, "The devil prowls around like a roaring lion looking for someone to devour" (1 Peter 5:8). In 2 Timothy, Paul lists a number of metaphors which compare to the Christian life: soldier, athlete, farmer, craftsman, dishes, and servant.

- Look also for interruptions in the expected patterns. When a discourse book is written in the epistle genre (see Appendix for guidelines), elements that are missing or repeated should be given special attention. For instance, in Galatians, Paul offers no thanksgiving to God on behalf of them, as is his custom in other epistles. This is not an oversight, however, because in their case, they have polluted and subverted the gospel message of grace through their erroneous doctrine. Paul isn't thankful for those who corrupt the gospel! Paul strategically breaks his form by omitting any thanks, and because of this, the alert reader is aware that there is something wrong from the very beginning of the epistle.

- Repetition is the single most-important device used by authors in organizing a text. This is actually true for all three types of literature; features that are repeated are the surest clue as to the point the author is trying to make, as well as indicators of the literary structure. It may involve recurrence, not only of the same word, but also of phrases, ideas, grammatical constructions, or types of sentence. For example, in Malachi, Yahweh (through the prophet) keeps putting questions in the mouths of the hearers/readers: "But you say, '[What/how] . . . ?'" Then Yahweh answers "their" arguments.[3] Here are examples of other kinds of repetition:

"flesh" and "spirit"	(word, Romans 7–8)
"love"	(word, 1 John)
"by faith"	(phrase, Hebrews 11)
"Give careful thought"	(phrase, Haggai)
"some to be apostles, some to be prophets, some to be evangelists . . ."	(grammatical construction, Ephesians 4:11)
"What then?" / "What shall we say then?" etc.	(rhetorical questions, Romans)
"Cursed is the person who. . . . Then all the people shall say 'Amen!'"	(sentence, Deuteronomy 27)

- Many biblical discourses signal the internal divisions through the use of a repeated introductory phrase: "dear friend" in 3 John, "thus says Yahweh" in the prophets, "this is a trustworthy saying" in 1 Timothy.

- How much text does the author devote to a particular subject? The amount of space is a good gauge for measuring the importance of the ideas presented in discourse literature—the more space, the more importance. "Love" receives a whole chapter's worth of attention (1 Corinthians 13), as does faith (Hebrews 11).

- Looking for themes and motifs is just as important in discourse as it is in narrative and poetry. Here are a few examples.

Theme:
Blood sacrifice (Leviticus, Hebrews)
Vanity (Ecclesiastes)
Sin / sinful nature (Romans 7-8)

Image:
Sword and famine (Jeremiah)
A lion preying on a lamb (Amos 3:12)
Stone (1 Peter 2)

Logical Relationships

If a discourse is a text that makes its point by presenting a logical sequence of thought, then it is of utmost importance to be able to identify *how* these thoughts are related to one another. Learning about logical relationships equips us to recognize and understand the ways that various thoughts, sentences, and paragraphs work together to connect ideas.

Fortunately, certain words and phrases are tip-offs to these logical relationships. Though the simple word "and" conjoins many of these, some connecting words tend to be specific to the kind of logical relationship. These key words act as signals to help us recognize which relationships are present in a passage. Here are some of the relationships that you'll find in discourse:

Logical Relationship	Explanation	Key Words	Example
Alternative	Two or more possibilities are presented that are mutually exclusive—implied "either . . . or."	either/or, however, neither/ nor, whether/ or	"this day . . . I have set before you life and death, blessing and curses" (Deuteronomy 30:19). "Do something, **whether** good **or** bad, so that we will be dismayed and filled with fear" (Isaiah 41:23). "To one there is given . . . the message of wisdom, to another the message of knowledge . . . to another faith by the same Spirit, to another gifts of healing . . ." (1 Corinthians 12:8ff).

Comparison	Two or more things are placed together to show their similarity.	as, even as, in the same way, just as, like, likewise	"Ephraim is **like** a dove, easily deceived and senseless" (Hosea 7:11). The tongue is **like** a horse's bit, a ship's rudder, and a spark igniting a forest fire (James 3:3-6).
Concession	An allowance or exception is made to what is normal or expected.	although, despite, even if, even though, nevertheless, yet	"**Even if** I caused you sorrow by my letter, I do not regret it" (2 Corinthians 7:8). "By faith Abraham, **even though** he was past age—and Sarah herself was barren—was enabled to become a father" (Hebrews 11:11).
Condition / Result	A condition is expressed, and then the result is given: "If [or since, or when] this, then that"—either stated or implied	Consequently, if [or], since / then, therefore	"**If** your heart turns away and you are not obedient . . . [then] I declare to you this day that you will certainly perish" (Deuteronomy 39:17-18). "**If** anyone is in Christ, [then] he is a new creation" (2 Corinthians 5:17). "**Since** you have been raised with Christ, set your hearts on things above" (Colossians 3:1).
Contrast	Two or more things are placed near each other to highlight their differences.	although, but, however, instead, nevertheless, on the contrary, on the other hand, rather, though, yet	"**Though** your sins are like scarlet, they shall be as white as snow" (Isaiah 1:18). "Consequently, you are no longer foreigners and aliens, **but** fellow citizens" (Ephesians 2:19).
Explanation	The idea or thought presented in the first part (a clause, sentence or paragraph) is somehow clarified in the next.	for, you see, that is	". . . we are no longer slaves to sin, **for** the one who has died is free from sin" (Romans 6:6-7). "**for** they drank from the spiritual rock that accompanied them, and that rock was Christ" (1 Corinthians 10:4).
Interruption	The author begins one thought and then breaks off onto a different thought before returning.	—	"As for those who seemed to be important—whatever they were makes no difference to me; God does not judge by external appearance—those men added nothing to my message" (Galatians 2:6).

Progression	Each clause or sentence builds upon the earlier. These may reflect temporal progress (movement through time) or logical progress.	again, also, and, first, further [more] finally, last, next, not only . . . but,now, then	"those he predestined, he **also** called; those he called, he **also** justified; those he justified, he ALSO glorified" (Romans 8:30 [Logical]). "that Christ died for our sins . . . that he was buried, that he was raised on the third day . . . and that he appeared to Peter and **then** to the Twelve . . . and **last** of all he appeared to me" (1 Corinthians. 15:3-7 [Temporal]).
Purpose	An explanation of the intent of an action or idea is given.	because, for, for this reason, in order that, so that, therefore, this is why, thus	"For I long to see you, **in order that** I might impart to you some spiritual gift with you." (Romans 1:11). "Therefore, even Jesus, **in order that** he might set apart a people for himself, died outside the city gate" (Hebrews 13:12).
Quotation	The author cites another text to prove or illustrate a point.	as it is written, as [for] the Scripture [God] says, this was to fulfill	"The man who obeys them will live by them" (Ezekiel 20:13, see Leviticus 18.5). "**Just as it is written**, 'The righteous will live by faith'" (Romans 1:17, see Habakkuk 2:4).
Reason	The rationale or basis for a statement is given.	because, for [this reason], therefore	"Christ's love compels us, **because** we are convinced that one died for all . . .'" (2 Corinthians 5:14).
Rhetorical question	The question is stated, and the answer immediately given.	---	"Who is wise? He will realize these things." (Hosea 14:9). "Who will rescue me from this body of death? Thanks be to God—through Jesus Christ our Lord!" (Romans 7:24-25).
Series	A list of equal but logically related items.	finally, first, next	"Cursed is the man who . . ." (Deuteronomy 27:15-26). "Be joyful in hope, patient in affliction, faithful in prayer" (Romans 12:12).

These relationships work on various levels: between phrases, between sentences, between paragraphs, and between larger sections within an entire book.[4] There isn't any easy answer to determining whether a logical connecting word (like "therefore") is connecting two sentences, two paragraphs, or even larger sections. But you need to remind yourself continually to think in terms of the bigger picture relationships. For example, the logical connecting word "therefore" in Romans 12:1 is pointing back, not merely to the previous sentence or paragraph, but to the whole argument that Paul has carefully developed in chapters one through eleven. In this case, bigger is better. The larger the level of logical relationship you are able to see, the better will be your grasp of the entire biblical book that you are studying.

Summary

Biblical discourse presents a network of ideas which are related to one another in order to achieve the author's master plan in communicating to us. It is often said that ideas have consequences, and this is certainly true in the case of God's Truth. Our goal is to understand how the text was put together by the author to build his case, and then to respond in the ways that are appropriate to those ideas.

When reading discourse, look for the following things. If you are able to see these, then you are well on your way toward grasping the Truth of the Scriptures.

- Identify the genre you're reading (e.g., prophecy, epistle, etc.)—and look at the Appendix for further guidelines appropriate to that genre.

- Look for introductory phrases that will assist you in seeing the structure of the book.

- Find the significant repeated terms, which will give you a good idea of the main points.

- Distinguish which topics brought up by the author receive the most emphasis, through the amount of space given to them; interruption of forms (missing or added elements); extended illustrations (e.g., figures, stories, poems); and/or repetition.

- At the paragraph level, determine the main idea of each paragraph, and identify what you understand the author to be doing with each paragraph—e.g., warning, blessing, comforting, challenging, urging, convincing, informing, etc. (see discussion on "intended purpose" in chapter five).

- Locate all the logical connecting words (see chart above) and then analyze the logical relationships of ideas within the text. Determine whether the connection is just between phrases, or operating at bigger levels such as entire paragraphs or more.

- Finally, state to the best of your understanding the main Truth of the whole passage or book.

CHAPTER ELEVEN

Narrative Illustration

Ruth

In these next few chapters, I'll be inviting you to look over my shoulder to see how all the guidelines and methods I've been recommending to you look when put into practice. For this chapter, I've selected a narrative passage—the book of Ruth—to use as a model. In the next two chapters, I will demonstrate the other two literary types: poetry and discourse. Obviously, far more could be presented on the passages I've selected than I plan to write here. But my goal is not to write a commentary or a sermon series. Instead, my hope for you is that in seeing it actually done, your quest to follow the Bible will seem less daunting and more do-able. In all three chapters, I will use the same four steps: **seeing, understanding, sharing,** and **responding**. However, what we are looking for varies, depending upon the literary type.

Seeing

The first step in *seeing* any passage of the Bible is to determine the literary type, in order to ensure that we are asking the right kinds of questions. Ruth is a narrative. All narratives are built of certain elements: setting, characters, plot, and style. Because these features are all present in Ruth, we know it is a narrative, and because it is a narrative, we know that these will be the most fruitful things to consider if we want to follow the author's intent. Let's look at Ruth with each of these elements in mind.

Setting

The setting for a narrative is the product of two factors: time and place. The beginning of the book of Ruth establishes the initial setting right away, both in terms of time and place, beginning with time. "In the days when the judges judged, there was a famine in the land. . . ."

Setting			
Time	Days of judges	From the book of Judges, it was a terrible time, characterized by failure, wickedness, disobedience, violence, brutality, immorality, idolatry; it was every man for himself—"every man did that which was right in his own eyes." Foreign oppressors frequently overran the people of Israel. The leaders they had were unstable, rash, and poor examples to the people.	Very bad
	Famine in the land	Obviously a difficult time of hardship and deprivation.	Very bad

In other words, this was an especially bad period during a very bleak era in Israelite history. A biblical story could hardly start off on a worse foot than it does in the very first verse of Ruth.

Setting			
Places	Bethlehem, in the land of Judah	From 1 Chronicles 2, we learn that Caleb, the heroic spy from the tribe of Judah, had a great grandson named Bethlehem. Presumably the town was named for him. The name means, "House of Food [bread]." During the famine, Elimelech and his family abandon God's land, and Bethlehem in particular, looking for a place where "the grass is greener."	From good . . .
	Moab	Moab is a *terrible* choice. When God called Abram, he told him to leave his people, yet Abram brought his nephew Lot along, which proved to be a big mistake; he was nothing but trouble. They finally parted ways, with Lot taking the more inviting plains of the Jordan. Eventually, Lot ended up getting drunk and having incestuous relations with his two daughters. One of them gave birth to a son whom she named "From Father" (= "Moab"). Centuries later, when the Israelites came up out of Egypt and were heading toward the land, the Moabites stood between them and the land (thanks to Abram and Lot!), and refused them passage. The Moabite king Balak hired a prophet named Balaam to curse the Israelites (Numbers 22-24). God turned the intended curses into blessings, so Balak changed strategies. The Moabites seduced the Israelites into spiritual idolatry and sexual depravity at Beth-Peor (Numbers 25). This place thus is stigmatized as a place of tragic failure. When Moses died, Yahweh buried him somewhere in this God-forsaken land: "in Moab, in the valley opposite Beth-Peor" (Deuteronomy 34:6)—a tragic place for this hero's burial site. As readers, then, we should be shocked at Elimelech's decision. Moab has never done anything good for Israelites. We're left to wonder what in the world Elimelech is thinking!	. . . to very bad

As we should expect, Elimelech's bad decision leads to disaster. The narrative pace moves so quickly that in the space of three verses (1:3-5), the father dies, the two sons get married, both sons die, and ten years pass.

The pace then slows substantially, and over the course of the rest of chapter one, Naomi resolves to return to Israel's land. She attempts to persuade the two Moabite daughters-in-law to remain in Moab. Orpah does stay behind in Moab, but Ruth prevails in going with Naomi. The two of them travel back to "the house of food" (Bethlehem), in the region of Judah. Naomi and Ruth arrive right at the time of barley harvest, which is a very good time. Harvest time is like payday, a time of abundance.

Chapter two is comprised of five scenes.

Ch. 2	Place	Time
Scene 1 2:1-2	Home of Naomi and Ruth	One morning
Scene 2 2:3-13	In the barley fields of Boaz (a relative of Naomi's late husband)	While working that morning: Boaz greets the harvesters (v. 4), then dialogues with his foreman about Ruth (v. 5-6). He and Ruth then converse (v. 8-13).
Scene 3 2:14-16	Unspecified, where the field workers were taking their lunch together	Mealtime: Boaz invites Ruth to partake of food he provides. Next he speaks to his men, telling them to pull out extra stalks for her to gather as she works.
Scene 4 2:17	Back in the fields	Time passes very quickly, and we fast-forward to the end of the day. After threshing, Ruth has gathered a large amount of grain.
Scene 5 2:18-23	Home of Naomi and Ruth	Mostly a single conversation between Ruth and Naomi at day's end. But in v. 23, Ruth harvests together with Boaz's girls until the end of barley and wheat seasons—very fast pace. The chapter concludes with Ruth living at home with Naomi.

In terms of narrative scenes in chapter two, we have a chiasm, with the emphasis falling on the midday meal, where Boaz shows Ruth remarkable favor. The episode ends by returning to its original site, with Naomi and Ruth together again.

A Home of Naomi and Ruth
    B In the fields
    →   C Mealtime interaction
    B' In the fields
A' Home of Naomi and Ruth

Chapter three also reflects symmetry with its five scenes divided by time intervals, involving two places.

Ch. 3	Place	Time
Scene 1 3:1-5	Home of Naomi and Ruth.	One day: Naomi advises Ruth about approaching Boaz, and Ruth agrees to do as she says.
Scene 2 3:6-7	Boaz's threshing floor	That evening: Boaz lies down after eating and drinking; Ruth lays down at his feet undetected.
Scene 3 3:8-13	Boaz's threshing floor	Middle of the night: Boaz discovers Ruth and, learning her identity, promises to redeem her if possible.
Scene 4 3:14-15	Boaz's threshing floor	Early the next morning: Ruth leaves unnoticed by anyone but Boaz, who loads her with more barley to take home.
Scene 5 3:16-18	Home of Naomi and Ruth	When Ruth gets home: She reports the night's events and conversation with Boaz to Naomi.

Once again, the scenes form a chiasm. The emphasis centers again upon the conversation between Boaz and Ruth, this time in the middle of the night instead of the middle of the day. And again, the episode opens and closes in the home of Naomi and Ruth.

A Home of Naomi and Ruth
    B At the threshing floor of Boaz: evening
     →   C At the threshing floor of Boaz: middle of the night
    B' At the threshing floor of Boaz: early morning
A' Home of Naomi and Ruth

Chapter four is composed of three scenes and an epilogue.

Ch. 4	Place	Time
Scene 1 4:1-12	At the town gate (the place where civil judgments are made)	The next morning: The next-of-kin who has first rights to redemption of Elimelech's property arrives, and Boaz dialogues with him (v. 1-6). In v. 7, the action *freezes* while the narrator offers an explanation of the custom concerning property transfer using a sandal. The dialogue resumes in v. 8. In v. 9-12, Boaz addresses those at the gate, calling them as official witness to the legal transaction made. The people acknowledge their role, and pronounce a blessing upon the marriage of Boaz and Ruth.

Scene 2 4:13-15	Unspecified. Presumably the home of Boaz, who has taken in Naomi as well as Ruth	Rapid movement: marriage (the wedding itself is not mentioned), conception, birth of a son, blessing upon Naomi by the women of the town of Bethlehem.
Scene 3 4:16-17	Unspecified. Presumably the home of Naomi	Unspecified duration of time, as Naomi cares for the child in her lap (v. 16). Again the women speak, crediting Naomi with a son (v. 17a). The child is named (v. 17b). In v. 17c the narrator includes a *preview*: Obed becomes the father of Jesse, who becomes the father of David.
Epilogue 4:18-22	Change of form into non-narrative—a descending (father-to-son) genealogy covering ten generations. It begins with Perez, includes Boaz (7th generation), and continues through David, the tenth generation.	

Because of the break in form from storyline to genealogy, the emphasis falls upon the interpretive ending of the book.

Characters

Here is a brief analysis of each of the characters within the book of Ruth, using categories introduced in chapter eight.[1]

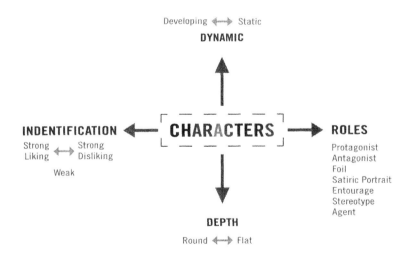

I will deal with the minor characters of the book first. The family of Elimelech is introduced at the start of the book: Elimelech, his wife Naomi, and their two sons Mahlon and Kilion. While Naomi will go on to become a major character, the other three may be treated together.

Elimelech, **Mahlon**, and **Kilion** are from Bethlehem, a town in the land allotment given to the tribe of Judah. We may infer that they are Judahites, both on the basis of where they live as well as the fact that Boaz, who is related to Elimelech (2:3; 3:12) is explicitly identified with the tribe of Judah (4:12). They are also identified as Ephrathites. The name Ephrah has two associations: one as the wife of Caleb (1 Chronicles 2:19, see chart on settings in chapter one), the other as a synonymous place name for Bethlehem (Genesis 35:19; 48:7), the burial place of Rachel. As Judahites, they are from the tribe from which the promised king is to come (Genesis 49:8-10), and the tribe to which the Israelites first looked for leadership during the period of the judges (Judges 1:1-19). These three Judahites are a disappointment.

We know Elimelech, whose name means, "My God is King," primarily for one thing: making a (literally) fatal decision. His choice to leave the land God chose for his people in favor of Moab, a traditional enemy of the Israelites, leads directly to his own death as well as that of his sons. They are *static* characters, undergoing no change. They are *weak* characters—readers do not identify with them because we only encounter them in a very few verses. For the same reason, they are *flat*, i.e., we know very little about them: they lived, moved to Moab, were married, and died of unspecified causes. They are too minor in the storyline to fulfill any role other than that of an *agent*.

Orpah is the Moabite wife of Kilion (see 4:10). She too is mostly a *static* character and is not developed (i.e., she is more *flat* than round) enough to elicit much identification. She initially plans to travel with Naomi to Israel, but then accepts Naomi's advice to remain in Moab. Her role is primarily that of a *foil* to Ruth—her decision to turn back contrasts Ruth's persistent resolve in going with Naomi. Orpah's decision is safe and sensible under the circumstances, while Ruth's is the riskier.

The **villagers** of Bethlehem appear in various places throughout the book. First, the women are incredulous when Naomi returns from Moab (1:19). Next, Boaz greets the harvesters in his field, and they return the greeting (2:4). Then the unnamed foreman is able to answer Boaz's inquiries about Ruth (2:6-7). Naomi cautions Ruth that she might not be safe working in the fields alone (2:22-23)—implying criticism of the village men.

It is customary for the village elders to come to the city gate to discuss civic matters. Boaz is able to gather ten of them—presumably a quorum—to witness and arbitrate the business transaction with the nearest relative of Elimelech (4:1-2). The elders and the others at the gate operate as a single entity (character) in 4:11-12, acknowledging their role as witnesses to the proceedings, then offering their blessing upon the marriage.

After Ruth bears a son, the women praise Yahweh and pronounce a blessing upon Naomi and the offspring. As Naomi cares for the son, the women curiously identify with her joy by claiming that *Naomi* has a son. The villagers function en masse, and they are *static*, *flat*, and *weak* in eliciting identification. They function merely as an *agent* in the storyline.

The relative next in line appears in 4:1-8. He is also a *flat* character, not even meriting a name. But in his case, he does a flip flop. At first he is eager to redeem the property. But when he learns that the woman Ruth is part of the deal, he reneges. He serves as a *foil* to Boaz. Like Orpah, he does the sensible thing, whereas Boaz takes the risk.

Several other names are mentioned within the book: Judah, Tamar, Obed, David, and those in the genealogy of 4:18-22. However, none of these function as characters within the story.

Ruth is a major character. As a Moabite, she inherits a tainted reputation, underscored within the narrative by the fact that the family's involvement with Moab brings death to three of the family's members. She does not undergo a change of character, but as the story unfolds, it is clear that her loyalty, humility, willing submission, industry, respectfulness, and commitment all combine to reverse the reader's negative associations with Moabites. The fact that she insists on accompanying Naomi demonstrates not only family fidelity, but also courage in accepting the social risks of relocating to the land of Israel, a nation that the Moabites had reduced to subservience for eighteen years during the period of the Judges (Judges 3:10f.), and where she could expect to face harassment, humiliation, and hostility.

Ruth is a *round* character, displaying numerous traits, all good. And while her character traits do not undergo change, her situation changes dramatically from widowhood and marginalized status (see 2:10) to marriage, motherhood, and inclusion into what will be the royal genealogy. For this reason, her character must be classified as *developing*. Identification is strong and very positive; the down-and-outer has been embraced, and readers are pleased to see that her commitment to God's people is rewarded. In seeking her refuge in Yahweh, the God of Israel (2:12), she is blessed for her faith. Boaz accords her the highest tribute in 3:12 when he says, "All my fellow townsmen know that you are a woman of noble character," using exactly the same Hebrew construction as the woman of noble character in Proverbs 31:10.

Boaz serves as Ruth's redeemer. He maintains a solid, exemplary character throughout the story, both in his gracious actions and his words. His obedience to God's commands is evident in the narrative.

- He makes provision for non-commissioned workers to gather for themselves the leftovers of the harvest, especially the poor and the alien—Leviticus 19:9-10; 23:22.

- He understands and follows the "flow chart" for inheritance of property—Numbers 27:8-11.

- He knows and accepts the responsibility of caring for and marrying the widow of a close relative—Deuteronomy 25:5-10.

He is kind (2:20), polite, gracious, self-effacing, responsible, devout, and a principled man of high standards. Because of these traits, he is a *round* character, and our identification with him is *strongly positive*. Like Ruth, his character doesn't change, but it is increasingly revealed throughout the story. His circumstances do change, involving both marriage to an "excellent woman," and fathering an heir who in turn will father David. Boaz is a developing character and a major player in the story.

Naomi is the main character of the whole story, regardless of the book's name. She is introduced in 1:2 as Elimelech's wife. After her husband and two sons die, she becomes simply "the woman" (1:5).[2] She takes center stage in 1:6, governing both the action and the dialogue (whereas Ruth does not even speak until 1:16). When Naomi and Ruth arrive in Bethlehem, the focus remains on Naomi (1:19-22). In her self-description, she has changed from Naomi ("pleasant") to "Mara" ("bitter"), though this name does not stick. The explanation of 2:1 presumes Naomi as the lead figure. And the episode ends with Naomi initiating conversation with Ruth, interpreting the events of the day for Ruth, and giving her instructions.

Naomi also initiates the action of chapter three by giving explicit directions to Ruth. Ruth compliantly follows what Naomi says (3:1-6), and the episode ends with Naomi once again both interpreting the events and advising Ruth. The storyline of the entire narrative ends by looking at Naomi. It is she (not Ruth) who is blessed by the women of the town, who owns the love of her daughter-in-law that is better than seven sons, and it is she who has been redeemed. Naomi is dandling the wonder child at the end of the story, and the women say, "*Naomi* has a son" (4:17). A strong case could be made for renaming this book "Naomi".

Naomi is a *round* and very complex character, grieving over the death of her men, torn in leaving her daughters-in-law, embittered, pleasantly surprised by Ruth's success in the fields, shrewd and calculating in her advice, and richly blessed in the end. Her character is *developing* throughout the story, and she recognizes the hand of God's blessing in restoring her from her earlier state of bitterness. Most readers will have a *strongly positive* sense of identification with her, especially those who have also experienced heart-wrenching loss and crushing disappointment. She is thus the story's *protagonist*, a fact seen more clearly by analyzing the plot, which is the next step.

Plot

In chapter eight, I explained that a narrative plot has a typical structure that looks like this:

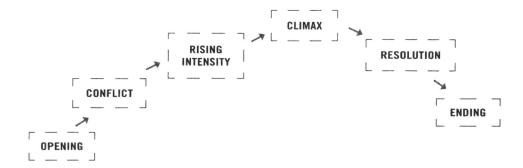

The opening verses of the book orient us to the setting of the events, which is typical. But in this case, the setting itself initiates tension and conflict. In the short space of just five verses of narration, the protagonist Naomi is thrust into overwhelming circumstances. Notice how this crisis happens so quickly within the story.

- Period of the judges: it starts off bad!

- Famine: it gets worse.

- Elimelech and his family go to Moab: a mind-boggling development. Of all places to seek security, why move to the land of a bitter adversary? The situation gets much worse.

- Elimelech dies: a crisis, even if not entirely surprising to the reader given Elimelech's decision.

- Mahlon and Kilion marry Moabite women: a dubious decision at best. According to Deuteronomy 25:3-6, the Moabites were excluded from God's people ten generations from the time of Moses' final speech. Clearly ten generations had not yet elapsed; in fact, Mahlon and Kilion were probably only the third generation.[3] Add disobedience to God's commands to Elimelech's foolishness.

- Mahlon and Kilion die: Elimelech's two heirs—and Naomi's "social security"—are eliminated. Naomi faces personal catastrophe.

- Naomi is left alone in Moab, bereft of all her loved ones. Tragic—or so it would seem.

Some relief of this tension comes when Naomi hears that the famine in Israel is over (good), and she resolves to return (also good). Tension re-emerges when Naomi is faced with a difficult choice: go back to her homeland utterly alone, or allow her daughters-in-law to accompany her at great risk to themselves. She fully recognizes the jeopardy and despair for them if they come with her, so she tells them to stay (mixed—good for them, bad for her). But Ruth insists on going with her (good for Naomi—bad for Ruth). Upon returning, Naomi acknowledges her bitterness and affliction. She is in a far worse state than when she had left. Nevertheless, the famine is over, barley harvest is beginning, she is back in the land where she is supposed to be, and she has a very loyal family member at her side. The first episode comes to a close, and it actually could function as a complete story in its own right, a bittersweet comedy, with Naomi restored to her home, sadder but wiser.

The second episode begins on an ambivalent note. Ruth proves her industriousness by taking the initiative to gather the grain left behind by the harvesters (good), though a Moabite woman doing so alone could be risky (uncertain). Boaz notices her, and clearly shows her favoritism, though no reason is offered by the text for this. Boaz ensures her success in gleaning, and her safety, both by allowing her to work with his servant girls (safety in numbers) and by ordering the men to leave her alone (very good). He affirms her and blesses her in the name of Yahweh (also good). He provides special food for her at mealtime, and makes further provision for her when she returns to her gleaning (good). Naomi is pleased with Ruth's success and the security offered to her, and Naomi now has both food (the initial problem of famine has now been solved) and a faithful and productive family member to provide for her (good).

In episode three, Naomi hatches a plan for Ruth that could result in a permanent solution for provision. Naomi advises Ruth to clean up, dress nicely, wear perfume, approach Boaz during the night and lie down next to him. It takes little imagination to understand what she is asking Ruth to do: Naomi is telling Ruth to seduce him (tension). Ruth agrees (more tension), and the narrative unfolds. When Boaz discovers her and learns her identity, he honors her, and vows to redeem her if at all possible (very good). However, there is someone else who has first claim to her (tension). Only the next day will anyone know whether or not Boaz can redeem her. This is actually very good news, because either way Ruth is going to be redeemed (good!). However, by now we have such a strong positive identification with Boaz that we don't want her to be redeemed by anyone except him (tension). He protects her identity from being discovered by others on the threshing floor, and gives her more grain (good). Ruth reports back to Naomi, who tells her (and us readers) to wait to see what will happen (suspense).

In the final episode, Boaz calls the nearest relative over to the city gate, making sure that there is a legally sufficient number of witnesses (mounting anticipation). He explains Naomi's intent to sell the family property, and specifies that the nearest relative owns first rights to purchase it. Boaz asks him if he would like to do so (high drama). The relative says yes (oh, no—that's not what we want!).

Boaz then adds, as if it were an afterthought, then the relative will also have the responsibility to marry Ruth, the Moabite, the widow. Notice how he now obscures what he really thinks of her, not mentioning her virtues this time as he has done in previous conversations. Instead he identifies her in two ways: as belonging to that other, despised people, and as a widow. Everything now rides on the relative's response (climax). The relative reverses his previous answer, claiming that to do so would jeopardize his estate. The real reason is not made explicit. Perhaps he believes that the foreign woman would pollute his household. Perhaps he is already married and doesn't want to upset his current marital situation. Or perhaps he's shrewd in thinking, *Mahlon got himself killed by marrying a Moabite, and so did Kilion. These women are bad news, and I don't want anything to do with them!*

The path is now open for Boaz to redeem Elimelech's property—and Ruth. The transaction is narrated quickly (resolution for Boaz and Ruth). The villagers at the gate pronounce their blessing on the marriage, and their favor underscores the reader's approval of how things have turned out. They marry, Ruth conceives, and then bears a son, but the focus shifts back to Naomi. The women state that *Naomi* has been provided with a redeemer, who will ensure her well being in her old age. They continue by saying *Naomi* has a son (resolution for Naomi), and this son becomes the grandfather of David, eventual king of Israel (evaluation). This is a key point in that it is also the solution to the implicit problem in 1:1, that this was "when the judges ruled."

Having traced the storyline, it is now possible to address the basic plot level questions within the narrative.

Who is the protagonist?	Naomi
	Her entourage includes Ruth the Moabite and, secondarily, a chorus of village women.
What are her calling, desires, or objectives?	She desires (1) food and physical security and (2) a lasting name for her family through her male offspring.
What is the source of the conflict? Who are the opponents?	The conflicts are not with human opponents, but entirely with her circumstances: instability (period of the judges), need for food during famine, threat of living in Moab, death of her husband and sons, loss of family name, need for redemption, need for an heir.

Are the initial objectives realized or exceeded in the narrative?	(1) She does receive food in plenty and her physical security is ensured through the marriage of Ruth and Boaz. (2) The family name is not only passed along, but the names of all her family members are "remembered" through this story forever. More importantly, however, is that her family lineage is connected to David, whose line will endure forever (2 Samuel 7:9ff.), and from whom Messiah will come.
What is the plot type: tragedy, comedy, or unresolved?	Without question, this is a comedy, ending far better than Naomi could ever have imagined.

Style

Here are several basic stylistic features that can be noted though much more could be developed here.

Genre and forms (see Appendix)	The genre is story.
	The overriding form of the narrative is history. Embedded within the history are other, smaller forms: prologue, irony, dialogue, command, chiasm, allusion, report, greeting, blessing, and covenant.
	There is also an epilogue (a genealogy), which is a clear break from the category of Narrative/Story/History. This interruption of the literary form should cause us to pay special attention.
Sentence types	The entire book alternates between storyline narration and speech, with only a few exceptions: parenthetical explanations necessary to the story in 2:1 and 4:7 and the genealogy of 4:18-22.
Allusions to other texts	Period of the judges: Judges
	Leaving the land during a famine: Genesis 12:10ff.; 26:1ff.; 41:57ff.; 43:1ff.
	Moab: the reader should be aware of Genesis 39:30-37; Numbers 22-25; Deuteronomy 23:3-6; Judges 3:12-30.
	Mara: Exodus 15:22-23
	Harvesting leftovers: Leviticus 19:9-10; 23:22
	Redeemer relative: Deuteronomy 25:5-10
	Redemption of property: Numbers 27:8-11
	Rachel and Leah: Genesis 29-30
	Perez, Tamar, and Judah: Genesis 38
	Jesse, David: 1 Samuel 16ff.
Repeated terms	Though many words are repeated, two of them merit special attention:
	return (Hebrew *šûb*), which occurs fifteen times in the book, twelve times in chapter 1.[4]
	redeem[er] (Hebrew *go'ēl*), which occurs fifteen times, all but once in chapters 3 and 4.

The significance of these features will be brought out later.

Understanding

Now that we have looked closely at the book of Ruth, we are ready for the second step for following the Bible, *understanding*. The following conclusions can be drawn from the observations made so far.

Structure of the Book

The structure of a narrative text may be based on several different factors: changes in setting, changes in characters, changes in literary form, or the elements of a typical plot structure. If we line these up for Ruth, they look like this.

	Prologue	S T O R Y L I N E					Epilogue
Reference	1:1-5	1:6-22	2:1-23	3:1-18	4:1-17		4:18-22
Setting	Period of judges, famine Bethlehem to Moab, in Moab ten years	From Moab to Beth-lehem	In the field, back home	Home, threshing floor, home again; one night	Next day, at the city gate 4:1-12, [home] one night		n/a
Characters	Elimelech's family	Naomi, Ruth and Orpah	Ruth and Naomi, Boaz and workers, Boaz and Ruth, Naomi and Ruth	Ruth and Naomi, Boaz and Ruth, Ruth and Naomi	Boaz, nearest relative, people in the gate, Boaz and Ruth, Naomi		n/a
Literary form		H I S T O R Y					Genealogy
Plot structure	Opening and initial conflict	Rising Intensity			Climax and resolution		Explana-tion

Ironies in the Opening

There are a number of situations and events at the beginning of the book of Ruth that surprise the reader, especially if the reader is familiar with other Bible stories. Irony is often the product of realities that contrast with our expectations.

- Irony: Leaving Bethlehem (the "House of Bread") during a famine, especially when readers know from other Bible stories what happens when biblical characters leave God's land during a famine (Abraham, Isaac, Jacob).

- Irony: Elimelech (= "my God is King") leaving the land that God has given to his people.

- Irony: Seeking security in Moab, the land of the enemy.
- Irony: Ruth is more committed to God's people than Elimelech's family, who abandoned them (1:16-17).

Narrative Tension

These factors contribute to a larger tension that emerges through the story, involving a moral and theological problem: what happens when obeying one of God's commands necessitates breaking another of his commands?

It is very clear that from Deuteronomy 23:3-6 that no Moabite or a descendent of a Moabite was to enter the assembly of God's people for ten generations. Mahlon should never have married Ruth to begin with. But he did, and she was left as his widow. However, according to Deuteronomy 25:5-10, the next of kin was to marry a childless widow and through her to produce offspring able to carry on the family name or bear the disgrace of "the unsandaled." The reader who is aware of these two commands sees this problem looming as the relationship of Boaz and Ruth blossoms.

The ending of the book——the genealogy——is what implicitly solves the theological problem. In keeping Deuteronomy 25, Boaz (and his descendents) broke Deuteronomy 23. Yet the blessing of the people, and especially of Yahweh, upon their union demonstrates that faithfulness to marriage covenant responsibilities is the weightier of the two commands, with the power to trump the other. Ruth's people will be Naomi's (and Yahweh's) people, and Ruth's God will be Naomi's God (1:16). She will be included in the assembly of God's people, as will her son. And not only will Ruth's grandson be allowed into the assembly of the people, he will be their greatest leader and the "father" of the Messiah himself!

There is one further endnote to this story; it may provide an important and surprising explanation for Boaz's openness to getting involved with a Moabite woman. This insight is also found in a genealogy, this one found in Matthew 1:3-6, where the identical genealogy of Judah through David is presented. And there we learn, for the first time, that Boaz's own mother was not a native Israelite either, but another "outsider" who had been allowed into the assembly, a woman of dubious reputation who was also honored for her courage and faith in the God of the Israelites. The woman's name is Rahab, the one who hid the spies in the city of Jericho. Boaz's own father had married her, and together they successfully reared this Torah-obeying, Yahweh-loving, Gentile-embracing "man of standing" (2:1), with the wisdom to treasure a woman of excellence. As Paul Harvey would put it, "and now you know the rest of the story!"

Linking to the Larger Context

In the Hebrew text of Ruth, the very first word (actually, the first prefix) of the story is "and." This is very significant, because it points to the fact that the story must be read against a larger, canonical mega-story. I have already pointed out many of the allusions to other passages. There are two more that need to be brought out now.

In the last section of the book of Judges there appears a repeated phrase: "In those days Israel had no king; every man did what was right in his own eyes." Civil unrest, immorality, idolatry, violence, and anarchy were rampant. The narrator's implicit, repeated solution is that Israel desperately needs a king. It is during this period that this historical story takes place. In the book(s) of Samuel, we discover that God concurs with their need for a king, and his choice for his people is David, the grandson of Boaz and Ruth. The book of Ruth, then, is an important connecting bridge between the narratives of Judges and Samuel. Ruth is a story of Israel on the road to kingship.

Ironically, however, this historical connection cannot be made until after the fact. Whenever I read the genealogy of Perez through David at the end of Ruth, I mentally supply a drum roll and a cheering crowd, building into a thundering crescendo with the final name, *David!* However, the biggest problem with reading the book of Ruth before reading Samuel is that you have no idea yet as to who David is. It is only after you have read of his life, passions, kingship, and his written psalms that you fully appreciate who David is and the role he plays in Israel's history. Interestingly, in the Hebrew order of the books of the Bible, in most manuscripts Ruth comes not only after Samuel and Kings, after the prophets, and after Psalms, but also immediately after the book of Proverbs, where the closing words extol the woman of excellent character (Proverbs 31:10-31), whose works bring her praise "in the city gates." Ruth is the ideal narrative embodiment of this "lady wisdom,"[5] while Boaz presents a best case scenario of the line from which Messiah will come, choosing wisdom over the seductive powers of foolishness.

Sharing

There are certain actions and qualities represented in the major characters of Naomi, Boaz, and Ruth that serve as examples across the generations of time (Romans 15:4) as we read this story. These are some of the main shared Truths the author appears to communicate through this narrative.

The first episode depicts devastating consequences of abandoning faith in God by leaving the land for Moab. Trust in God is a major theme throughout the Bible. Elimelech's decision to leave his people and forsake his land stands in complete contrast to Ruth, who seeks her refuge in Yahweh, the God of Israel (2:12), and affiliates herself with God's people. The author is encouraging us not to give up on God when things in life get tough. Choosing to live in knowing defiance to God's command leads to disappointment, frustration, and heartache. Though our natural tendency may be to seek our security independently of God's commands, patient, obedient faith in God will be rewarded.

As mentioned above, an important repeated term in the first chapter is "return." The Hebrew term may be translated as "go back" and also is the main Hebrew term for the English word "repent." The implied shared Truth underlying the use of this term in Ruth is that when we have "blown it" through sin or simple foolishness, there is always hope for those who turn back to faith in God. As tragic as the circumstances were for Naomi, she does receive redemption; blessing is found through returning.[6]

Ruth and Boaz are both examples of excellence of character for readers of this narrative. Ruth is explicitly identified in the narrated speech of Boaz as such in 3:11. What virtues make her excellent? Her first (and last) defining characteristic is the loyalty of her love (1:16-17; 4:15). She is wholly committed to her relationship to Naomi, Naomi's people, and Naomi's God. Secondly, she demonstrates her love for Naomi through her willingness to work to provide for their needs. It is she who initiates the idea to harvest in the fields (2:2), and her industriousness captures the attention of others (2:7). Third, she is commended for seeking her refuge in Yahweh, placing her faith in him above remaining with her family members back in Moab (2:12). Fourth, she displays genuine humility when recognized by others (2:10, 13). And fifth, she respectfully complies with advice given her by Naomi and Boaz (2:22-23; 3:3ff, 13ff).

Boaz is also an upright man. He is gracious and generous toward others, showing kindness toward them. He repeatedly shows his goodness toward Ruth by ensuring her safety and by providing food for her and Naomi. He is also a man who upholds God's commands; this quality is seen in his obedience to the instructions on allowing marginalized people to glean in his fields, and in following the proper protocol for redeeming family and property. He is an object lesson in being a redeemer. Whereas in many other biblical passages it is we who are the objects of redemption, an important shared Truth in Ruth is Boaz's role as a redeemer that serves as a pattern for us to follow: assuming the "costs" for bringing freedom to others (compare Philemon).

A further value affirmed by the book of Ruth is that God desires non-Israelites to be included in his redemptive plan. God uses his covenant people to bring salvation to a person who is otherwise "excluded from citizenship in Israel and [a foreigner] to the covenants" (Ephesians 2:12). His grace here extends beyond ethnic and social bounds. If it is large enough to incorporate a Moabite, then it is large enough for anyone. In other words, we must be prepared to accept and embrace people who are otherwise not "one of us." The early church faced the "Gentile problem" very early on (see Acts 13-15), and Ruth provides a clear example that covenant loyalty is much more significant than race or nationality. In Christ, the barrier between Jew and Gentile has been erased (Ephesians 2:13-22), but we are still prone to view God's acceptance of people as limited to those that we think are "worthy." The parameters of God's kingdom are frequently larger than our prejudices.

A final shared Truth emerges as we look more carefully at the wording of Ruth 4:14-15.

> The women said to Naomi, "Bless Yahweh, who today has not left you without a **redeemer-relative**, and may **his** name be called out in Israel. **He** will restore[7] your life and sustain you in your old age. For your daughter-in-law, who loves you and who is better than seven sons to you, has given birth to **him**."

Up to this point in the story, all of us have assumed that it is Boaz who is Naomi's redeemer-relative. (Remember, *she* is the protagonist!) Surprisingly, we learn that, in the women's perspective, Naomi's redeemer is not Boaz, but the one who has been born to her daughter-in-law. The last scene in the story looks not at Ruth, nor at Boaz, but at Naomi, with the redeemer-son in her lap.

Yet the last scene of the narrative is not how the author wishes to close the book. Instead, we have a break in literary form, a speed bump at the very end of the book. The son Obed is not the ultimate solution to all of the problems that Naomi faces. Her immediate problem is provision for food and security, a problem that has been solved by Boaz's and Ruth's faithfulness. The larger, though underlying, problem is desire for a lasting family name. And the genealogy with which the book closes points to a name very familiar to all Bible readers: David, whose name has forever been made great. Instead of this love story ending anticlimactically with a boring genealogy, it ends with a triumphant flourish. Naomi's family name will forever be memorialized through David and his royal line, which will lead to the Messiah-Son-Redeemer, Jesus. In the ultimate sense, he is the only relative able to restore our lives, whose name is to be called out in Israel and beyond.

The crisis set up by the first line of the book, "And in the days when the judges ruled . . ." will only be solved by a new order. Kingship needs to come to God's people. God had already planned for a king to come, and specifically one from the line of Judah (Genesis 49:8-12). Ruth starts with a problem—judges—and ends with the solution—David, their king. This is not merely a story of boy meets girl, they overcome challenges to their love, and eventually get married. The larger mega-story of the Bible points to its key role in the narrative of national and spiritual redemption, a story in which the "Son of David" stars, and of which we ourselves are a part.

Responding

The final step in following God's Word is to respond in ways that fit with and are appropriate to its message and purpose. Encountering this narrative should change and affect my life personally and practically. Here are some suggestions for appropriate ways to imagine living out these Truths.

- We shouldn't give up on God when things in life get tough. Elimelech and his family left God's land and his people when the circumstances got difficult. None of us are likely to be tempted to book a flight to Moab (present-day Jordan) to escape our problems. But exactly how do we try to escape our problems?

  I might try, like Elimelech's family, to run from my problems. Rather than reconciling a difficult relationship, maintaining personal integrity when under attack, or taking responsibility for doing the right thing when it is hard, I may be tempted to abandon it. I might want to literally leave the situation, thinking that life must be better elsewhere. In desperate situations, perhaps even suicide might seem like a better option than dealing with my "stuff."

  Or I might just quit believing in God. All of us have experienced hardships in our lives, or know personally those who have faced personal tragedy: loss of health, death of a family member, a financial crisis, suffering abusive treatment by those claiming to follow God. Some simply cannot accept that an all-powerful God who is responsible for bringing suffering to our lives could possibly be good, and so they stop believing that he exists at all.

  Or perhaps I don't seriously consider becoming an atheist, but do become an anti-theist—getting angry with God for doing this to me. Rather than bringing my frustrations, disappointment, and needs to him, I simply cease all prayer, and silently seethe.

  Or maybe I just want to quit. Life is too tough, and I don't even want to think about my problems, much less do anything about them.

  Perhaps I might not even try to follow God's Word, but instead try to do things my own way, thinking that it couldn't be any worse, and at least I could do what I feel like for a change.

Any one of these might be combined with attempting to live a double life by keeping up the outward appearances of having things under control, or at least maintaining a "spiritual" façade.

Any attempt at burying, running from, ignoring, or seizing control of the problems of our lives that is done independently of or defiantly toward God will ultimately result in disappointment, alienation, frustration, and bitterness. One way to respond to the shared Truths of the book of Ruth, then, is to do a personal inventory of my own life, reflecting on unhealthy ways I am handling the hardships within my own life. In what circumstances and in what ways am I prone to head off to my own equivalent of "Moab"?

- As I identify the ways that I attempt to function independently of God, I recognize my need to turn back to God. In Naomi's case, this involved physically returning to Bethlehem. In my case, returning is accomplished through repentance. This is done through prayers of confession and adopting new attitudes and behaviors. There is freedom and joy in removing any barriers that I might have erected between myself and God through my selfishness and sin. Turning away from my self-orientation and willfulness puts me in a better position to experience the redemptive blessings of God in my own life.

- The author of Ruth also promotes living a life of excellent character, exemplified in the behaviors of Ruth and Boaz. Their traits are patterns for me to follow.

Loyalty in love: I may seek special ways to show my love toward others, and by standing alongside them, especially when they are struggling through difficulties.

Graciousness: I can also demonstrate love by providing for the needs of others, showing generosity and kindness.

Industriousness: In my work habits I should be productive and responsible. Not only does this benefit me and my dependents, but it may also be a positive testimony to others in my workplace.

Trust in Yahweh: Faith in God is exhibited by "cooperating" with him, making a priority of knowing and following his Word, and being confident that his will revealed in the Bible is actually what is best for me.

Redeeming: I can look for opportunities to act redemptively on behalf of others. This involves knowing their needs and helping them by sharing or shouldering the costs for them to experience freedom. The costs may be financial, in helping to support people or ministries that share the gospel, or they may include time spent with troubled teens or struggling coworkers, or efforts in assisting the needy with homecare or medical needs.

- We are all called to have compassion and show mercy toward others, including (and especially) those we might think are somehow unfit. I confess that there have been categories of people that I have struggled to accept. I must constantly monitor whether I am guilty of wanting to limit God's grace only to those that I approve.

- And finally, I should respond to the promise of the future, coming Son of David with hopeful expectancy. This King has provided the final redemption for all believers and as such is the object of my hope, affection, and worship

Though this survey of the steps for studying the book of Ruth has been relatively brief, I hope that you can see that reading biblical narratives can be a rich and rewarding experience. Following through on all four steps, **seeing, understanding, sharing**, and **responding**, can lead to exciting insights and to life changes that are powerful and significant.

CHAPTER TWELVE

Poetry Illustration
1 Samuel 2:1-10

In the previous chapter we looked closely at how the four steps of **seeing**, **understanding**, **sharing**, and **responding** look when studying a narrative text, the book of Ruth. I would now like to do the same for another literary type in the Bible: poetry. We will look at the text of the prayer-song of Hannah in 1 Samuel 2:1-10.

Seeing

Once again, the place to begin in *seeing* any scriptural passage is by identifying the literary categories, so that we ask the most appropriate questions as we study. The literary type found in this passage is poetry. The genre is a psalm. And the main form is a psalm of thanksgiving.

The Immediate Context

This psalm is inserted within a book (1-2 Samuel) that is mostly narrative. In the first chapter, we are introduced to some of the characters: Elkanah, his two wives Hannah and Peninnah, and the high priest Eli. We learn that Peninnah had multiple children, but Hannah has had none, though Elkanah loved her. The anguish caused by her childlessness is compounded by Peninnah, who tormented her for many years. Hannah prayed to Yahweh, vowing that if Yahweh gave her a son, she would give him back to Yahweh. While pouring out her heart to Yahweh in the temple, Eli the priest approached her. After initially misjudging her fervor as drunkenness, Eli blessed her by expressing his desire that her prayers be answered. In due time, Hannah conceived and gave birth to a son, Samuel.

So the occasion for the thanksgiving psalm here is the coming of a long-awaited child. In a very real sense, then, this is a birthday song.

Thanksgiving Form

Typically, a psalm of thanksgiving will include most or all of these elements (see Appendix):

- a call to give thanks
- a description of distress before deliverance
- praise to God for his compassion, faithfulness, etc. in delivering
- generalizing statement about how God cares for all his people
- promise to fulfill one's vows
- final statement of praise

Here is how the text of 1 Samuel 2:1-10 lines up with these elements:[1]

1. *Call to give thanks (2:1)*

   Then Hannah prayed and she said: "My heart rejoices in Yahweh; my horn is exalted in Yahweh. My mouth boasts over my enemies, for I delight in your salvation."

2. *Praise to God for his compassion, faithfulness, and so forth, in delivering (2:2)*

   "There is no one holy like Yahweh; for there is no one besides you; and there is no Rock like our God."

3. *Generalizing statement about how God cares for all his people (2:3-9)*

   "Do not boast in proud talking or speak from your mouth proud arrogance, for Yahweh is a God who knows, and before him deeds are measured. The bows of the mighty are shattered, but those who stagger are armed with power. Those who are full hire themselves out for food, but those who are hungry are filled [fattened]. Even the childless has given birth to seven, while the one with many sons languishes. Yahweh brings death and makes alive; he brings down to the grave and resurrects. Yahweh grants wealth and destitution. He even raises up. He lifts from the dust the destitute and he lifts from the refuse the needy, to seat them with nobility and a throne of honor. For unto Yahweh belong the foundations of the earth; upon them he has set the world. The feet of the most pious he will guard, but the wicked will perish in darkness."

4. *Final statement of praise (2:10)*

   "It is not by strength that one becomes mighty; Yahweh will shatter the most contentious. He will thunder against them from the heavens. Yahweh will judge the ends of the earth. He will give strength to his king and he will lift high the horn of his anointed one."

Several observations can be made from looking at this.

1. In the call to praise there is not an invitation for others to join in, but rather it is self-focused: *my* heart, *my* horn, *my* mouth, *I* rejoice.

2. There is no section of this psalm that describes Hannah's distress before deliverance. From the context, it is clear that her inability to bear children, together with being provoked by her husband's other wife for years, was a source of grief for her. It is strange and surprising that she doesn't even mention these particular struggles (1:16).

3. There is no promise to fulfill one's vows. Typically, the psalmist will pledge to give public thanks, frequently accompanied by an offering. Again, this personal element is absent, although readers know from the context that she does make a pledge (1:11)—to give her offspring back to Yahweh. And in the narrative that follows, she does indeed keep that vow. Nevertheless, her vow oddly does not appear in the psalm, where you would expect it.

Parallelism

In the Bible, poetry is distinguished primarily by the use of parallelism, the "rhyming" of ideas and grammatical forms in lines directly parallel to one another (see chapter nine). To review, the main types of parallelism are:

- synonymous, where the ideas and/or forms are nearly the same
- synthetic, where the second line builds on the first by adding something different
- antithetic, where the second line contrasts with the first, usually indicated by the word "but"
- inverted, where the elements in the second line appear in reverse order from the first

While the distinctions between these are not always completely clear in every case, it can still be profitable to see this poem more closely and carefully by analyzing its parallelism. Once again, I use vertical lines and spacing to make it easier to see these patterns.

[1] Then   Hannah   prayed
     and   she   said: } synonymous

[2]   "My heart   rejoices | in Yahweh;
       My horn   is exalted | in Yahweh.   } synonymous

       My mouth   boasts | over my enemies,
for I   delight | in your salvation.   } synthetic

       There is no one holy | like Yahweh;
for there is no one | besides you;   } synonymous
and there is no Rock | like our God.

[3]   Do not boast | in proud talking
or [do not] speak from your mouth | proud arrogance,   } synonymous

for Yahweh is a God | who knows,
and before him | deeds are measured.   } synonymous

[4]   The bows of the mighty | are shattered,
BUT those who stagger | are armed with power.   } antithetic

[5]   Those who are full | hire themselves out for food,
BUT those who are hungry | are filled [fattened].   } antithetic

       Even   the childless | has given birth to seven,
       While   the one with many sons | languishes.   } antithetic

[6] Yahweh brings death | and makes alive;
       he   brings down to the grave | and resurrects.   } synonymous

7 Yahweh grants wealth	and destitution;		synthetic
He even	raises [them] up.		

8 He	lifts from the dust	the destitute	synonymous
and he	lifts from the refuse	the needy;	

to seat them	with nobility	synonymous
and a throne	of honor.	

For unto Yahweh [belong]	the foundations of the earth;	inverted
upon them	he has set the world.	

9 The feet of the most pious	he will guard,	antithetic
BUT the wicked	will perish in darkness.	

It is not by strength	that one becomes mighty;	synthetic
10 Yahweh will shatter	the most contentious	

He will thunder against them	from the heavens;	synonymous
Yahweh will judge	the ends of the earth.	

He will give strength	to his king	synonymous
and he will lift high the horn	of his anointed one" [Messiah]	

A variety of kinds of parallelism appear in this section. Ordinarily in a psalm, synonymous parallelism is dominant, though that is not the case here. A higher than normal amount of antithetic parallelism appears (a feature typically seen only occasionally in thanksgiving psalms).

Understanding

In comparing this passage to a typical psalm of thanksgiving, I pointed out that there were several differences. The call to praise does not invite others to join in, but rather Hannah speaks about herself: *my* heart, *my* horn, *my* mouth, *I* rejoice. This should lead you into thinking that the psalm as a whole will be very personal to her situation of childlessness, persecution by the "other woman," and grief, together with joy over having just borne a son. But surprisingly, the "I"-troubles cease after this introduction—there is not a single first person reference for the rest of her prayer. By starting off so personally, the fact that the rest of her poem is not personal stands out in contrast.

There are two typical elements of a thanksgiving that are missing. First, there is no description of Hannah's distress before her deliverance. Instead of talking about her own crises of childlessness and provocation by her rival Peninnah, the psalm focuses on how Yahweh reverses the fortunes of everyone, lifting up the lowly and humbling the proud. And second, the psalm makes no mention of Hannah's previous vow, nor her resolve to keep that vow. We would especially expect her to mention the vow if this prayer were a thanksgiving for her individual situation. However, in contrast to opening words, it turns out that this psalm isn't really about her and the birth of her son Samuel at all.

Reversal

The usual form of a thanksgiving includes a description of the psalmist's circumstances before deliverance, and often some details (with poetic language) of how God delivered him or her. But this psalm doesn't refer to any specifics of Hannah's situation. Instead, there is an unusually high amount of descriptions of reversals: the downtrodden are suddenly blessed, while the oppressors—rich, powerful, and wicked—are just as suddenly humbled. This double reversal is the dominant theme of the entire psalm. Notice the number of contrasts here.

Oppressors humbled		Downtrodden blessed
The bows of the mighty are shattered	But	those who stagger are armed with power
Those who are full hire themselves out for food	But	those who are hungry are filled
the one with many sons languishes	While	Even the childless has given birth to seven
Yahweh brings death	And	makes alive
he brings down to the grave	And	resurrects
Yahweh grants . . . destitution	And	Yahweh grants wealth . . .
		He even raises up.
		He lifts from the dust the destitute.
		He lifts from the refuse the needy, to seat them with nobility and a throne of honor.
the wicked will perish in darkness.	But	The feet of the most pious he will guard
Yahweh will shatter the most contentious.		
He will thunder against them from the heavens.		
		He will give strength to his king
		he will lift high the horn of his anointed one

Yahweh Raises a Horn of Salvation

The psalm of thanksgiving begins and ends with a reference to God "exalting," that is, lifting up high, a horn. In 2:1, Hannah says, "My horn is exalted in Yahweh." At this point it is not clear what Hannah means by this term. However, at the end of the poem there is a synonymous parallelism that clarifies the identity of this horn:

He will give strength | to his king
and he will lift high the horn | of his anointed one [Messiah]

{ synonymous

Hannah is looking to a horn for her hope of salvation, but it is not her son. It is a future, coming king, the anointed one (Hebrew, *meššîah)*. The book of (1–2) Samuel begins many years before Israel's first king with the birth and ministry of Samuel. It continues through Samuel's life until his own sons are adults (and have proven themselves as bad characters). The book presents Samuel installing Saul as Israel's first king, together with his own forty-year, very checkered career. It continues with the selection of David as Israel's second king, also a forty-year tenure, with all its ups (e.g., military victories, escaping close calls, and Yahweh making an eternal covenant with him) and downs (e.g., adultery with Bathsheba, murder of Uriah, and family turmoil and violence). The book of Samuel, then, is a post-Davidic retrospective look back over this tumultuous time period. And the reader's hope, just like Hannah's, is that Yahweh will raise up the ultimate king, the one who carries the title of "horn." The use of the term "horn" for this messianic hope is seen in other passages throughout Scripture as well.

Psalm 89 is a poetic reflection on the covenant that God made with David's offspring, questioning Yahweh's continued faithfulness and love to the Davidic heir to the throne. I pick up with the psalmist quoting Yahweh:

My faithful love will be with him, and through my name his horn will be exalted. I will set his hand over the sea, his right hand over the rivers. He will call out to me, "You are my Father, my God, the Rock my Savior." I will also appoint him my firstborn, the most exalted of the kings of the earth. (Psalm 89:24)

Psalm 132 also reflects on the promises Yahweh made to David and his royal line, especially how the throne of a Davidic heir would be established, and his rule will be both eternal and over all the earth:

For the sake of David your servant, do not reject your anointed one [Hebrew, *meššîah*]. The LORD swore an oath to David, a sure oath that he will not revoke, 'One of your own descendants I will place on your throne. . . . Here [in Zion] I will make a horn grow for David and set up a lamp for my anointed one [Hebrew, *meššîah*]. (Psalm 132:10-11, 17)

Luke 1:67-79 records the prophetic song of Zechariah on the occasion of the birth of his own son, John the Baptist. Like Hannah's song, however, the main focus of his song, especially the first half, has to do with God saving his people from their enemies. Zechariah's hope also is centered in the future, coming "David":

Praise be to the Lord, the God of Israel, because he has come and has redeemed his people. He has raised up a horn of salvation for us in the house of his servant David (as he said through his holy prophets of long ago), salvation from our enemies.

It seems very clear, then, that the references to horn at the beginning and end of Hannah's thanksgiving shifts attention away from merely the birth of her own son and centers her own hope for ultimate reversal and redemption on the future king.[2] In other words, her problem (i.e., her situation of distress) was not as personally limited or self-oriented as her childlessness.

Instead, her fortunes were wrapped up with the greater needs of all her people, which required a sweeping change of administration: "in those days Israel had no king; every man did what was right in his own eyes." The reversal she hoped for looked far beyond bearing her own son, looking with eyes of faith toward a future savior-king.

Structure of the Psalm

From the first to the end, Hannah's song praises Yahweh, both for his character (holy, all-knowing, just, all-powerful) as well as his actions, especially in (a) reversing the fortunes of those needing deliverance and (b) doing so by providing an anointed king (i.e., horn). This is how the psalm appears to be structured, emphasizing these points:

Then Hannah prayed and she said:

Yahweh exalts the horn

> *My heart rejoices in Yahweh; my horn is **exalted** in Yahweh. My mouth boasts over my enemies, for I delight in your salvation.*

Description of Yahweh

> *There is no one HOLY like Yahweh; for there is no one besides you; and there is no Rock like our God.*

> *Do not boast in proud talking or speak from your mouth proud arrogance, for Yahweh is a God who KNOWS, and before him deeds are measured.*

Reversal

> *The bows of the mighty are shattered, but those who stagger are armed with power. Those who are full hire themselves out for food, but those who are hungry are filled [fattened]. Even the childless has given birth to seven, while the one with many sons languishes.*

Yahweh's power over everything

> *Yahweh brings death and makes alive; he brings down to the grave and resurrects. Yahweh grants wealth and destitution. He even raises up. He lifts from the dust the destitute, and he lifts from the refuse the needy, to seat them with nobility and a throne of honor. For unto Yahweh belong the foundations of the earth; upon them he has set the world.*

Reversal

> *The feet of the most pious he will guard, but the wicked will perish in darkness.*

Description of Yahweh

> *It is not by strength that one becomes mighty; Yahweh will shatter the most contentious. He will thunder against them from the heavens. Yahweh will JUDGE the ends of the earth.*

Yahweh exalts the horn

> *He will give strength to his king and he will **lift high the horn** of his anointed one.*

The Bigger Picture: Context

While it might be natural to assume that 1 and 2 Samuel are separate biblical books (we usually count them as two books), traditionally they were counted and read together as a single book. The literary patterns, styles of writing, flow of thought, and theological emphases all point to a single (unnamed) author and point of view. When viewed in this way, the book of Samuel reflects a larger structure in which the poetic prayer of Hannah in 1 Samuel 2 and the psalm of David in 2 Samuel 22:2–23:7 merit special attention. Not only does the poetry in these places stand out by interrupting the narrative background, but it also interprets the rest of the story.

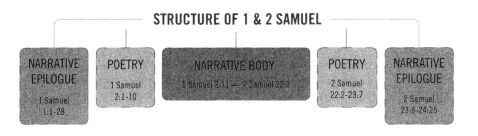

STRUCTURE OF 1 & 2 SAMUEL

| NARRATIVE EPILOGUE | POETRY | NARRATIVE BODY | POETRY | NARRATIVE EPILOGUE |
| 1 Samuel 1:1-28 | 1 Samuel 2:1-10 | 1 Samuel 2:11 — 2 Samuel 22:1 | 2 Samuel 22:2-23:7 | 2 Samuel 23:8-24:25 |

The two poetic sections turn the reader's attention away from the immediate circumstances—the birth of Samuel and the last words of David—to a description of Yahweh as a Rock (1 Samuel 2:2; 2 Samuel 22:2-3, 32, 47; 23:3), as the One who delivers and saves the righteous (1 Samuel 2:1; 2 Samuel 22:3-4, 32, 47; 23:3), and who has established an anointed king to rule (1 Samuel 2:10; 2 Samuel 22:44, 48, 51; 23:1, 3).

Motif

The narrative storyline of Hannah echoes several other stories in the Bible. Abraham's wife Sarah was also childless. Abraham loved her, but her desire for the family name to be carried on prompted her to offer to her husband another woman, her servant. This other woman was Hagar, and the birth of her son Ishmael to Abraham became a sore spot for Sarah. But she received assurance from other men (the three visitors) that God would give her a son. Eventually, Sarah's fortunes were miraculously reversed, and she did conceive, giving birth to Isaac (Genesis 16-21).

Jacob (Israel) also had two wives, Leah and Rachel. Though Jacob loved Rachel, she was childless, while Leah did bear children—six sons and a daughter. Like her grandmother Sarah, Rachel offered her servant girl Bilhah to her husband, and following her lead, Leah gave her servant girl Zilpah to Jacob. Leah, Bilhah, and Zilpah all bore sons, while Rachel's grief was compounded (Genesis 30). Finally, miraculously, Rachel did have a son, Joseph, who became the pride of his father and the envy of all his half-brothers (and later a second son, Benjamin). And it was through this favored son Joseph that God brought salvation to the rest of the family.

There are also several more stories that appear later in the storyline of the Bible that also reflect this motif of the reversal of childlessness with a son being born who will play a special role in God's plan for his people: Manoah's wife, who gives birth to Samson (Judges 13), and Zechariah and Elizabeth giving birth to John the Baptist (Luke 1). However, in only two cases does the birth of the miraculous child give rise to a song of thanksgiving to God: here in 1 Samuel 2 and in Zechariah's song of Luke 1:68-79. These two poems share common terms and themes (raising up a horn, salvation, deliverance from enemies). In addition, and more importantly, in neither case is the song of thanksgiving at the birth of the child merely a birthday song; instead, both poems look more broadly at what God is doing to bring kingship and salvation to all his people.

Sharing

We should always look to the broadest context first before trying to identify the shared Truths of a specific passage. Here are some emphases of the book of (1-2) Samuel as a whole.

- Without a king, Israel continues its downward spiral of apostasy and decadence (1 Samuel 2:12-36; 4-6): corruption of temple worship, Eli's wicked sons, the ark of the covenant captured, Samuel's wicked sons, perversion of justice.

- A kingly rule is established, though Saul, whose name means "the one asked for," is emotionally unstable and spiritually inert. Saul is clearly not the kind of king who can deliver the Israelites.

- Israel's problems will only be solved by a king who is devoted to Yahweh and who obeys God's commands (1 Samuel 13-31). "If both you and the king who reigns over you follow the LORD your God—good! But if you do not obey the LORD, and if you rebel against his commands, his hand will be against you, as it was against your fathers" (1 Samuel 12:14-15).

- Each subsequent leader suffers the consequences of his sin, pointing to the need for a new leader.

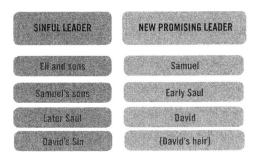

SINFUL LEADER	NEW PROMISING LEADER
Eli and sons	Samuel
Samuel's sons	Early Saul
Later Saul	David
David's Sin	[David's heir]

- Jerusalem (Zion) emerges as God's special dwelling place, both for worship and for establishing his rule, though the temple is still not yet built.

- God chooses David's line for blessing his people, and guarantees his promise to David's line through making an eternal covenant (2 Samuel 7) which offers the following: a great name, a place in the land, rest (i.e., peace from enemies), a house (i.e., David's line is a royal dynasty), a descendent who will build the temple, a Father/Son relationship, an eternal kingdom, and an eternal throne. While individual kings could disqualify themselves from the blessings of this covenant, the covenant with David's line itself was eternal. David was a case study illustrating this. David's sins against Bathsheba and Uriah (and hence God) did not invalidate the Davidic Covenant, but they did result in personal and political upheaval for him.

- God uses prophets to hold Israel's kings accountable: Samuel stands in power over Saul (1 Samuel 9-13, 15, 28) and David (1 Samuel 16), and both Nathan (2 Samuel 12) and Gad also stand over David (2 Samuel 24).

- The messianic king, i.e., the ultimate deliverer for Israel, has not yet come, but remains a future hope.

With the larger context now in mind, we now have a better basis for identifying the shared Truths that the author of Samuel intends for us as readers to know and to which we should respond. Here are Truths that are communicated through 1 Samuel 2:1-10.

1. We should delight in God's deliverance. In Hannah's case, the occasion of the delivery of her son brought her a delivery of another sort—from the shame and humiliation of childlessness in her society. But this is not what the poem is talking about. The deliverance concerns people more broadly and generally—delivery from poverty, hunger, enemies, and ultimately death itself.

2. Hannah's words serve as an example to all of us, causing us to identify with the larger problems of society. Her own personal problems are eclipsed by much bigger issues, ones that plague humanity.

3. Closely connected to deliverance is the future hope and anticipation of reversal. God's justice will fall upon those who are proud, boastful, oppressive, wicked, and oppose God. Conversely, God's mercy will revive and restore all those who are poor, needy, and unfortunate. In God's future kingdom, roles will be reversed and justice established throughout the earth.

4. The only final answer to any of our problems requires nothing less than God sending a royal, saving Messiah. Through her praise, Hannah lifts high this king—one who remains entirely a future hope for her—just as Yahweh will exalt him before all the earth.

Responding

For each of the shared Truths identified above, I would like to offer suggestions for how the author intends us to respond.

1. We should delight in God's deliverance. In Hannah's case, the occasion of the delivery of her son brought her a delivery of another sort—from the shame and humiliation of childlessness in her society. But this is not what the poem is talking about. The deliverance concerns people more broadly and generally— delivery from poverty, hunger, enemies, and ultimately death itself.

   This is a song of thanksgiving, spoken to Yahweh in response to Hannah's recognition that God is the source of deliverance. We too are encouraged by this passage to take delight in his salvation. We may do so in prayers of thanksgiving, in writing poetry, singing songs, offering testimony to others, causing them to remember that God does "guard the feet of his most pious" ones. Thus our first response to 1 Samuel 2:1-10 is to join our hearts with Hannah and the author of Samuel in announcing our deepest gratitude to God for saving us.

2. Hannah's words serve as an example to all of us, causing us to identify with the larger problems of society. Her personal problems are eclipsed by much bigger issues, ones that plague humanity.

    It is easy for any one of us to become so preoccupied with our own problems that we neglect to see ourselves as part of a larger picture. It takes more globally-focused eyes to see beyond our little world of personal finances, relationships, needs, and goals to an entire world that is aching for justice, hope, and redemption. We are not so independent of others as we are prone to think—especially those of us whose cultural context cherishes democratic politics, capitalistic economics, special interest groups, rugged individualism, and self-determination. Without intending to attack these norms here, honesty requires that we acknowledge that they have created a climate of autonomy where we are often reluctant to identify with others. This prayer may encourage us to think, pray, and act on broader levels. It's not "all about me," and my own concerns for deliverance should embrace and include the very real and pressing needs of others.

3. Closely connected to deliverance is the future hope and anticipation of reversal. God's justice will fall upon those who are proud, boastful, oppressive, wicked, and oppose God. Conversely, God's mercy will revive and restore all those who are poor, needy, and unfortunate. In God's future kingdom, roles will be reversed and justice established throughout the earth.

    God's kingdom has been described as upside-down. People's success and failure should not be judged by the short-term here-and-now, before God's kingdom standards have been established on earth. My best allies may well be those who are now poor, hurting, and needy. And I should not be seduced by the apparent success of those who take credit for their own riches and accomplishments. Only the rest of story will reveal final rewards and success according to God's standards of righteousness. This recognition should affect how I view others, whom I choose as role models, and the kind of character I strive toward myself.

4. The only final answer to any of our problems requires nothing less than God sending a royal, saving Messiah. Through her praise, Hannah lifts high this king—one who remains entirely a future hope for her—just as Yahweh will exalt him before all the earth.

Hannah lived at a time when there was no king in Israel, a time of moral and spiritual chaos. Yet her prayer began and ended with the announcement that God will someday establish a king whose reign would initiate a whole new world order. She saw something as mundane (!) as the birth of her son as a foreshadowing of the fulfillment of all our hopes and expectations. Unfortunately, when my own prayers are answered by God, I too rarely thank him only for that blessing, failing to see the bigger picture of redemption that he is working out on earth, made possible by the coming of the Messiah-King. I need to envision my entire life, with all of its little ups and downs, in the greater context of what God is doing for me in Christ.

CHAPTER THIRTEEN

Discourse Illustration

3 John

We have now looked at illustrations of how to use these four steps of Bible study—*seeing*, *understanding*, *sharing*, and *responding*—for two different literary styles in the Bible, narrative and poetry. In this chapter I will illustrate how the four steps of Bible study look when we turn to the third and final literary type, discourse. The passage I've selected for this is a short, one-chapter book, 3 John.

Seeing

As with every passage of Scripture, the place to begin in *seeing* is identifying the literary categories present in the text. At the end of chapter ten, I offered a series of guidelines to follow when reading a discourse. The first of these guidelines is to identify the genre you're reading (e.g., prophecy, epistle)—and look at the Appendix for further guidelines appropriate to that genre.

In this case, the literary type found in this passage is discourse. The genre is an epistle.

Epistle Genre

In the Appendix, I have devoted a section to each of the genres of the Bible, with several pages of discussion of things to look for when reading an epistle. There I present a standard outline for an epistle, one that looks like the one below. While it is possible for there to be variations or missing elements, this is the standard form; when there are exceptions to the pattern, it is usually for a good reason.

OPENING
    Name of the Sender
    Name of the Recipients
    Greetings

PRAYER OF THANKSGIVING / BLESSING

BODY
    Teaching (Doctrinal Exposition)
    Urging (Exhortation)

TRAVEL LOG / SENDING OF SOMEONE ELSE TO VISIT

CLOSING [the order of these two may be reversed]
    Greetings
    Blessing

Let's see how well 3 John fits to this pattern:[1]

OPENING   v. 1
    Name of the Sender
        The elder,
    Name of the Recipients
        to beloved Gaius, whom I love in the truth.
    Greetings

PRAYER OF THANKSGIVING / BLESSING   vv. 2-4
            [2]Beloved, I pray that you may enjoy good health and that all
        may go well with you, even as your soul is getting along well. [3]It
        gave me great joy to have some brothers come and tell about your
        faithfulness to the truth and how you continue to walk in the truth.
        [4]I have no greater joy than to hear that my children are walking
        in the truth.

BODY
    Teaching (Exposition)

Urging (Exhortation) vv. 5-13

> [5]Beloved, you are faithful in what you are doing for the brothers, even though they are strangers to you. [6]They have told the church about your love. You will do well to send them on their way in a manner worthy of God. [7]It was for the sake of the Name that they went out, receiving no help from the pagans. [8]We ought therefore to show hospitality to such men so that we may work together for the truth. [9]I wrote to the church, but Diotrephes, who loves to be first, will have nothing to do with us. [10]So if I come, I will call attention to what he is doing, gossiping maliciously about us. Not satisfied with that, he refuses to welcome the brothers. He also stops those who want to do so and puts them out of the church. [11]Beloved, do not imitate what is evil but what is good. Anyone who does what is good is from God. Anyone who does what is evil has not seen God. [12]Demetrius is well spoken of by everyone—and even by the truth itself. We also speak well of him, and you know that our testimony is true. [13]I have much to write you, but I do not want to do so with pen and ink.

TRAVEL LOG / SENDING OF SOMEONE ELSE TO VISIT v. 14

> [14]I hope to see you soon, and we will talk face to face.

CLOSING v. 15

Blessing

> Peace to you.

Greetings

> The loved ones here send their greetings. Greet the loved ones there by name.

— —

As you can see, John has followed the standard epistle form quite closely, though in the body of this very short, personal letter there is not the customary two-part structure of teaching first, followed by urging. Instead the context focuses primarily on urging, with teaching interspersed.

Repetition

The second guideline for reading biblical discourse is this: Look for introductory phrases that will assist you in seeing the structure of the book.

In 3 John, the author uses an introductory phrase (a formula, see Appendix under "Forms") to divide the book into sections. The phrase is "beloved" (Greek *agapēte*; NIV: "dear friend").

Once again, here is the epistle genre outline, with this word "beloved" highlighted. It signals the recipient of the book (v. 1), the beginning of the prayer (v. 2), the beginning of the body (v. 5), and a section break later in the body (v. 11).

OPENING v. 1
    Name of the Sender
        v. 1 The Elder,
    Name of the Recipients
        v. 1 . . . to beloved Gaius . . .
    Greetings

PRAYER OF THANKSGIVING / BLESSING vv. 2-4
        v. 2 Beloved, I pray that you . . .

BODY
    Teaching (Exposition)

    Urging (Exhortation) vv. 5-13
        v. 5 Beloved, you are faithful . . .
        v. 11 Beloved, do not imitate

TRAVEL LOG / SENDING OF SOMEONE ELSE TO VISIT v. 14

CLOSING v. 15
    Blessing
    Greetings

The payoff for having looked for at introductory phrases here in 3 John is that we see that the body has two parts: verses 5-10 and 11-13.

We read the third guideline at the end of chapter ten: Find the significant repeated terms which will give you a good idea of the main points.

There are two words repeated by the author of 3 John that are especially prominent: (be)love(d) and truth. Here is where these words occur in the text.

OPENING   v. 1

¹The elder, to **beloved** Gaius, whom I love in the **truth**.

PRAYER OF THANKSGIVING/BLESSING   vv. 2-4

²**Beloved**, I pray that you may enjoy good health and that all may go well with you, even as your soul is getting along well. ³It gave me great joy to have some brothers come and tell about your faithfulness to the **truth** and how you continue to walk in the **truth**. ⁴I have no greater joy than to hear that my children are walking in the **truth**.

BODY

Teaching (Exposition)

Urging (Exhortation)   vv. 5-13

⁵**Beloved**, you are faithful in what you are doing for the brothers, even though they are strangers to you. ⁶They have told the church about your **love**. You will do well to send them on their way in a manner worthy of God. ⁷It was for the sake of the Name that they went out, receiving no help from the pagans. ⁸We ought therefore to show hospitality to such men so that we may work together for the **truth**. ⁹I wrote to the church, but Diotrephes, who **loves**² to be first, will have nothing to do with us. ¹⁰So if I come, I will call attention to what he is doing, gossiping maliciously about us. Not satisfied with that, he refuses to welcome the brothers. He also stops those who want to do so and puts them out of the church. ¹¹**Beloved**, do not imitate what is evil but what is good. Anyone who does what is good is from God. Anyone who does what is evil has not seen God. ¹²Demetrius is well spoken of by everyone—and even by the **truth** itself. We also speak well of him, and you know that our testimony is **true**. ¹³I have much to write you, but I do not want to do so with pen and ink.

TRAVEL LOG   v. 14

¹⁴I hope to see you soon, and we will talk face to face.

CLOSING v. 15

    Blessings

        Peace to you.

    Greetings

        [15]The **loved**[3] ones here send their greetings. Greet the **loved** ones there by name.

- -

As pointed out above, the primary function of the repetition of *(be)love(d)* is to indicate structural divisions. The two exceptions to this are in verse 6, describing Gaius' love (noun) and in verse 9, where what Demetrius loves (verb)——being first——contrasts with Gaius.

The other important repeated term is *truth*: appearing once in the opening (verse 1), three times in the prayer (verses 3-4), once in the first section of the body (verse 8) and twice in the second section of the body (verse 12). It does not tell us anything about the structure, but it is does indicate that it John is stressing this idea throughout this text.

Understanding

We move to the second step of Bible study, **understanding**, as we consider the fourth guideline from the chapter ten summary, which is to distinguish which topics brought up by the author receive the most emphasis, through the amount of space given to them, interruption of forms (missing or added elements), extended illustrations (e.g., figures, stories, poems), and/or repetition.

Truth and *love* are the only two topics that stand out for special emphasis through repetition. John does bring up other ideas: joy (verses 3-4), faithfulness (verses 3 and 5), good versus evil (twice each in verse 11). However, none of these have much space given to them and instead serve the larger themes of love and truth.

There are no additional elements to the epistle genre, though two are missing. There is no explicit greeting in the opening, but in this case the letter is very short, it is personal throughout, John is very warm and supportive of Gaius, and there is a greeting at the end.

Secondly, the body of the epistle does not have a section of teaching (exposition) before turning to urging (exhortation). The reason for this is that while most often epistles written to churches present teaching before moving to urging, in epistles written to individuals (1-2 Timothy, Titus, Philemon, 2 John, 3 John) this is not the case.

John does not use any extended figures of speech or poems. However, he does use two real life figures to illustrate his point. Diotrephes is a negative example: unwelcoming, self-promoting, exclusive, and maliciously gossiping. By contrast, everyone, especially those on the side of truth, speaks well of Demetrius.

The next guideline at the end of chapter ten was as follows: At the paragraph level, determine the main idea of each paragraph, and identify what you understand the author to be doing with each paragraph: e.g., warning, blessing, comforting, challenging, urging, convincing, and informing. (See discussion on "intended purpose" in chapter five).

The paragraphs for 3 John line up with the different sections of the epistle genre, with one additional paragraph division in the body, signaled by "**Beloved**" (verse 11).

Paragraph	Verse	Purpose
1 Opening	1	To **greet**, expressing love which is grounded in truth
2 Prayer	2-4	To **affirm** Gaius: (a) expressing prayer for his continued well-being, and (b) the joy that John has in Gaius' commitment to the truth
3 Body	5-10	To **urge** Gaius to receive and support others who are committed to the truth. He does this in several steps: (a) he affirms Gaius for already expressing love for those strangers, (b) he asserts that all believers ought to support coworkers on behalf of truth, and (c) he critiques Diotrephes for loving self-promotion and for gossiping rather than welcoming other brothers.
4 Body	11-13	To **urge** Gaius toward good rather than evil. He explains the direct connection between goodness and God, then offers Demetrius as a positive example of the truth.
5 Travel Log	14	To **inform**, communicating John's wish to see Gaius in person.
6 Closing	15	To **close**, expressing greetings from John's cohorts, toward Gaius and his cohorts as well.

The next guideline for reading discourse literature in the Bible that I offered in chapter ten was this: Locate all the logical connecting words and then analyze the logical relationships of ideas within the text. Determine whether the connection is just between phrases or operating at higher levels such as entire paragraphs or more.

OPENING v. 1

PRAYER

²Beloved, I pray that you may enjoy good health and that all may go well with you, **even as** your soul is getting along well . . . .

Comparison: John expresses his desire that Gaius' physical well being is comparable to the well being that his soul already enjoys in the truth.

BODY vv. 5-13

⁵Beloved, you are faithful in what you are doing for the brothers, **even though** they are strangers to you.

Concession: Gaius' support of fellow believers extends to those he does not know previously.

⁸ . . . We ought **therefore** to show hospitality to such men

Result: Because these men went out for the sake of Jesus (i.e., the Name), they are deserving of respect given to God.

so that we may work together for the truth.

Purpose: The reason they should be given respect is because they, like John and Gaius, are mutually in the service of truth.

⁹I wrote to the church, but Diotrephes, who loves to be first, will have nothing to do with us.

¹⁰ . . . **So if** I come, I will call attention to what he is doing, gossiping maliciously about us.

Condition/Result: If John does come to Gaius, then he will expose Diotrephes.

¹¹ . . . Beloved, do not imitate what is evil **but** what is good.

Contrast: doing evil versus doing good.

¹³I have much to write you, **but** I do not want to do so with pen and ink.

Contrast: Though he wants to say more, he prefers not to do so in writing.

TRAVEL LOG   v. 14

CLOSING   v. 15

In keeping with John's other writings (sometime scholars refer to this as "Johannine dualism"), he presents several contrasts in this epistle, especially contrasting evil Diotrephes with Demetrius, who is good, loving, and committed to truth. These two figures, along with the positive pattern of Gaius, are live object lessons that illustrate John's points in this book.

Diotrephes:	Versus	Gaius:
• Loves to be first • Has nothing to do with John and his cohorts. • Maliciously gossips • Refuses to welcome partners in the truth • Prevents others from welcoming brothers by removing them from the church		• His soul prospers • He is faithful to the truth and walks in it • Faithful in showing support to brothers in the truth. • He has shown them love. Demetrius: • Everyone speaks well of him • The truth also commends him. • John and his associates speak well of him.
Evil: done by those who have not seen God		Good: from God

Sharing

This brings us to the final guideline that I offered in chapter ten for reading discourse literature in the Bible: State to the best of your understanding the main Truth of the whole passage or book.

John's epistle to Gaius commends him for his faithfulness to the truth, which is displayed by his love and gracious support of other believers. This is love in action, positive proof of goodness that comes from God himself. This has earned him a reputation for being on the side of love, truth, and goodness. Likewise, those belonging to the truth also speak favorably about Demetrius, another role model for them. By contrast, Diotrephes is the very opposite. Instead of loving others, he promotes himself. He does not affiliate himself with truth lovers——he avoids them and verbally attacks them behind their backs. Furthermore, Diotrephes pressures others within the church likewise to reject traveling representatives of the truth, threatening to kick them out of the church if they don't.

The shared Truth that the author intends for the benefit of all readers of this epistle is stated in verse 8: "We ought therefore to show hospitality to such men so that we may work together for the truth." The "we" envisioned here includes everyone who is aligned with truth: those who love God and who demonstrate God's goodness to others. In John's view, love, truth, goodness, and God all come in one package. To be committed to one of these necessarily involves all the others, with God as the ultimate source of the other three. God is love, and love comes from God (1 John 4:7-8). Jesus is the truth wrapped in a human body (John 14:6), bringing truth to humanity (John 1:17). Likewise, everything that is good comes from God (3 John 11).

It is therefore not only inconsistent but unthinkable that someone could claim to know or love God without knowing, loving, and caring for all those who are with him, fellow workers for the truth. Lack of love for other believers ("brothers") is clear evidence that one is not a child of God (1 John 3:10), while loving the brothers is equally clear evidence that we have experienced new life (1 John 3:14) and that God is in us (1 John 4:12). So loving God is inseparable from loving those who belong to God (1 John 4:21).

More particularly, this love of God, good, and truth is demonstrated by how we treat brother (and sister) believers as they bring the truth to others. While this will include showing hospitality (NIV), a survey of other translations of verse 8 broadens this idea to include receiving, welcoming, helping, and supporting those who are fellow workers for the side of truth.

Responding

Because the entire body of this epistle is primarily urging the reader, the response that it calls for is more action oriented. Rather than, for example, building a case here that loving God entails following Jesus' example as well as keeping his commands, and that the heart of God's commands is that we love one another (points John makes elsewhere in his gospel and in 1 John), he assumes all this. This epistle focuses on the practical consequences of these truths; it's a "So what?" kind of book.

As readers, then, we "walk out" (verses 3-4) this shared truth of the importance of loving and supporting others. Here are some suggested ways to consider in order to make your love for other believers tangible.

- Showing kindness: cultivating a sensitivity to recognize and care for other believers who are needy. Doing so might involve helping them with physical problems, or encouraging by listening to those who are emotionally or spiritually hurt or weary.

- Praying: offering regular, intercessory prayer on behalf of them. Following John's example, this would include praying for both the well being of their physical health and prosperity as well as their souls.

- Opening our homes: opening our hearts to other believers is also practically shown by opening our homes to them, sharing meals together, perhaps sleeping accommodations, and more importantly, our own selves.

- Supporting them financially: helping meet their material needs by giving them the money necessary to enable them to share in the work of teaching others the truth.

- Recognizing the need for working together: in our contemporary culture which is prone to operate individualistically, we need to reprogram our thinking. We should strive to see ourselves as connected to a larger whole, and to seek our personal identity in relation both to Christ and to others who are in Christ. Since we are fellow workers, we should look for ways to build team spirit—a unity that is empowered by the Spirit.

- Learning and obeying God's truth: loving God is also manifested in loving truth. We should therefore be diligent in seeking his truth. This will include continual, careful reflection on God's Word and a willingness to receive it by following it.

EPILOGUE

Through the Forest

It's my hunch two kinds of people will read the last chapter of a book like this. First, there are those who have read the entire book up to this point and now are in effect finishing the last lap. If you fit into this category, my sincerest congratulations for your commitment, perseverance, and continued interest.

The second kind are those who want a sneak peek at the ending, to see how it all comes out, and perhaps whether or not it is worth reading in entirety. Many math textbooks contain the correct answers to the problems at the end so that students can compare their answers and, if there is a discrepancy, work backward from the answer to the original problem. If you fit into this category, then this chapter may not fit your expectations very well. You see, this epilogue raises more questions than it gives answers. In reality, the whole book is about asking questions.

The Quest for Questions

Learning to read the Bible better is largely a matter of refining the best questions to ask of the text. Actually, our learning about any topic is mostly dependent upon the questions that come to our minds as we think about things. In chapter seven, I introduced the provocative writer and thinker Neil Postman. Here are some of his thoughts, taken from a different book, on the role of questions.

> [A]ll knowledge we ever have is a result of questions. . . . We do not see *anything* as it is except through the questions we put to it. . . . For example, that a vaguely formed question produces a vaguely formed answer; that every question has a point of view embedded in it; that

for any question that is posed there is almost always an alternative question that will generate an alternative answer; that every action we take is an answer to a question, even if we are not aware of it; that ineffective actions may be the result of badly formed questions; and most of all, that a question is language, and therefore susceptible to all the errors to which an unsophisticated understanding of language can lead.[1]

What we see in the Bible, how we understand it, the shared Truth that we recognize in it, and the way that we respond to it, hinge entirely on what kinds of questions come to our minds when we read it.

LEARNING TO
READ THE BIBLE BETTER IS LARGELY A MATTER OF REFINING THE BEST QUESTIONS TO ASK OF THE TEXT.

A common maxim says, "There's no such thing as a wrong question." Of course this is correct, because only statements, not questions, can be demonstrated as true or false. However, not all questions are created equal. Some questions are simply better than others, because they are more appropriate to gaining useful understanding. Suppose you're considering purchasing a car, and you've limited your choices to three different models. To select between them, you decide to ask some questions of the salesperson. Some questions you could ask might be very helpful in making a wise choice, while other questions might be irrelevant, or even nonsensical.

Helpful questions	How much does it cost? What kind of gas mileage can I expect? What security features does it have? How long does the standard warranty last, and what is covered? What financing options are available?
Unhelpful questions	Why are the tires black? How does the radio know how to play only one station at a time? Where did Chevrolet get its name? How many employees work for this auto manufacturer? If you need vision correction, is it better to drive this car wearing contacts or glasses? Couldn't you call a carburetor an admixturator instead?
Nonsensical questions	How far can I go between tune-ups if I only drive in reverse? What kind of fuel would this car run on if gas weren't combustible? How fast can this car accelerate in cubic pounds per acre? Is there enough oxygen in the atmosphere at 42,000 feet elevation for this car to drive?

We have precisely the same situation when studying the Bible. Some questions are critically important. Other questions may not be very helpful because, even if they can be answered, they don't give us the information necessary to help us to determine the author's intentions.

In this book, I've laid out what I believe to be the most helpful questions to ask when the goal is seeking to follow Scriptures as a guide to God's Truth, and responding in ways that honor him and bring us greatest joy.

Wonder Management

Perhaps another profitable way of considering the questions we ask is to recognize that we need to recapture, cultivate, and train a childlike sense of wonder at the world around us, including the world of the Bible. As Conrad Hyers perceptively points out:

> The great enemy of religion is not godlessness so much as matter-of-factness . . . . There are those for whom life is alive and ringing with great wonders and those for whom life is largely a ho-hum parade of trivia. Instead of a world filled with incredible creations—like the childhood marvels on Old MacDonald's farm, with a pig, goat, horse, cow, chicken, duck, and goose here, there, and everywhere—it becomes for many a world of blah: "here a blah, there a blah, everywhere a blah, blah!" The basic problem in education [is a] lack of fascination . . . . Both religion and education are fundamentally an awakening of a profound sense of mystery . . . . Actually, wonder is one of the more fundamental religious virtues, perhaps *the* most fundamental of all.[2]

If this is the case, then following the Bible is a journey that begins with wonder, a desire to understand reality from a God's-eye viewpoint. We travel through the world of Bible, now equipped with a set of questions to help us navigate its terrain. Then, having experienced it by agreeing with, responding to, and participating in the Truth claims that we encounter, our lives undergo transformation. We ultimately think and behave more like Jesus, our mentor and model. And that is a great, exciting, and wonder-full mystery!

Summary

What questions have we learned to ask that help us to follow the Bible more closely? Well, the methods of Bible study that I have recommended to you involve four steps, each of which concerns a particular question.

Step one is *seeing*. *Seeing* asks the question, "What does it say?" There are a number of secondary questions that are very helpful, beginning with the literary categories of the text being studied.

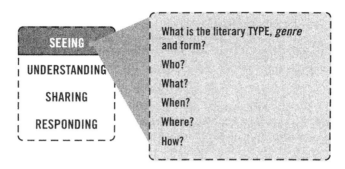

Because there are three different types of literature in the Bible, all the ensuing questions for what to look for in this first step of seeing depend on the literary type.

Type	Things to look for
Narrative	What *genres* and **forms** does the author use? What is the setting (time and place)? Who are the characters, and how does the author want us to view them? What plot conflict(s) appear(s), and how are the problems resolved? What techniques does the author use to emphasize his points?
Poetry	What *genres* and **forms** does the author use? What types of parallelism? What images and metaphors appear? What other stylistic features occur (inclusion, chiasm, acrostic, etc.)? What is the emotional tone of the passage?
Discourse	What *genres* and **forms** does the author use? What is the main topic, and what is the author saying about it? What repeated terms appear? How does the author argue his case? What logical connections exist that relate the units of thought together? Is the author drawing upon other texts to strengthen his argument?

The second step is *understanding*. *Understanding* asks the question, "What does it mean?" Most essentially, it takes all the answers from the previous step, and asks how all this fits together into a whole?

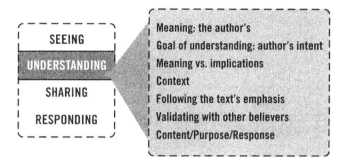

The third step is *sharing*. *Sharing* asks the question, "What truths is it teaching?" This step investigates what ideas and content the author intends his readers to understand. It also considers the question, "What is the author's purpose for writing?"

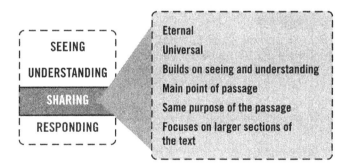

The fourth step is **responding**. **Responding** asks the question, "So what?" How does the author ideally intend his readers to respond? If the Truths that the author claims to be true are indeed true, what consequences would that have for my practical, daily life? How would I think differently? Feel? Imagine? Behave? Act, and react?

An Encouraging Word

Do you have this all down pat? Not yet? Don't be too anxious about it—studying the Bible is a skill we learn over a lifetime of walking with the Lord. Work at it bit by bit. Start with a commitment to study a small book or passage, using these methods. Then do it again . . . and again. Try it with different types and genres in the Bible. Each time, you'll find yourself becoming more comfortable with the methods and more skillful at getting positive results.

I once met a young lady in a one-week Bible class that I was teaching. She shared with my wife and me the bizarre and incredible story of how she had been abducted from her native Africa, brought to the United States, and subsequently abandoned. Homeless, rejected, and utterly desperate, without another person to turn to, she had found refuge in a church that happened to have an unlocked door and a very compassionate and sympathetic pastor to welcome her. His family ultimately adopted her. She told us how she had come to meet Jesus through her own reading of the Bible.

She also tried to describe to us, in her broken English, how deeply she treasured God's Word. With face radiating, she exclaimed, "I just can't take the Bible off my eyes!"

Though her English grammar may be less than perfect, that phrase perfectly describes my own deepest wish for you, dear reader. May you, too, so fall in love with Jesus and value his Words that you can't take the Bible off your own eyes.

APPENDIX

Digging Deeper

Genres and Forms

In chapter two, I identified three main types of literature in the Bible: narrative, poetry, and discourse. I then devoted a chapter to describing each of these types. I presented seven genres as well. A genre is a category of writing with its own kind of structure and message. Just as there are different kinds of stores (tire, candy, shoe, sporting goods) or departments in a department store (boys' clothes, hardware, cosmetics, appliances), so there are different "departments" within the Bible. In the Bible, the "departments" are apocalyptic, epistle, gospel, prophecy, psalm, story, and wisdom. Here are some guidelines for reading each of these genres.

Genres

Apocalyptic

Apocalyptic literature is a style of biblical writing that reflects a unique "mood" toward the world and human history. Apocalyptic uses a lot of symbolism and vivid language to talk about the conflict between good (God, angels, and the righteous) and evil (Satan, evil spirits, and the wicked). You'll find apocalyptic in Daniel, Zechariah 9-14, and Revelation.[1] This apocalyptic "mood" is seen in the following literary features.

1. *Heavenly perspective*: In apocalyptic literature, the message usually comes from heaven to the human author by way of a dream, a vision, or an angel.

2. *Universal scope*: Unlike the prophets whose messages concern Israel, Judah, and particular nations (e.g., Edom, Assyria), the

apocalyptic writers are concerned with *all* humanity, as well as the angels, the earth, the stars, the sun and moon, and heaven.

3. Vivid and *strange language*: Bizarre creatures, dreamlike happenings, and other unusual objects and events are used to excite our imagination.

4. *Symbolic* use of things (e.g., scroll, tree, horns, lampstands, bowls), places (e.g., Babylon), animals (e.g., goat, dragon, beast), and numbers (e.g., 7, 12, 666, 144,000). Time is also divided into numerically significant periods, e.g., seventy "sevens," "time, times, and half a time," 1,260 days, Revelation 11.

5. Constant use of *imagery from the Hebrew Bible* (e.g., plagues, trumpets).

6. *End times focus*: Apocalyptic looks not only to the future, but especially to the end of time, the final page of the history of the universe. There is a general pessimism about the world—the world is in such bad shape that it is beyond hope for reformation. The world's problems are so great that nothing less than a complete destruction and a new beginning will solve them. Apocalyptic reflects belief in two separate ages in God's plan: *Now*: a time of rampant evil with suffering for the saints, and the *future*: a completely different time period free from the ravages of evil. The expectation is that God's coming is just around the corner, followed by eternal, conscious experience of individual judgment and rewards, e.g., Revelation 19.

7. *History is pre-planned*: All events in human history are following one pre-determined, master plan which reaches from the creation and Fall to its future climax, the "eschaton".

8. *Cosmic conflict*: History is building toward the great showdown between good and evil, with Jesus (the Messiah, the Lamb, the Son of Man) as the ultimate winner.

9. God will ultimately save the righteous. Because of this, God is praised in numerous songs of *worship*.

10. Common literary forms found in apocalyptic include blessings, commands, curses, dialogues, doxologies, formulas, lists, quotations, and visions (see "Forms" below).

Contrasting Prophecy with Apocalyptic [2]	
Prophecy	Apocalyptic
Author's view:	*Author's view:*
Things are bad → obey *Torah!*	*Things are bad* → new creation coming!
Focus → Israel and Judah	*Focus* → the universe
Message: Repent!	*Message:* Endure!
Hope: healing of the nation	*Hope:* a new kind of existence

Here are some guidelines for understanding apocalyptic:[3]

- Apocalyptic draws heavily upon other Scriptures for its symbolism. The best way to understand apocalyptic, then, is to become as familiar as possible with all the rest of the Bible, from which it draws its symbolic vocabulary. At the very least, the serious student should keep a concordance ready to look up the background texts behind the symbolism.

- Recognize the purpose of apocalyptic and adjust your genre expectations accordingly. Often readers approach apocalyptic writings with the goal of identifying present-day people, places, and events as the "fulfillment" of these "prophecies." To do so is to *misread* these texts at the most fundamental level.[4] Their purpose is not for us to uncover the possible modern-day referents, but to accomplish greater purposes.[5]

- Apocalyptic is meant to foster our faith and give us hope, encouraging us to faithful, expectant living. It assures us of God's ultimate, sovereign control, especially at times when he may seem distant due to the evil and suffering we encounter in this life. Apocalyptic serves to warn us that this world bears the indelible stain of sin, and that we can expect to suffer as a result. It teaches us about the patient justice of God: God will ultimately ensure that justice is meted out upon the wicked.

- The importance of apocalyptic writings is for our *present-day* life. It always contains specific ethical admonitions we need to hear and heed *now*.

- Apocalyptic reminds us of the ultimate supremacy of Christ, and thus evokes a response of *worship*. If a Bible study of apocalyptic passages fails to produce worship, it has been stillborn.

Epistles

The epistle[6] genre refers to the books of the Bible that are letters. Since epistles are discourse, everything we look for in discourse literature we should expect to find in an epistle (see chapter 10). In addition, there are some other features unique to epistles that influence our interpretation of them. These include:

(1) *Structure*: Most of the epistles follow a basic structure:

OPENING
    Name of the Sender
    Name of the Recipients
    Greetings

PRAYER OF THANKSGIVING / BLESSING

BODY
    Teaching (Doctrinal Exposition)
    Urging (Exhortation)

TRAVEL LOG / SENDING OF SOMEONE ELSE TO VISIT

CLOSING [the order of these two may be reversed]
    Greetings
    Blessing

(2) *General movement*: In most epistles, the author first gives information (teaching) and then calls for action (response). It moves from explaining different Truths to how to live out those Truths.

(3) Reference to *the other Scripture*: The epistles speak plainly about Jesus Christ. As the authors teach about him, they constantly refer back to the rest of Scripture. What is written there often helps us understand Jesus better.

(4) The features listed in the outline above set out the predictable pattern of certain forms we can expect in an epistle. In addition, epistles commonly use a number of other forms. We might even think of an epistle as a collage or a jigsaw puzzle in which the overall message emerges through how the author arranges

all the different parts (forms). Common literary forms include blessing, closing, command, doxology, epilogue, exhortation, exposition, formula, greeting, hymn, list, motif, opening, prayer, quotation, rhetorical question, and travel log (see "Forms" below).[7]

(5) As in all genres of biblical literature, looking for repetitions is vital to understanding the text. Repetitions are used to *emphasize* a point (e.g., the word "one" is used seven times in Ephesians 4:4-6 to underscore Paul's discussion of the unity of the church in 4:1-16). They are also used to indicate *structural patterns*. Certain phrases are often used in the epistles that indicate divisions as the author moves from one thought to the next. In other words, these phrases provide us with the "chapter" divisions the author had in mind (rather than our present chapter divisions that were provided hundreds of years later). A few examples of these phrases (formulas) are:

> *"What shall we say? . . ."*
>
> *"Brothers . . ."*
>
> *"[Dear] Children . . ."*
>
> *"Dear friends . . ."*
>
> *"Here is a trustworthy saying . . ."*

Repetition also can provide cohesion.[8]

Reading an epistle is *not* like reading a business letter. The writers employ *many* creative techniques and patterns to make their arguments more effective and memorable. Be on the lookout for poetic features (especially parallelism, figures of speech, chiasm, and inclusio), illustrations, and examples. For example, when Paul describes to Timothy how to live, he does not merely give him a list of tasks, but uses the images of a son, a soldier, an athlete, a craftsman, a dish, and a servant (2 Timothy 2).

Sometimes an author will write about a particular thought to different readers in separate letters. It can be very useful, then, to compare *parallel passages*, because often one passage clarifies what may be obscure in the other. For example, we may gain some insight into the command to "be filled with the Spirit" by comparing it to its parallel:

Ephesians 5:18-19	Colossians 3:16
Instead, *be filled with the Spirit*. Speak to one another, with psalms, hymns, and spiritual songs . . . always giving thanks to God the Father for everything.	*Let the word of Christ dwell in you richly* as you teach and admonish one another with all wisdom, and as you sing psalms, hymns, and spiritual songs with gratitude in your hearts to God.

Gospels

The gospel genre is actually a kind of biography, yet each one is more than that. They are carefully constructed narratives (see chapter 8) about the earthly life, ministry, and death of Jesus and his mission of salvation, designed to challenge the reader's thinking and lifestyle. They are not merely informational or historical—they are also persuasive. The Christ-story is used as the vehicle for attempting to change the reader's understanding of God, the world, and self in light of what Jesus has done.[9] Thus the purpose of the gospels is to proclaim the "good news" (Greek *euangelion*) of what God has done in and through Jesus Christ so that people will respond by repentance. A key issue that separates the genre of gospel from mere biography is that it demands a *response* from the reader.

Because of the distinctive content and concerns of the gospels, there is no true parallel to this genre outside of the Bible.[10] Starting with biography, the gospel writers "broke the mold" to fit their unique message and needs.

The books of Matthew though Acts[11] contain the gospel story of Jesus and his followers. Everything that characterizes narrative and story are applicable to gospel, so be sure to read those sections. In addition to what I've said in those sections, there are additional, special features:

- Dependence upon the Hebrew Bible: The gospel narratives link the story of Jesus Christ with the story begun in Genesis and continuing throughout the Scriptures. The gospel writers seek to demonstrate how this "new thing" is clearly anticipated in the plan of God all along, and so locate their message within the storyline of the entire Bible. Their story is seen as the continuation of a larger story begun centuries before by other biblical writers, i.e., what they share is a new act to a pre-existing drama described in earlier biblical literature.[12] Therefore, the gospels draw upon the Hebrew Bible for direct quotations, allusions to similar phrases, motifs, vocabulary, and style, as well as parallel forms, characters, scenes, and events.

- Unique emphasis: Each gospel approaches the story of the good news about Jesus from a different perspective, highlighting different aspects of Jesus' character or actions. For example, in Matthew, Jesus is compared to someone who is similar to but greater than Moses.

- Key motifs: There are a number of motifs that occur throughout the gospels: Jesus as the promised Messiah, the fulfillment of the Scriptures, Jesus as God's Son, the kingdom of heaven/God, the disciples' misunderstanding of who he is, miracles, the Holy Spirit, opposition from Jewish leaders, etc.

- Same basic pattern: Each gospel has its own form of the following elements: prologue, ministry of John the Baptist and baptism of Jesus, ministry of Jesus (teaching, miracles, parables, etc.), identification of Jesus as the Messiah (the long-awaited individual through whom Yahweh will redeem his people), Jesus' triumphal entry into Jerusalem, his arrest, trial and crucifixion, resurrection, epilogue.

- Focal point: The cross and resurrection of Jesus are seen as the "high point" of Jesus' ministry and mission on earth. However, each gospel writer also had his own unique purpose and style. Each one carefully arranged, adapted, combined, edited, and thus interpreted the details of Jesus' life to produce a work specifically designed to accomplish his goals.[13]

- Common literary forms: These include birth announcement, commission, dialogue, epilogue, genealogy, history, parable, prayer, prologue, and quotation.

- Strategy: The story-teller is "omniscient," i.e., the narrator can tell us details of his characters' inner life (including Jesus'). This may include what they are thinking and feeling, what they are doing when nobody else is present (e.g., Matthew 4:1-11; Luke 24:13-14; John 8:6; 12:6; Acts 24:26), and things we would not be able to know if we had actually been bystanders at these events. They are also written from a clearly Christian perspective of belief and post-resurrection understanding (i.e., there is no attempt to disguise what we would call subjectivity).

Matthew emphasizes Jesus as the greater-than-Moses, Scripture-fulfilling Messiah claiming his right to the throne of the kingdom of heaven (kingdom of God).[14]

Mark is a *dramatic irony*; that is, the reader knows more about the identity of Jesus as the story unfolds than any of the human characters do. It emphasizes the mystery and misunderstanding surrounding Jesus' earthly ministry and suffering, made sensible only by retrospectively looking at his earthly life from the viewpoint of knowing that he was and is the Messiah, the Son of God (1:1).[15]

Luke-Acts presents how in Jesus, God kept his past promises to extend his saving plan beyond the Jews to all the people, and how by the Holy Spirit this plan continues beyond Jesus' earthly life to include the ongoing mission[16] of the church.[17]

John compels belief in Jesus by presenting witnesses and proofs to back up Jesus' claims for himself[18] and his offer of eternal life to those who remain faithful to him.

I have one final note for studying the gospels. Please do not confuse "Life of Christ" studies with studies in the gospels—they are two entirely separate things. While various "harmonies" of the life of Christ are available in print, the whole point in reading the *gospels* as written is to determine what distinctive perspective is provided by each of the biblical authors. As Gordon Fee has correctly pointed out, "the Gospels *in their present form* are the word of God to us; our own reconstructions of Jesus' life are not."[19]

Prophecy

Contrary to common thinking, prophecy is not primarily about predicting the future. Prophecy is any message given by God through a certain person to other people. Sometimes this message involves declarations about the future, but not always. In fact, most often it does not. Prophecy simply refers to anytime a biblical writer says (or implies), "Thus says Yahweh." The 10 Commandments (Exodus 20:2-17; Deuteronomy 5:6-21) and the other biblical laws are prophecy, as well as Isaiah through Malachi (except Lamentations). When reading prophecy, you will encounter all three different types of literature: narrative, poetry, and discourse. Here's what to look for when reading prophecy.

- The phrase, "Thus says Yahweh.": This indicates the claim made by the prophets that they are actually speaking for God. Of equal importance is the fact that this phrase, along with "says

Yahweh" and "An oracle: the word of Yahweh" (Zechariah 9:1; 12:1; Malachi 1:1), usually marks a new literary section as well.

- Quoted speech of God: There is a lot of first-person frame of reference, i.e., "I," "me," "my," and "mine" referring to Yahweh (rather than the prophetic author). Most often when God speaks, it is in poetic verse.

- Common topics: These include commands of God, accusations of sin, covenant breaking by God's people, calls to repentance,[20] threats of punishment, and promises of future blessings.

- Lawsuit: A legal charge is brought against Israel/Judah by Yahweh through the prophets for having broken the terms of their covenant with God (see "Forms" below).

- "The day of Yahweh": This describes a future time (from the prophet's perspective) when God will enter into human history in a decisive way. Sometimes the emphasis is on salvation, peace, and blessing. At other times it sounds terrible, filled with foreboding, darkness, war, and devastation. The day of Yahweh does not refer to a single day, but rather to anytime when God specially intervenes in human affairs, restoring the fortunes of a righteous remnant who are preserved through even the most severe judgment. Thus the day of Yahweh is a time of cosmic house cleaning.

- Future kingdom: The prophets speak of a time when Yahweh will establish a peaceful, universal kingdom under a co-rulership shared between himself and his Messiah. The Messiah is a specially anointed son-king from the line of David, who, after he delivers his people and conquers his enemies, will initiate an eternal reign of peace, sealed by a renewed covenant with his people.[21] The Gentile nations will also undergo a conversion to Yahweh-worship, and they are gathered in and included in the blessings of Yahweh's reign. The Holy Spirit will be poured out on people, bringing power and the comfort of his constant, indwelling presence. This future age will also be a time of glory, joy, and peace in God's presence, together with the removal of sin, curses, and death.

- Ethical commands: The hearers/readers are told both to cease specific sinful activities and to seek righteous, God-honoring behavior. Often the prophets condemn merely "going through the motions" of religion to challenge the hearts and inward motivations of the listeners.

- Main characters: The chief characters within the prophets of Isaiah through Malachi are Yahweh, the prophets themselves,

Israel/Judah, the righteous remnant, and the nations—
especially Edom, Egypt, Assyria (Nineveh), and Babylon.

- Common pattern: Several of the prophetic books share common, large-block elements.

	Isaiah	Jeremiah	Ezekiel	Zephaniah
Judgments against Israel	1-12	1-25	4-24	1:1-2:3
Judgments against nations	13-23	46-51	25-32	2:4-15
Announcements of salvation	40-55	26-35	33-48	3:9-20

- Common literary forms include blessing, commission, diatribe, lament, lawsuit, oracle, promise, and rhetorical questions.

- The prophets are frequently called upon to perform symbolic actions. These include Zedekiah's horns (1 Kings 22); Isaiah's 3-year nakedness (20); Jeremiah's belt (13) and buying a field (32); Ezekiel lying on his left side, and then his right (4); Hosea's marriage to Gomer (1, 3); Amos' ripe fruit (8); Jonah's flight toward Tarshish (1); Zechariah's shepherding (11).

- There is also extensive use of satire and irony: A very effective way to cut the proud and arrogant down to size is to mock them through these techniques. Thus, "prophecy which seeks to instruct, amend, and reform also seeks to offend."[22]

Here are some basic guidelines that you can follow in order to read and respond to biblical prophecy with greater understanding:

1. Determine the literary type you are dealing with in each section. The prophetic genre may contain narrative, poetry, and discourse all mixed within a single book. Once you have identified the type(s) of literature encountered in your passages, adjust your reading expectations to fit that type.

2. Decide whether you are dealing with a prophetic passage that is apocalyptic. If it is, then apply the apocalyptic guidelines.

3. Identify the various forms within the passages being studied. Because prophecy can come in any of the three literary types (narrative, poetry, and discourse), there is a greater variety of forms in prophecy than in any other genre.[23]

4. Recognize that prophecy is organized topically rather than chronologically or sequentially. Some describe its movement as "symphonic." Like a musical score of a play or movie, there are melodic themes, harmonizing elements, counterpoint sub-

themes, stanzas, and movements. All these terms seem to do justice to the structure better than attempting to outline the text. Then seek to understand its structure and the arrangement of the parts on the basis of either theme (content) or literary patterns.

5. Identify the figurative language. As a general rule, the Bible will interpret its own symbols either in the immediate context or elsewhere in the Bible. The best way to interpret symbols is to look carefully at the main points being developed by the author in the passage, and then to compare that symbol with other passages by using a concordance.

6. Investigate whether the passage is referring to other Scriptures. Very frequently the prophets build on or allude to prior passages (especially from Genesis through Deuteronomy). They also commonly contest how the priests, leaders, and false prophets have (mis)interpreted the earlier promises of God to their forefathers. When this is the case, make sure that you understand these background passages.

7. Determine the author's purpose from the text. Ask questions like: What kind of response from the reader is the author trying to elicit? Joy? Hope? Comfort? Repentance? Fear? Shock? Awe? Worship? etc. What kinds of sins are exposed, and what would be modern-day equivalents? What is the basis of its hope? What is the content of its hope?

8. Be on the lookout for dramatic literary techniques. The prophets, generally speaking, stood over against the status quo of society. Their message was seen as radical and usually offensive to the listeners. The prophets can be characterized as unwanted, annoying interrupters of the lives of their contemporaries. As a result, be especially alert to the presence of satire and irony, two favorite tactics used by critics of society.

9. On the basis of the structure of the passage, the author's purpose, and the main points that the author develops, identify the Truths that the author is sharing and the responses most appropriate to those Truths.

Psalms

The first and most important feature to recognize when reading biblical psalms is that they are always poetry. Not all poetry fits into the genre category of psalm, but all psalms are poetry. As C. S. Lewis puts it:

Psalms are poems, and poems intended to be sung: not doctrinal trea-
tises, nor even sermons. . . . Most emphatically the Psalms must be
read as poems; as lyrics, with all the licenses and also the formalities,
the hyperboles, the emotional rather than logical connections, which
are proper to lyric poetry.[24]

The place to begin your study of a psalm is by reviewing the guidelines
I gave for studying poetry. Psalms are found throughout the entire Bible—
within larger narrative sections (e.g., Judges 5), discourse (Philippians
2:6-11) and, of course, poetry (Habakkuk 3). Here's what to keep your eyes
on:

- A psalm will usually have a single, overriding form that provides
  its structure and outline. These include lament, praise, and
  thanksgiving. Most psalms fit into one of these three categories.
  In each of these, certain elements are usually present, though
  the order may be slightly different, or one or two elements
  omitted.

In the **lament** form, the author complains to God about what he is
going through and asks God to deliver him. The usual elements of a
lament psalm are:

An opening cry or question (e.g., "Have mercy on me, O God" in
Psalm 57:1)

A description of the situation or enemies (57:3-4, 6)

A call for God to intervene (57:2)

Statement of confidence in God (57:7-8)

A vow to give thanks when delivered (57:9-10)

A **praise** psalm exalts God for his character or awesomeness. The
usual parts include:

A call to praise (Psalm 149:1)

Listing of those who should praise (149:2-3)

Reasons for praising are given (149:4-9)

A concluding "Praise the Lord!" (149:9)

A psalm of **thanksgiving** gratefully recognizes God for his particular
gracious acts of salvation toward his people. The usual parts are:

A call to give thanks (Psalm 116:1-2, 7)

A description of the former problems or predicament (116:3-4)

Praise to God for delivering (116:8-11)

A general statement about God's care for his people (116:5-6)

A promise to fulfill vows (116:12-14, 17-19)

A final statement of praise (116:15-16)

Some psalms do not fit these three forms (for example, Psalm 133), but these are the exceptions. It's possible to group these psalms into other formal structures, like royal psalms that celebrate kingship (Psalms 2, 72, 93-100, 110) or psalms focusing on God's Word (Psalms 1, 119).

- The basic feature of biblical poetry is parallelism. Be sure to check back in chapter nine for an introduction to how parallelism works. Here are some other features of parallelism that supplement that material.

Ellipsis: Frequently the second line will omit an implied element from the first line.

| May Yahweh | cut off | all flattering lips |
| and --- | --- | every boasting tongue |

Psalm 12:3

Here you naturally understand the implied subject (Yahweh) and verb (will cut off) from the first line and "import" it to the second line. This omission is called an *ellipsis*. Most often, when one or two elements are missing, they are compensated for by an added, different element in the second line.

| to bind | their kings | with fetters | --- |
| --- | their nobles | with shackles | **of iron** |

Psalm 149:8

| For you | O God | tested us | --- |
| you | --- | refined us | **like silver** |

Psalm 66:10

These added words serve to balance out the length of the two lines, and are sometimes referred to as "ballast." Sometimes the corresponding elements are simply lengthened to compensate for the missing element.

Yahweh is	gracious	and compassionate
---	**slow to anger**	and **rich in love**

Psalm 145:8

Other common poetic features that appear in psalms include:

Refrain: a repeated phrase or line that indicates either emphasis (e.g., "His love endures forever" is the second line in every verse of Psalm 136) or divides the psalms into literary sections, like Psalm 57:5, 11: "Be exalted, O God, above the heavens; let your glory be over all the earth."

Selah: a word indicating a pause, usually significant in indicating literary units as well.

Change of images: such as from "man" to "tree" to "chaff" in Psalm 1, or "green pastures" to "valley of the shadow of death" to banqueting "table . . . in the house of Yahweh" in Psalm 23.

Common literary forms seen in psalms include: acrostics (alphabet psalms), blessings, formulas, imprecation (praying for God's judgment on someone), inclusio, lament, praise, prayers, quotations, rhetorical questions, refrain, and thanksgiving.

- *Superscriptions*: Many of the psalms, especially in the book of Psalms, have superscriptions, that is, brief notes at the beginning that give information about that psalm.

Here are some guidelines that should help you when you read psalms.

1. Recognize the type of literature you are dealing with: poetry (see chapter nine). Since poetry uses a different format to communicate a different kind of truth, we should not look for either the "moral of the story" (narrative) nor a central proposition or argument (discourse), but rather how we should encounter and respond to the various word pictures and creative perspectives on reality that we encounter.

2. Identify the overall form of the psalm you are studying. Your choices are Hymn, Lament, Praise, and Thanksgiving (see "Forms" below).

3. Group the parallel lines together, and note what kinds of parallelism are used (e.g., synonymous, antithetic) throughout the psalm, looking for any patterns. Check also for chiasm, inclusio, and refrain.

4. Determine the structure of the psalm you are studying. There are several clues to how the units are divided.

    *   Use of a refrain: a repeated word, line, or verse that introduces or closes off a section (e.g., Psalm 42:5,11; 46:7, 11; 59:6, 9, 14, 17; 73:1, 13, 18; 107:6-8, 13-15, 19-21, 28-31).

    *   Use of *Selah*: nearly always a division-marker.

    *   Use of chiasm.

    *   Change of images: from one set of metaphors to another.

    *   Change of voice: psalmist speaking about God versus speaking to God or to others; psalmist speaking versus God or someone else speaking; etc.

5. Determine the meaning of the images and figures of speech.

6. Read the psalm in light of its *context*. Every psalm is in a context, whether embedded in a story, a gospel, or within the book of Psalms. Contrary to the common practice of approaching each chapter in Psalms as an independent literary work, there is very clear evidence that each psalm has been carefully placed where it is to form sub-units, "books," and an overarching plot with various themes developed. As with every passage of Scripture, pay attention to the contextual "neighborhood."[25]

7. Consider the possibility of messianic references——the New Testament writers saw clear messianic applications to psalms we frequently do not (e.g., Ps. 8:4-6; 1 Corinthians 15:27; Hebrews 2:6-9).

8. Determine the main theme of the psalm and how each of the images, sub-themes, and variations contributes to the overall picture the author is presenting. Also determine the mood or tone of the psalm and what emotions and responses it is seeking to elicit.

Story

Earlier, I said that there is not an automatic connection between literary types and literary genres. A genre like prophecy may appear as narrative, poetry or discourse, and a literary type like poetry may occur in apocalyptic, epistle, gospel, prophecy, psalm, story, or wisdom.

However, nowhere is the connection between a type and a genre as close as between narrative and story. Because all stories are narrative (and vice versa), everything that I have already said about the literary type of narrative applies to the genre of story. Actually, the only good reason I have for keeping the term story as a genre is to distinguish it from the special category of gospel. In studying stories, keep in mind everything stated in the chapter on narrative (chapter eight).

Wisdom

The last genre that we come to is wisdom. Wisdom is the human search for how to live well——what can a person do to maximize his or her own well-being? Thus "wisdom" is not intelligence but a particular attitude toward reality, i.e., a worldview.

The wisdom literature of the Bible deals with living well, and as a genre is different from other categories of Scripture in building on distinctive foundations. Wisdom literature offers insights for life, gained from the author's observations of the world around us. There is universal agreement that the biblical books of Job, Proverbs, and Ecclesiastes belong to the wisdom category. Other books, such as Song of Songs (Song of Solomon), Ruth, Esther, certain psalms,[26] and James, are sometimes also categorized as wisdom. Some common characteristics of wisdom literature include the following:

- Use of all three literary types: narrative, poetry and discourse.
- Wisdom presumes a divine order behind nature; in other words, because God governs all aspects of life, all of creation and human experience points to God's plan and to his character.

Wisdom also assumes the unity of life. There is no distinction between what is "religious" and what is "secular"; God governs every aspect of reality. Brueggemann states: "I submit that it is the discovery, premise, assumption, and conviction of the *interconnectedness of life* that is the central substance of the wisdom teachers."[27]

- Life experience is the authority and the teacher. These insights are gleaned from years of having "been there, done that." Wisdom "explicitly claims no authority beyond the weight and persuasion of insight into the shape of the world. . . . Its authority depends on the appeal to good sense made by the statement itself."[28] Truth is discovered by reflecting on creation rather than by receiving a direct revelatory word from God. In other words, its authority is not the binding "Thus says Yahweh," but rather the advice of "Listen, my son, to your father's instruction." (Proverbs 1:8).

- The starting point of biblical wisdom is "the fear of Yahweh."[29] This is not merely the first step, but is the very essence of what it means to be wise, that is, to submit to God and his way.

- Pragmatism: The focus in wisdom literature is very practical. Righteousness is preferable to unrighteousness not only because it pleases God, but also because it works. Foolishness is criticized not only because it is morally wrong, but also because it brings frustration and misfortune. The question is not, "What does God want?" but, "What can I do to achieve true happiness and success?"

- Earthly focus: This genre primarily dwells on life in the here and now, not on the afterlife. The wise can expect reward in this life, and the foolish can expect punishment in the here-and-now as well.

- Universal scope: The Truths of wisdom apply to all people universally. Because these lessons are learned from experience in the world, they are wise for all the people of the world. It doesn't matter whether you live in ancient Israel, ancient Egypt, or present-day Iowa, foolish living hurts your chances for living well. For this reason, there is no mention of many features prominent in the other parts of the Bible: the covenant, the exodus, the temple, Jerusalem, the Messiah, sacrifices, the priesthood, prophecy, etc. The curious lack of these elements has been a vexing problem for scholars trying to establish the relationship of wisdom literature to the rest of Scripture.

- Either/or perspective: Most of the Bible's wisdom literature is either very hopeful and optimistic or cynical. Proverbs seems to be confident in human wisdom, while Job and Ecclesiastes point out the limitations of human wisdom and what it can do. The wisdom books, taken together, give us both sides of the coin, providing a balance between the benefits and the limitations of wisdom. In addition, wisdom literature makes extensive use of contrast between wisdom and foolishness, often seen in parallelism (e.g., Proverbs 10-15).

- There is extensive use of metaphor, simile, and other figures of speech.

- Common literary forms include allegory, command, encomium, formula, instruction, list, motif, proverb, and rhetorical question (see "Forms" below).

Here are important features to keep in mind when reading wisdom literature.

1. The role of wisdom in human life is presented in many different facets. Its benefits are frequently highlighted: for example, "Wisdom is supreme; therefore get wisdom; though it cost all you have, get understanding" (Proverbs 4:7). Yet even wisdom has its limits, as in, Job 28; Ecclesiastes.

2. Wisdom and foolishness are described as two different ways or paths (Hebrew, *derek*) of life.

3. God is the ruler over all aspects of creation, and he is free to do as he pleases (Proverbs 16:1, 4, 9, 33; 19:21; 20:24; 21:30-31; Job 42:1-6).

4. Other prominent themes that appear in wisdom literature include fidelity in marriage; the tongue; perils of drinking; the problem of suffering; unfairness of life; parental advice for children; the blessing of work; wealth; discipline and moderation.

5. Although proverbs are meant to tell us how to live our lives, because they draw on commonly-accepted truth, they do not come across as confrontational or judgmental. It is hard to argue with truth that *everyone* knows and accepts.

6. Proverbs also appeal to the reader because they don't come right out and say things but let the reader draw his own conclusions.

We get to figure out "the moral of the story" for ourselves and how we think the proverb should be applied to life. And since the author and the reader "share" this common truth together, the reader is more apt to be on the author's side in agreement.

7. The dual focus: wisdom invites the reader to think *backward* by imagining what kinds of experiences led to the formation of the proverb. They also summon the reader forward to think about how the proverb might apply to future situations.

Forms

Every biblical passage belongs to a given type (for example, narrative), genre (e.g., gospel), and form (e.g., genealogy). Forms change frequently as you read along, and it is even possible to have several different forms present simultaneously. For example, Proverbs 6:16-19 reads:

> "There are six things Yahweh hates,
> seven that are detestable to him:
> haughty eyes,
> a lying tongue,
> hands that shed innocent blood,
> a heart that devises wicked schemes,
> feet that are quick to rush into evil,
> a false witness who pours out lies
> and a man who stirs up dissension among brothers.

Here the type is poetry, the genre is wisdom, and the forms are both proverb and list. In the book of Hebrews, the type is discourse (except when poetry is quoted from Psalms), and the genre is epistle. But look at the variety of forms in just the final four verses: exhortation (verse 22), travel log (23), greeting (24), and closing (25).

Below is a list of some of the most common literary forms in the Bible, along with a description of their features and some biblical examples. Remember that different forms can overlap or coexist in a single verse or in a longer passage. In narrative texts, for example, the story will be moving along in the history form when suddenly some character engaged in a dialogue utters a curse. When this happens, the history form is not suspended; it merely is sharing space with the curse and dialogue.

In poetic texts, specifically in the genre of psalm, the lament, praise, and thanksgiving forms allow other forms, such as imprecation or prayer, to coexist within their structure. In discourse, especially in the genre of epistle, forms such as command, doxology, formula, list, and quotation pop in and out of the backdrop exposition or exhortation forms.

There are many forms of biblical literature. It is important to know these for two reasons. First, they give us a built-in outline of the structure of the passage we are studying and inform us of what we should look for. Second, whenever the predictable form is somehow interrupted, we should look very closely, for this is where the author has emphasized an important theological point. These forms include the following:

1. **Acrostic**: A pattern in which successive poetic lines begin with consecutive letters of the alphabet (line 1 with "a", line 2 with "b", etc.). See Psalm 119, where the first eight verses begin with the first Hebrew letter, "Aleph"; the next eight begin with the second Hebrew letter, "Beth"; etc. Other acrostic poetry includes: Psalms 9-10 (taken together); 25; 34; 37; 111; 112; 145; Proverbs 31:10-31; Lamentations 1-4; Nahum 1:2-8.

2. **Allegory**: A story whose true meaning lies in identifying what each figure represents (see Galatians 4:21-31, especially v. 24). Biblical examples are rare (Psalm 80:8-16; Ecclesiastes 12:1-6; Isaiah 5:1-7; 1 Corinthians 10:1-11, though these are debated).

3. **Allusion**: The author is drawing a clear intertextual (i.e., text within a specific context, such as a biblical book) relationship with an earlier passage but without any attempt to quote it word-for-word. Example: in Acts 7:2-52, Stephen is summarizing the story of the Hebrew Bible, which includes some direct quotation but is primarily Stephen's own retelling of the events. Other examples: Acts 13:16-40; Ezekiel 4:9—6:10 alluding to Leviticus 26.

4. **Announcement of birth**: A message (usually given by an angel) that predicts the birth of an important child. Typical features include:

(1) previous barrenness

(2) a parent prays

(3) a messenger comes

(4) fear or disbelief

(5) prediction of birth

(6) prediction of the son's future ministry

(7) birth

(8) competition between mothers and/or siblings

(9) the younger child ends up ruling the older

(10) growth of the child

Examples include Isaac, Esau and Jacob, Joseph, Samson, Samuel, John, and Jesus.

5. **Aphorism**: A specific kind of proverbial saying than originates from a particular person (rather than common folk wisdom) and is tied to a given situation (rather than primarily being guidance for daily living). Aphorisms are not like proverbs that are unattached and thus applicable to innumerable situations. Examples: 1 Samuel 10:11-12; Matthew 7:7-8; Luke 6:29-30.

6. **Apophthegm**: Also referred to as a pronouncement story, an apophthegm is a brief story or event that leads directly into a block of teaching. The episode's primary function is simply to provide the occasion for the teaching. Examples: the dialogue between the legal expert and Jesus in Luke 10:25-29 gives the opportunity and context for the parable of the Good Samaritan which follows (v. 30-37); see also Mark 12:13-17; John 8: 1-11; Acts 16:25-31.

7. **Aretalogy**: see **Miracle**.

8. **Archetype**: see **Motif**.

9. **Autobiography**: First-person, historical memoirs. See Ezra 7ff; Nehemiah; Acts 16:10ff.

10. **Blessing** (or **Benediction**): A pronouncement of well-being or honor upon someone; a wish for someone's good, either upon God or another person. Example: "Blessed are you who are poor, for yours is the kingdom of God" (Luke 6:20; Deuteronomy 33; Revelation 5:13).

11. **Body**: The central part of an epistle, including exposition and/or exhortation.

12. **Chiasm(us)**: Parallel elements of a passage that occur in reverse order (a>b; b>a):

> A Make the **HEART** of this people calloused
>> B Make *their ears* dull
>>> C And close their eyes
>>> C Otherwise they might see with their eyes
>> B Hear with *their ears*
> A Understand with their **HEARTS**   Isaiah 6:10

When a chiasm has a center, unparalleled element (called the "pivot"), it is in an emphasized position. For example, Psalm 67:

A vv. 1-2

  B v. 3

    C May THE NATIONS be glad and sing for joy,

      for you rule the peoples justly   v. 4

    and guide THE NATIONS of the earth

  B v. 5

A vv. 6-7

13. **Chronicle**: Used to summarize the reign of a king (e.g., 2 Kings 15:1-7). Typically, it includes:

(1) the age he began to reign

(2) the length of his reign

(3) whether he did right or evil in Yahweh's eyes

(4) "he walked in the ways of ____"

(5) the major events during his reign

(6) who succeeded him as king

(7) "[Are not] The other events of his reign [are] recorded in the book(s) of ____[?]"

14. **Closing**: The conclusion of an epistle which includes two or three elements (in any order):

(1) Greetings

(2) Blessing upon the readers: "grace"

(3) Blessing upon God

15. **Command**: A direct order given from a superior to a subordinate. These include both orders from one human to another (e.g., 1 Kings 21:9-10) as well as from God to humans (1 Kings 19:15-16).

16. **Commission**: Yahweh appoints a particular person to a specific task or ministry. Typical features include:

(1) Yahweh gives a command to a particular person.

(2) The person raises objections based on their inadequacies.

(3) Yahweh reassures them of his presence and power.

(4) A prediction concerning the success of the ministry is given.

(5) The person obeys, and success is granted.

Examples include: Abraham, Moses, Gideon, Samuel, King Saul, Isaiah, Jeremiah, Saul/Paul.

17. **Confession**: Voluntary admission of sin in prayer (e.g., Psalm 51:3-6; Daniel 9:5-11; Nehemiah 1:6b-7).

18. **Covenant**: A contract or an agreement between two parties. Features include:

>   (1) stipulations that each party agrees to

>   (2) the presence of witnesses

>   (3) the formalizing of the agreement, often through animal sacrifice

These agreements may involve one human with another (Genesis 31:44-54) or Yahweh with humans (Genesis 15:7-20). See **Treaty**.

19. **Curse** (or **Malediction**): An utterance which wishes misfortune upon someone. The term "cursed" usually appears right in the text (e.g., Genesis 3:14-19; Revelation 22:18-19).

20. **Dialogue**: A conversation between two or more persons (e.g., 1 Samuel 15:12-33; John 3:2ff.).

21. **Diatribe**: The writer engages the reader in a "conversation" in which he anticipates the reader's possible objection or response to his argument, puts their objection/response into their mouths, and then responds to it. Example: after extolling God's grace in Romans 5, Paul has readers saying, "Shall we go on sinning so that grace may increase?" But he immediately responds to this argument: "By no means!" (6:1-2). The most extended example of the diatribe is in Malachi 1-3 with the repeated use of "But you say . . ."/"But you ask . . ." followed by Yahweh's answer (cf. Ezekiel 33:10-20).

22. **Doxology**: Giving praise or glory to God; it is usually found at the end of a prayer, a discourse unit, or a book (e.g., 1 Chronicles 16:36; Romans 11:33-36; Jude 24-25). It usually begins with, "Blessed are you . . ."; "Praise be to you [him]."; "To him who . . . be blessing."; etc.

23. **Dream**: The dream form usually contains some or all of the following elements:

>   (1) a divine message which is revealed through a dream

>   (2) vivid recollection of the dream upon awakening

>   (3) a desire to understand its meaning

>   (4) a prophetic interpretation of the dream

(5) appropriate action by the dreamer and/or its fulfillment

Example: Genesis 28:10-19.

24. **Encomium**: A text that praises a particular virtue or quality. Examples include Song of Songs (love); Proverbs 2:12-19; 3:13-20 (wisdom); Hebrews 11 (faith).

25. **Epilogue**: The concluding section of a literary unit which retrospectively reinterprets all the preceding material. Examples: Deuteronomy 34; Joshua 24; Judges 21:24-25; 2 Kings 25:27-30; Jeremiah 52:31-34; Amos 9:11-15; Habakkuk 3:16-19; Malachi 4; Job 42:7-17; Ecclesiastes 12:13-14; Esther 10; 2 Chronicles 36:20-23; Matthew 28:16-20; John 21:24-25; Revelation 21-22.

26. **Exhortation**: A call or urging of people to respond with a change of behavior. Found commonly in the epistles, it is often introduced with "therefore" and is distinguished by phrases such as "I urge you . . . ," "I appeal to you . . . ," "I beseech you . . . ," "Let us . . . ," "Make every effort to . . . ," "I admonish you. . . ." Example: Ephesians 4:1-3.

27. **Exposition**: A detailed explanation that presents information or doctrinal truths in a logical fashion (in contrast to, for example, imaginative or figurative). In most cases, the author is identified in the text itself. Examples: Deuteronomy 1:1-31:29; Romans 1:11-11:32; Galatians 1:6-5:1a; Colossians 1:15-2:23; Hebrews 1-11.

28. **Farewell Address**: A final speech that is given at the end of the career of a leader shortly before his death or departure. Frequently seen features include:

(1) announcement of departure

(2) listeners' sorrow and leader's comfort

(3) leader recalls ministry highlights

(4) urges them to keep God's commands

(5) urges them to love one another

(6) predicts their future persecution, yet joy

(7) assures them of God's presence

(8) leader names his replacement

(9) blesses them / wishes their peace

(10) prayer

Examples include: Jacob (Genesis 47:29-49:33), Moses (Deuteronomy), Joshua (22-24), David (1 Chronicles 28-29); Jesus (John 14-17); Paul (Acts 20:17-38; 2 Timothy 3:10-4:22); Peter (2 Peter).

29. **Formula**: A short, fixed, stereotyped phrase that signals either a new thought unit or a different source. Examples include: "The word of Yahweh came to . . ." (indicates prophecy); "This is what Yahweh says, 'For three sins of [. . .], even for four, I will not turn back my wrath" (Amos 1-2, indicates different nations to be judged); "I tell you the truth . . ." (John, indicating emphasized truths Jesus taught); "As it is written . . ." (Romans, introducing scriptural quotations); "Here is a trustworthy saying . . ." (1 Timothy, indicates divisions); "By faith . . ." (Hebrews 11, new characters); "To the angel of the church in [. . .] write: 'These are the words of . . . '" (Revelation 2-3, indicates divisions).

30. **Genealogy**: A listing of the names of the ancestors of a particular person or family. Examples: Genesis 10-11 (Abraham); Luke 3:23-38 (Jesus). There are several kinds of genealogies:

> a. *Broad*, listing all the descendents (e.g., "These were the sons of Israel: Reuben, Simeon, Levi, Judah . . ." 1 Chronicles 2:1); the purpose is to emphasize that all are included.

> b. *Deep*, listing just the eldest offspring of each generation (e.g., "Solomon's son was Rehoboam, Abijah his son, Asa his son . . ." 1 Chronicles 3:10); the purpose is to legitimate an heir.

> c. *Descending*, moving from parent to child (1 Chronicles 9:39-44 cf. Matthew 1:1-16).

> d. *Ascending*, moving from child to parent (1 Chronicles 9:14-16 cf. Luke 3:23-37).

Genealogies have different functions as well:

- They show that God's plan extends to all mankind.
- They trace the line of descent from the offspring of the woman (Gen. 3:15) to Jesus.
- They inform us who the "good guys" and the "bad guys" are.
- They anchor the story of the Bible into the story of history, that is, real space and time.

31. **Greetings**: A form common at the beginning and end of many epistles. At the beginning, it is part of the opening, and usually involves some form of "grace and peace." At the conclusion of the epistle, the author and his companions greet the recipients and their companions (e.g., Colossians 4:10-15).

32. **History**: A factual, third-person, written account of past events (e.g., 2 Samuel 8; Acts 14:1-7). History belongs to the genre of story, but is more limited in that it assumes a correspondence with facts and events that actually occurred. It includes both the storyline itself and narrative descriptions and explanations. Basic things to look for include:

(1) setting: both place and time

(2) characters: major and minor, and how they are presented by the author

(3) plot, or the creation of conflict(s): between humans and God, humans and humans, humans and nature, humans and spirits, inner conflict within an individual's conscience, etc., and how resolution is reached (see chapter eight).

(4) style: repetition, irony, allusion, narration vs. dialogue, narrator's point of view, etc.

33. **Household Codes**: Three biblical passages (Ephesians 5:22-6:9; Colossians 3:18-4:1; 1 Peter 2:18-3:7) lay out guidelines for home relationships (husband/wife, parents/children, masters/slaves), all built upon the principle of Christ-like submission.

34. **Hymn**: A song (i.e., poetry) which praises God either for his character (see **Praise**) or for his acts on our behalf (see **Thanksgiving**). There are frequent examples throughout the Bible: Judges 5; Isaiah 61:10-11; Colossians 1:15-20; 1 Timothy 3:16; Revelation 5:9-13.

35. **Imprecation**: A poetic prayer found in a lament that asks God specifically to punish the wicked. Examples include Psalms 69:22-28; 109:6-20; 137:8-9; Jeremiah 18:21-23; Lamentations 3:64-66 (see **Lament** and **Petition**).

36. **Inclusio**: The opening word, phrase, or idea is repeated at the end of the literary unit. Examples: "horn" (1 Samuel 2:1, 10); "Praise Yahweh, O my soul" (Psalm 103); "Praise Yahweh" [="Hallelujah!"] (Psalm 113); "grace" in the opening and closing of Paul's epistles.

37. **Instruction**: Instruction is sustained teaching (either poetic or narrative) on moral wisdom. Focusing on practical, ethical behavior, it is found widely in the wisdom literature. It is different from exhortation in that it adopts a teaching tone rather than an urging tone.

38. **Irony**: (see "Narrative: Style") Irony occurs whenever any of the following apply:

(1) there is a discrepancy between what is said and what is actually meant

(2) what occurs is the opposite of what you expect

(3) certain characters know more than the others but don't let on

(4) the reader knows more than the characters (called *dramatic irony*)

39. **Kerygma** (or **Gospel Sermon**): A sermon presentation of the gospel which usually contains the following:

(1) prophecy concerning the Messiah

(2) a presentation of Jesus' preaching and healing power

(3) the fact of his crucifixion, resurrection, and exaltation

(4) the promise of Christ's return

(5) a call to repentance

(6) an offer of God's forgiveness

Examples include: Acts 3:13-26; 4:10-12; 5:30-32; 10:36-43; 13:17-41; 1 Corinthians 15:1-7.

40. **Lament**: A particular form of poetry in which the author complains to God about his current hardships and calls upon him to deliver. Typical elements include:

(1) opening cry or question (e.g., "How long, O Yahweh . . . ?")

(2) description of circumstances or enemies

(3) petition for God to intervene (sometimes with an *imprecation* and/or reasons why God should act)

(4) statement of confidence and faith in God

(5) vow to give thanks when deliverance comes

Examples: Ezekiel 19; Psalm 3-7; 42-43; 140; Lamentations.

41. **Law**: Legal codes given by God (see Prophecy) for governing his people (e.g., Exodus 22; Leviticus 1-7).

42. **Lawsuit** (Hebrew, *rîb*): A legal case between two parties, seen in the prophets as follows: Judge: Yahweh; jury: heavens and earth; defendant: Israel/Judah; prosecuting attorney: Yahweh through the prophet; crime: rebellion, idolatry, covenant-breaking.

Examples: Isaiah 1; Ezekiel 8; Micah 6.

43. **List** (or **Catalogue**): A series of items or names. Examples: Numbers 13:4-15 (list of spies); Galatians 5:19-23 (acts of the flesh versus fruit of the Spirit).

44. **Miracle** (or **Aretalogy**): The recording of an event that runs counter to the normal operations of nature. There are five distinct elements that may be present in the telling of biblical miracles:

(1) The need for divine intervention is explained.

(2) Help is sought out.

(3) Faith or obedience is expressed.

(4) The miracle is performed.

(5) Humans respond to the miracle.

45. **Motif**: (1) A repeated pattern, (2) a dominant theme, or (3) a dominant image.

(1) Example of a repeated pattern: The basic structural pattern for Matthew is:

- Jesus' ministry, including healing
- Jesus' teaching
- the phrase, "When Jesus had finished [saying these things/instructing/these parables]."

(2) Example of a dominant theme: "flesh" versus "spirit" in Romans 7–8.

(3) Example of a dominant image: courtroom ("forensic" terms in John, e.g., "witness," "verdict," "judge," "testimony," "[legal] Counselor," "condemn," "convict")

Motifs also include "archetypes" (i.e., a familiar image, character, or event that recurs throughout the Bible) such as:

(a) the contrast of light [=good] versus darkness [=evil] in John's writings

(b) the journey (e.g., Numbers, Luke, Acts)

(c) passing through water from the old life to the new (e.g., Noah, Red Sea, crossing the Jordan, Naaman, Christian baptism)

(d) the woman at the well (Isaac and Rebekah, Jacob and Rachel, Moses and Zipporah, Jesus and the Samaritan woman)

(e) fire as a symbol for judgment

In these cases, any deviations in later occurrences from the established pattern are highly significant.

46. **Opening**: The beginning of an epistle. There is a standard pattern which includes:

(1) Identification of the sender (author and sometimes associates)

(2) Identification of the recipient(s): an individual, a church, or a group of people

(3) Greeting: containing "grace and peace"

47. **Oracle**: A prophetic utterance which contains an announcement of doom (Numbers 23:7-10, 18-24; 24:3-9, 15-24; 2 Samuel 23:1-7; Isaiah 13:1-14:23; 14:28-32; 15:1-16:12; 17:1-14; 19:1-15; 21:1-10,11-12,13-15; 22:1-19; 23:1-16; 30:6-11; Ezekiel 12:10-16; Nahum; Habakkuk 1-2; Malachi; Psalm 36). It is frequently, but not always, associated with the judgment that the Messiah will bring upon the wicked nations.

48. **Parable**: A short, usually fictitious story which teaches or illustrates spiritual truth. Parables always involve a surface level using everyday objects or events and a deeper, more obscure level of reality. "At its simplest the parable is a metaphor or simile drawn from nature or common life, arresting the hearer by its vividness or strangeness, and leaving the mind in sufficient doubt about its precise application to tease it into active thought."[30]

Frequent introductory phrases are, "The kingdom of heaven is like . . ."; "A certain man . . ."; "There was a [. . .] man who . . ." In Luke, threefold repetition within parables is common (e.g., a priest, a Levite, a Samaritan in 10:25-37; lost sheep, lost coin, lost son in Luke 15; the three servants in 19:11-27; the three servants plus the son in 20:9-19), with the third (or fourth) providing a different "twist." Jesus' parables sometimes draw on features from historical events in the Bible: Luke 10:25-37 cp. 2 Chronicles 28:14-15; Luke 15:11-32 cp. Genesis 37-43; etc.

49. **Paraenesis**: see **Exhortation**.

50. **Petition**: A particular kind of prayer in which the speaker calls upon God (in second-person address) to act on behalf of human need (e.g., Psalm 7:1-2; Acts 4:29-30).

51. **Postscript**: A very brief addendum to the end of a passage that provides musical or historical information. Examples: "For the director of music. On my stringed instruments" (Habakkuk 3:19); "This concludes the prayers of David son of Jesse" (Psalm 72:20). Do not confuse postscript with epilogue. (See **Superscription**).

52. **Praise**: A specific kind of hymn that exalts God for his character and attributes. It is different from a doxology in that it is an entire poetic

unit on its own rather than a worshipful "addendum" to what precedes (e.g., Psalms 113; 117; 146-150). Elements include:

(1) Summons to praise

(2) List of those who should praise

(3) Reasons for praise

(4) Concluding "Praise Yahweh!" [="Hallelujah!"]

53. **Prayer**: Human direct (quoted) speech addressed to God (e.g., Matthew 6:9b-13). Prayers include confession, petition, praise, prayer log, and thanksgiving.

54. **Prayer Log**: The author indicates that he (and sometime others) have prayed or regularly do pray for those reading the text. It does not address God in the second-person, but does inform readers of the content of the prayer. Examples: "Dear friend, I pray that you [you = readers, not God] may enjoy good health and that all may go well with you, even as your soul prospers" (3 John 2; see also 2 Thessalonians 1:11; Colossians 4:12).

55. **Prologue**: The opening section of a book that presents material essential to understanding all that follows. Examples: Job 1-2; Proverbs 1:1-7; Luke 1:1-4; John 1:1-18; Acts 1:1-2; 1 John 1:1-4; Revelation 1:1-3.

56. **Proverb**: A short, poetic maxim that expresses succinctly a truth about "the way things are." A proverb has been described as, "The wisdom of many, the wit of one" and, "Short sentences drawn from long experience." Proverbs are based on observing patterns within God's created order, distilling a general principle from these experiences, and expressing its truth in a concise, memorable, and poetic style (see "Wisdom" above). The process of how a proverb is formed can be seen in Proverbs 24:30-34: observation (verses 30-31), contemplation (32), and a generalized proverbial saying (33-34). For example, "One who puts on his armor should not boast like one who takes it off" (1 Kings 20:11).

57. **Quotation**: Citing directly from a previously written work. It may include the Hebrew Bible quoting the Hebrew Bible (e.g., Exodus 34:6[-7] in Numbers 14:18; Joel 2:13; Jonah 4:2; Nahum 1:3; Psalm 86:15; 103:8; 145:8; Nehemiah 9:17), the Greek Bible quoting the Hebrew Bible (e.g., Isaiah 7:14 in Matthew 1:23), or the Greek Bible quoting the Greek Bible (Luke 10:7 in 1 Timothy 5:18; John 6:39 in John 18:9). Occasionally the Bible quotes other, outside sources (e.g., Acts 17:28 [Aratus/Cleanthes], and Titus 1:12 [Epimenides]). Biblical quotations sometimes have introductory formulas: "[As, for] it is written . . . ," "This was to fulfill what was written [spoken, said] in . . . ," and "For God [He, the Holy Spirit, the

Scriptures, David, Moses, the prophet] says . . . ." Occasionally there are "clusters" of quotations (Acts 7; Romans 3:10-18; 9:7-11:10; 15:9-12; Galatians 3:6-13; Hebrews 1:5-13; 2:6-13; 1 Peter 2:6-8).

58. **Refrain**: A line or series of lines which are repeated in a poetic work to indicate divisions (similar to the "chorus" of many of our hymns). Examples: "And there was evening, and there was morning—the ___ day" (Genesis 1); "His love endures forever" (the second line of every verse of Psalm 136); Psalms 42-43 (42:5, 11; 43:5); Psalm 80:3, 7, 19.

59. **Report**: A "news flash" delivered by a messenger about events taking place elsewhere (e.g., 1 Samuel 4:12-22).

60. **Rhetorical Question**: An artistic use of a question in which the speaker does not seek a direct answer, but uses it for dramatic effect and/or emphasis (e.g., "Where can I go from your Spirit?" Psalm 139:7; see also Job 41:1-14; Romans 10:14-15).

61. **Riddle**: A short, cryptic "verbal puzzle" which requires ingenuity to solve (e.g., Judges 14:14-18; Daniel 5:25-28; Matthew 12:40).

62. **Royal Edict**: An official, written message made by a king or governor (e.g., 2 Kings 18:19-25; Daniel 6:25-27; Ezra 1:2-4; John 19:19; Acts 23:25-30).

63. **Satire**: More of a stylistic device or tone of writing than a specific form, satire holds up a particular person or human characteristic to ridicule. Examples: Job 38, which derogates Job's ability to understand God's purposes, and 2 Corinthians 10f, where Paul belittles his opponents. The aim of satire is to change people's attitudes or behavior (see "Narrative: Style").

64. **Story** (see chapter eight and "**History**" above).

65. **Superscription**: A short introduction to a passage which presents either historical information or musical notations. An example of an historical superscription: "The word of Yahweh that came to Hosea son of Beeri during the reigns of Uzziah, Jotham, Ahaz and Hezekiah, kings of Judah, and during the reign of Jeroboam son of Jehoash king of Israel:" (Hosea 1:1; see Psalms 3, 51, etc.). A musical superscription: "For the director of music. With stringed instruments. According to *sheminith*. A psalm of David." (Psalm 6; see Psalms 69, 75; Habakkuk 3:1; etc.). The superscription may also indicate purpose: "A song of ascents" (Psalms 120-134).

66. **Thanksgiving**: A specific kind of hymn which honors God for his gracious acts toward people (e.g., Psalms 105-106). Elements include:

(1) a call to give thanks (e.g., "Praise Yahweh") or a direct statement to God ("I will exalt you, O Yahweh" Psalm 30:1; "I love Yahweh, for he heard my voice; he heard my cry for mercy" Psalm 116:1)

(2) a description of distress before deliverance

(3) praise to God for his compassion, faithfulness, etc., in delivering

(4) generalizing statement about how God cares for all his people

(5) promise to fulfill one's vows

(6) final statement of praise

Examples include: Exodus 15; 1 Samuel 2; Jonah 2:2-9; Psalms 30, 34, 66, 73, 103-104, 111-118; Luke 1:46-55.

67. **Travel Log**: An itinerary of either a journey taken (e.g., Numbers 33:2-49; Acts 27:1-12), or plans for a future journey (e.g., 1 Corinthians 16:5-12). The Pauline epistles contain either a travel log in which Paul states his plans to visit or, in the cases where he is in prison, his intention to send someone else to them on his behalf (e.g., Ephesians 6:21-22; Philippians 2:19-30). The single exception to this rule is in 1 Timothy, where Paul "passes on the torch" to Timothy as his replacement, that is, Timothy no longer needs Paul's supervision (6:11-21a).

68. **Treaty**: A form common in the ancient Near East, it is most clearly seen in Deuteronomy. It consists of the following:

(1) preamble: 1:1-5

(2) historical prologue: 1:6-4:49

(3) treaty stipulations: 5:1-26:19

(4) curses and blessings: 27:1-30:20

(5) reading of the treaty before witnesses: 31:1-29

69. **Vision**: Usually found in apocalyptic literature, it is the account of a visual experience of the supernatural (e.g., Zechariah 1:7-17; Revelation).

70. **Woe**: A particular kind of oracle in which the word "Woe!" actually appears. It differs from a curse in that it does not express a wish for destruction, but states that others are already in an accursed state (e.g., Isaiah 5:8-30; 31:1-3; Jeremiah 22:13-23; Ezekiel 13; 24:6-12; Amos 6; Habakkuk 2:6-20; Matthew 23:13-32). Typical elements include:

(1) beginning with the word, "Woe!" [Hebrew: *hoy*; Greek: *houai*]

(2) a description of the offense [in Hebrew: using a participial clause]

(3) the announcement of judgment, usually introduced with "therefore" [Hebrew: *lakēn*].

71. **Word Chain**: A list in which each word is the cause of the following word. Example: "Not only so, but we also rejoice in our *sufferings*, because we know that *suffering* produces perseverance; perseverance, CHARACTER; and CHARACTER, hope. And hope does not disappoint us, because God has poured out his love into our hearts by the Holy Spirit, whom he has given us" (Romans 5:3-5). Other examples include Romans 8:29-30; James 1:2-6 and 2 Peter 1:5-7.

BIBLE AS
Literature Summary

Three Types of Literature

Narrative	Poetry	Discourse
The text makes its point by telling a story.	The text makes its point by modifying and intensifying normal language.	The text makes its point by presenting a logical sequence of thoughts.

Seven Genres in the Bible

Story	Psalm	Prophecy	Wisdom	Apocalyptic	Gospel	Epistle
Telling of an event(s)	A poetic song	A message given directly from God	Insights for living learned from observing the world (Job, Proverbs, Ecclesiastes)	Highly symbolic, universal text focusing on end-times	Good news concerning Jesus' mission of salvation (Matthew–Acts)	A New Testament letter (Roman–2 Peter; 2 John–Jude)

Common Forms in the Bible

Form	Definition	Form	Definition
Acrostic	Each stanza begins with the next letter of the alphabet.	Autobiography	First-person historical account
Allegory	Characters and events symbolically refer to someone/something else.	Blessing	Pronouncement of honor or well-being on someone.
Announce. of Birth	Prediction of birth of an important child.	Chiasm	Parallel parts are in reverse order (mirror image).
Aphorism	Proverb originating from a specific situation.	Covenant	A contract between parties.
Apophthegm	A brief story which directly leads into a teaching block.	Curse	Wishing misfortune upon someone.

Dialogue	A conversation between parties.	**Command**	A direct order.
Chronicle	Summary of a king's reign.	**Commission**	Appointment to a task by God.
Closing	Conclusion of an epistle.	**Confession**	Admission of guilt.
Diatribe	A one-sided conversation.	**Miracle**	Event which supersedes nature.
Doxology	Giving praise / glory to God.	**Motif**	Repeated pattern, theme, or image.
Dream	Message from God given in a dream.	**Opening**	The beginning of an epistle.
Encomium	Praise of a virtue or quality.	**Oracle**	Prophetic announcement of doom.
Epilogue	Conclusion of a literary unit.	**Parable**	Short story teaching/illustrating truth.
Exhortation	An urging to change behavior	**Petition**	A prayer requesting God's help.
Exposition	Detailed explanation of truth.	**Praise**	A hymn exalting God's character.
Farewell Address	Final speech given by a leader.	**Prayer**	Human speech directed to God.
Formula	Fixed phrase signaling a new unit or change of thought.	**Prologue**	Opening to a narrative which gives essential information.
Genealogy	List of names of ancestors.	**Proverb**	Short, poetic, general truth.
Greetings	Greeting given at end of epistle.	**Quotation**	Citation from a previous writing.
History	Factual, third-person account of past events.	**Refrain**	Line(s) repeated in poetry to indicate divisions.
Household Code	Guidelines for specific relationships within the home.	**Report**	Delivery of a message about recent events elsewhere.
Hymn	A psalm praising God's character or specific acts.	**Rhetorical Question**	Question not expecting an answer.
Imprecation	Poetic prayer that the wicked be punished.	**Riddle**	A verbal puzzle.
Inclusio	Similar first and last lines in a unit	**Royal Edict**	Proclamation by governing official.
Instruction	Teaching about moral wisdom.	**Satire**	Ridicule of a person or trait.
Irony	Difference between surface meaning and a deeper meaning.	**Thanksgiving**	Hymn honoring God for specific acts of grace.
Kerygma	A gospel sermon.	**Travel Log**	Itinerary of a journey taken or planned.
Lament	Psalm of complaint and plea for help.	**Treaty**	A diplomatic agreement.
Law	Legal codes governing people.	**Vision**	Viewing of heavenly realities.
Lawsuit	Legal contest between two parties.	**Woe**	Oracle containing the word "woe."
List	A series of names or items.	**Word Chain**	A list where each term logically relates to the next.

BIBLIOGRAPHY
of Works Cited

Adams, Douglas. *The Prostitute in the Family Tree: Discovering Humor and Irony in the Bible*. Louisville, Ky.: Westminster John Knox Press, 1997.

Alter, Robert. *The Art of Biblical Narrative*. New York: Basic, 1981.

Andersen, Hans Christian. *The Emperor's New Clothes*. Translated by R. Lanning. New York: North-South Books, 2000.

Arnold, Jeffrey. *Discovering the Bible for Yourself*. Downers Grove, Ill.: InterVarsity, 1993.

Auerbach, Erich Mimesis. *The Representation of Reality in Western Literature*. Princeton: Princeton Univ., 1953.

Austin, J. L. *How to Do Things with Words*. 2nd ed. Oxford: Oxford Univ. Press, 1975.

Bailey, James L., and Lyle D. Vander Broek. *Literary Forms in the New Testament: A Handbook*. Louisville, Ky.: Westminster John Knox Press, 1992.

Bar-Efrat, Shimon. *Narrative Art in the Bible*. Translated by Dorothea Shefer-Vanson. Sheffield, England: Almond, 1984.

Barr, James. *The Bible in the Modern World*. London: SCM, 1973.

Bartholomew, Craig, Colin Green, and Karl Möller, eds., *After Pentecost: Language and Biblical Interpretation, Scripture & Hermeneutics Series* Vol. 2. Grand Rapids, Mich./London: Zondervan / Paternoster, 2001.

Baylis, Albert H. *On the Way to Jesus: A Journey Through the Bible*. Portland, Oreg.: Multnomah, 1986.

Berlin, Adele. *Poetics and Interpretation of Biblical Narrative*. Sheffield, England: Almond, 1983.

Birkerts, Sven. *The Gutenberg Elegies: The Fate of Reading in an Electronic Age*. Boston: Faber and Faber, 1994.

Boone, Kathleen C. *The Bible Tells Them So: The Discourse of Protestant Fundamentalism*. New York: State Univ. of New York Press, 1989.

Booth, Wayne C. "The Pleasures and Pitfalls of Irony: or, Why Don't You Say What You Mean?" *Rhetoric, Philosophy and Literature: An Exploration*, edited by Don M. Burks. West Lafayette, Ind.: Purdue Univ. Press, 1978.

———. *The Rhetoric of Irony*. Chicago: Univ. of Chicago Press, 1974.

Brichto, Herbert Chanan. *Toward a Grammar of Biblical Poetics*. New York: Oxford Univ. Press, 1992.

Brooks, Peter. *Reading for the Plot: Design and Intention in Narrative*. New York: Vintage, 1985.

Brown, Joanne Carlson and Rebecca Parker. "For God So Loved the World?" *Christianity, Patriarchy, and Child Abuse: A Feminist Critique*, edited by Joanne Carlson Brown and Carol R. Bohn. New York: Pilgrim, 1989.

Brueggemann, Walter. *The Creative Word: Canon as a Model for Biblical Education*. Philadelphia: Fortress, 1982.

Carroll, R. P. "Is Humour Also Among the Prophets?" *On Humour and Comic in the Hebrew Bible*, edited by Yehuda T. Radday and Athalya Brenner. Sheffield, England: Almond, 1990.

Childs, Brevard S. *Introduction to the Old Testament as Scripture*. Philadelphia: Fortress, 1979.

———. *The New Testament as Canon: An Introduction*. Philadelphia: Fortress, 1984.

Clements, R. E. *Wisdom in Theology*. Grand Rapids, Mich.: Eerdmans, 1992.

Clines, David J. A. "Possibilities and Priorities of Biblical Interpretation in an International Perspective," *Biblical Interpretation* 1/1 (1993), 67-97.

Crenshaw, James L. *Old Testament Wisdom: An Introduction*. Atlanta: John Knox, 1981.

Culpepper, R. Alan. *Anatomy of the Fourth Gospel: A Study in Literary Design*. Philadelphia: Fortress, 1983.

Curtis, Brent and John Eldridge. *The Sacred Romance: Drawing Closer to the Heart of God*. Nashville: Thomas Nelson, 1997.

Dodd, C. H. *The Parables of the Kingdom*. London: Fontana, 1961.

Doriani, Daniel M. *Putting the Truth to Work: The Theory and Practice of Biblical Application*. Phillipsburg, N.J.: P & R, 2001.

Duvall, J. Scott and Daniel J. Hays. *Grasping God's Word*. Grand Rapids, Mich.: Zondervan, 2001.

Exum, J. Cheryl and J. William Whedbee. "Isaac, Samson, and Saul: Reflections on the Comic and Tragic Visions," *Semeia* 32 (1984), 5-40.

Fee, Gordon and Douglas Stuart. *How to Read the Bible for All It's Worth*. Grand Rapids, Mich.: Zondervan, 1982.

Finzel, Hans. *Unlocking the Scriptures: A Fresh, New Look at Inductive Bible Study*. Wheaton, Ill.: Victor, 1986.

Fish, Stanley. *Is There a Text in This Class?* Cambridge: Harvard Univ. Press, 1982.

Fisher, Walter R. *Human Communication as Narration: Toward a Philosophy of Reason, Value, and Action*. Columbia, S.C.: Univ. of South Carolina, 1989.

Fokkelman, J. P. *Reading Biblical Narrative: An Introductory Guide*. Translated by Ineke Smit. Louisville, Ky.: Westminster John Knox Press, 1999.

Gemeren, Willem A. Van. *Interpreting the Prophetic Word*. Grand Rapids, Mich.: Zondervan, 1990.

Golding, William. *Lord of the Flies*. London: Faber & Faber, 1954.

Goldingay, John. *Approaches to Old Testament Interpretation*. Downers Grove, Ill.: InterVarsity, 1981.

Gottcent, John H. *The Bible: A Literary Study*. Boston: Twayne, 1986.

Goulder, Michael. "The Pauline Epistles," *The Literary Guide to the Bible*, edited by Robert Alter and Frank Kermode. Cambridge: Harvard, 1987.

Greidanus, Sidney. *The Modern Preacher and the Ancient Text: Interpreting and Preaching Biblical Literature*. Grand Rapids, Mich.: Eerdmans, 1988.

Guinness, Os. *Fit Bodies, Fat Minds: Why Evangelicals Don't Think and What to Do About It*. Grand Rapids, Mich.: Baker, 1994.

Guinness, Os and John Seel, eds. *No God But God*. Chicago: Moody, 1992.

Gunn, David and Danna Nolan Fewell. *Compromising Redemption: Relating Characters in the Book of Ruth*. Louisville, Ky. Westminster John Knox Press, 1990.

————. *Narrative in the Hebrew Bible*. New York: Oxford Univ. Press, 1993.

Hanson, Paul. *The Dawn of Apocalyptic*. Philadelphia: Fortress, 1975.

Hardy, Barbara, "Toward a Poetics of Fiction: An Approach through Narrative," *Novel* 2 (1968), 5-14.

Hayes, John H. *Old Testament Form Criticism*. San Antonio, Tex.: Trinity Univ. Press, 1977.

Hendricks, Howard G. and William D. Hedricks. *Living by the Book*. Chicago: Moody, 1991.

Hill, Jim and Rand Cheadle. *The Bible Tells Me So: Uses and Abuses of Holy Scripture*. New York: Anchor / Doubleday, 1996.

Hirsch, E. D., Jr. *Validity in Interpretation*. New Haven: Yale, 1967.

House, Paul R. *The Unity of the Twelve*. Sheffield, England: Almond, 1990.

Hyers, Conrad. *And God Created Laughter: The Bible as Divine Comedy*. Atlanta: John Knox, 1987.

Iser, Wolfgang. *The Act of Reading: A Theory of Aesthetic Response*. Baltimore: John Hopkins Univ. Press, 1978.

Jemielity, Thomas. *Satire in the Hebrew Prophets*. Louisville: Westminster John Knox Press, 1992.

Jensen, Irving L. *Independent Bible Study*. Chicago: Moody Press, 1963.

Johnson, Cedric B. *The Psychology of Biblical Interpretation*. Grand Rapids, Mich.: Zondervan, 1983.

Kaiser, Walter C., Jr. "The Old Promise and the New Covenant," *Journal of the Evangelical Theological Society* 15 (1972), 11-23.

————. *Toward an Exegetical Theology*. Grand Rapids, Mich.: Baker, 1980.

————. *Toward an Old Testament Theology*. Grand Rapids, Mich.: Zondervan, 1978.

————. *The Uses of the Old Testament in the New*. Chicago: Moody, 1985.

Kearney, Richard. *The Wake of Imagination*. Minneapolis, Minn.: Univ. of Minnesota Press, 1988.

Kingsbury, Jack Dean. *Conflict in Luke: Jesus, Authorities, Disciples*. Minneapolis, Minn.: Fortress, 1991.

————. *Matthew as Story*. Philadelphia: Fortress, 1986.

Klein, William W., Craig L. Blomberg, and Robert L. Hubbard. *Introduction to Biblical Interpretation*. Waco, Tex.: Word, 1993.

Knight, George W., III. "The Scriptures Were Written for Our Instruction," *Journal of the Evangelical Theological Society* 39/1 (1996), 3-13.

Kugel, James. *The Idea of Biblical Poetry*. New Haven, Conn.: Yale, 1981.

Kurz, William S. *Reading Luke-Acts: Dynamics of Biblical Narrative*. Louisville, Ky.: Westminster John Knox Press, 1993.

Lewis, C. S. *A Preface to Paradise Lost*. London: Oxford, 1959.

————. *Reflections on the Psalms*. Reprint, Glasgow: Collins / Fontana, 1976.

Liefeld, Walter. *New Testament Exposition: From Text to Sermon*. Grand Rapids, Mich.: Zondervan, 1984.

Lindbeck, George A. *The Nature of Doctrine, Religion and Theology in a Postliberal Age*. Philadelphia: Westminster, 1984.

Long, Thomas G. *Preaching and the Forms of the Bible*. Philadelphia: Fortress, 1989.

Lubeck, Ray. "Dusting Off the Old Testament for a New Millennium," *Preaching to a Shifting Culture: 12 Perspectives on Communicating that Connects*, edited by Scott Gibson. Grand Rapids, Mich.: Baker, 2004.

MacArthur, John, Jr. "Frequently Asked Questions about Expository Preaching," *Rediscovering Expository Preaching*, edited by John MacArthur, Jr. Dallas: Word, 1992.

McCann, J. Clinton. *A Theological Introduction to the Book of Psalms*. Nashville: Abingdon, 1993.

————, ed. *The Shape and Shaping of the Psalter*. Sheffield, England: JSOT Press, 1993.

MacIntyre, Alasdair. *After Virtue: A Study in Moral Theory*, 2nd ed. South Bend, Ind.: Univ. of Notre Dame Press, 1983.

Mains, Karen Burton. *Lonely No More*. Waco, Tex.: Word, 1993.

Marshall, I. Howard. "Luke and His 'Gospel,'" *The Gospel and the Gospels*, edited by Peter Stuhlmacher. Grand Rapids, Mich.: Eerdmans, 1991.

Mencken, Henry Louis. *A Mencken Chrestomathy*. Reprint, New York: Vintage, 1982.

Miller, Calvin. *The Finale*. Downers Grove, Ill.: InterVarsity, 1970.

Morgan, Robert and John Barton. *Biblical Interpretation*. Oxford: Oxford Univ. Press, 1988.

Newbigin, Lesslie. *The Open Secret: An Introduction to the Theology of Mission*. Grand Rapids, Mich.: Eerdmans, 1995.

O'Toole, Robert F. *The Unity of Luke's Theology: An Analysis of Luke-Acts*. Wilmington: Michael Glazier, 1984.

Osborne, Grant R. *The Hermeneutical Spiral: A Comprehensive Introduction to Biblical Literature*. Downers Grove, Ill.: InterVarsity, 1991.

Otto, Rudolf. *The Idea of the Holy*. Translated by John W. Harvey. 2nd ed. Oxford: Oxford Univ. Press, 1950; from Das Heilige, 1917.

Perrine, Laurence. *Sound and Sense: An Introduction to Poetry*. 2nd ed. New York: Harcourt, Brace & World, 1963.

Petersen, N. R. *Rediscovering Paul: Philemon and the Sociology of Paul's Narrative World*. Philadelphia: Fortress, 1985.

Postman, Neil. *Amusing Ourselves to Death: Public Discourse in an Age of Show Business*. New York: Viking, 1985.

————. *Conscientious Objections*. New York: Vintage, 1988.

———— and Steve Powers. *How to Watch TV News*. New York: Penguin, 1992.

Radday, Yehuda T. "On Missing the Humour in the Bible: An Introduction," *On Humour and Comic in the Bible*, edited by Athalya Brenner and Yehuda T. Radday. Sheffield, England: Almond, 1990.

Rhoads, David and Donald Michie. *Mark as Story: An Introduction to the Narrative of a Gospel*. Philadelphia: Fortress, 1982.

Ricoeur, Paul. "Arts, Language and Hermeneutic Aesthetics [herméneutique esthétique]: An Interview with Paul Ricoeur" by Jean-Marie Brohm and Magali Uhl. Translated by R. D. Sweeney. September 20, 1996. http://www.philagora.net/philo-fac/ricoeur-e.htm .

————. *Conflict of Interpretations*. Evanston, Ill.: Northwestern Univ. Press, 1974.

Roberts, Edgar V. *Writing Themes about Literature*. 3rd ed. Englewood Cliffs, N.J.: Prentice-Hall, 1973.

Rommetveit, Ragnar. *On Message Structure: A Framework for the Study of Language and Communication*. New York: John Wiley and Sons, 1974.

Rusch, Gebhard. "Comprehension vs. Understanding of Literature," *The Systemic and Empirical Approach to Literature and Culture as Theory and Application*, edited by Steven Tötösy de Zepetnek and Irene Sywenky. Siegen: Siegen Univ. Press, 1997.

Ryken, Leland. *Words of Delight: A Literary Introduction to the Bible*. Revised edition, Grand Rapids, Mich.: Baker, 1992.

Sailhamer, John H. *The Pentateuch as Narrative: A Biblical-Theological Commentary*. Grand Rapids, Mich.: Zondervan, 1992.

Schaeffer, Francis. *Art and the Bible*. Downers Grove, Ill.: InterVarsity, 1973.

Schreiner, Thomas R. *Interpreting the Pauline Epistles*. Grand Rapids, Mich.: Baker, 1990.

Searle, John R. *Speech Acts: An Essay in the Philosophy of Language*. Cambridge: Cambridge Univ. Press, 1969.

Simon, Uriel. "Minor Characters in Biblical Narrative," *Journal for the Study of Old Testament* 46 (1990), 11-19.

Stein, Robert H. *A Basic Guide to Interpreting the Bible: Playing By the Rules*. Grand Rapids, Mich.: Baker, 1994.

Steinmetz, David C. "Uncovering a Second Narrative: Detective Fiction and the Construction of Historical Method," *The Art of Reading Scripture*, edited by Ellen F. Davis and Richard B. Hays. Grand Rapids, Mich.: Eerdmans, 2003.

Sternberg, Meir. *The Poetics of Biblical Narrative: Ideological Literature and the Drama of Reading*. Bloomington, Ind.: Indiana Univ. Press, 1985.

Strom. Mark. *The Symphony of Scripture*. Downers Grove, Ill.: InterVarsity, 1990.

Stuhlmacher, Peter, ed. *The Gospel and the Gospels*. Grand Rapids, Mich.: Eerdmans, 1991.

Tannehill, Robert C. *The Narrative Literary Unity of Luke-Acts: A Literary Interpretation*. 2 vols. Minneapolis, Minn.: Fortress, 1990.

Tozer, A. W. *The Pursuit of God*. Reprint, Wheaton, Ill.: Tyndale House, 1982.

Traina, Robert A. *Methodical Bible Study*. 1952. Reprint, Grand Rapids, Mich.: Zondervan, 2002.

Turner, Mark. *The Literary Mind*. New York: Oxford Univ. Press, 1996.

Vanhoozer, Kevin J. "From Canon to Concept: 'Same' and 'Other' in the Relation Between Biblical and Systematic Theology," *Scottish Bulletin of Theology* 12/2 (1994), 96-124.

——. "From Speech Acts to Scripture Acts," *After Pentecost: Language and Biblical Interpretation*, edited by Craig Bartholomew, Colin Greene and Karl Moller. Grand Rapids, Mich.: Zondervan, 2001.

——. *Is There a Meaning in This Text? The Bible, the Reader, and the Morality of Literary Knowledge*. Grand Rapids, Mich.: Zondervan, 1998.

Wall, Robert W. "Canonical Context and Canonical Conversations," *Between Two Horizons: Spanning NT Studies & Systematic Theology*, edited by J. B. Green and M. Turner. Grand Rapids, Mich.: Eerdmans, 2000.

Warrnock, Mary. *Imagination*. Berkeley, Calif.: Univ. of California, 1976.

Watson, Francis. *Text, Church and World: Biblical Interpretation in Theological Perspective*. Grand Rapids: Eerdmans, 1994.

Westermann, Claus. *Basic Forms of Prophetic Speech*. 1967. Reprint, Louisville: Westminster John Knox Press, 1991.

Wilcock, Michael. *The Message of the Psalms*. 2 Vols. Downers Grove, Ill.: InterVarsity, 2001.

Witherington, Ben, III. *Paul's Narrative Thought World: The Tapestry of Tragedy and Triumph*. Louisville, Ky.: Westminster John Knox Press, 1994.

Wright, N. T. *The New Testament and the People of God*. Minneapolis, Minn.: Fortress, 1992.

Youngblood, Ronald. "A Holistic Typology of Prophecy and Apocalyptic," *Israel's Apostasy and Restoration*, edited by Avraham Gileadi. Grand Rapids, Mich.: Baker, 1988.

About the **AUTHOR**

Ray Lubeck is Professor of Bible and Theology at Multnomah Bible College in Portland, Oregon. He also serves as an adjunct faculty member at Western Seminary. He holds a Bachelor of Science in Biblical Education from Multnomah, a Master of Arts in Old Testament from Trinity Evangelical Divinity School in Deerfield, Illinois, and a Doctor of Theology degree in Old Testament from the University of South Africa. Additional graduate work has been taken at Regent College in Vancouver, British Columbia, Jerusalem University College, and Multnomah Biblical Seminary. He has written articles and contributed chapters to several books and commentaries, including the *Starting Point Study Bible* and *Preaching at the Crossroads: Evangelical Preaching at the Dawn of a New Millennium*. His book reviews have appeared in the *Journal of the Evangelical Theological Society* and *Cultural Encounters Journal*. He also directs the World Seen ministry at Multnomah, which examines contemporary worldviews, postmodernism, and pop culture.

Contact Information

For more information about Multnomah Bible College, you may visit Multnomah's website at http://www.multnomah.edu.

For information on World Seen, visit http://www.multnomah.edu/worldseen/main.asp.

To correspond with Ray Lubeck, please send your letter via e-mail to rlubeck@multnomah.edu or via mail c/o MBC, 8435 N.E. Glisan St., Portland, OR 97220, U.S.A.

NOTES

Chapter One

1. George A. Lindbeck makes this same point: "To become a Christian involves learning the story of Israel and of Jesus well enough to interpret and experience ourselves and our world in its terms." See *The Nature of Doctrine, Religion and Theology in a Postliberal Age* (Philadelphia: Westminster, 1984), 34.

2. Erich Auerbach pushes the point further when he says: "The world of Scripture stories is not satisfied with claiming to be historically true reality—it insists that it is the only real world. . . . The Scripture stories do not court our favor, they do not flatter us that they may please us and enchant us—they seek to subject us, and if we refuse to be subjected we are rebels." See Erich Auerbach, *Mimesis: The Representation of Reality in Western Literature* (Princeton, N.J.: Princeton Univ., 1953).

3. Kevin J. Vanhoozer points out that the "privilege of biblical interpretation . . . finally leads to the responsibility of hermeneutics: to the call to become not masters but 'martyrs' on behalf of meaning, not only hearers but doers, and perhaps sufferers, of the Word." See "From Speech Acts to Scripture Acts," in Craig Bartholomew, Colin Greene and Karl Moller (eds), *After Pentecost: Language and Biblical Interpretation* (Grand Rapids, Mich.: Zondervan, 2001), 46.

4. I owe the expression "receive . . . on the right wavelength" to J. P. Fokkelman, *Reading Biblical Narrative: An Introductory Guide*, Eng. Tr. Ineke Smit (Louisville, Ky.: Westminster John Knox Press, 1999), 8.

5. Frequently attributed to G. K. Chesterton, though he never said it in this form.

6. Kathleen C. Boone chronicles in a disturbingly accurate way how evangelicals ("fundamentalists") abuse Scripture in her book *God Tells Them So: The Discourse of Protestant Fundamentalism* (New York: State University of New York Press, 1989). While I disagree with her hermeneutical conclusions, I readily grant the validity of many of her arguments against the legitimacy of evangelicals' use of the Bible. I agree with her on many of the problems, yet this present book seeks to offer different solutions than hers.

7. See Robert W. Wall, "Canonical Context and Canonical Conversations" in J. B. Green and M. Turner (eds), *Between Two Horizons: Spanning NT Studies*

and Systematic Theology (Grand Rapids, Mich.: Eerdmans, 2000), 167.

8. Os Guinness and John Seel (editors) have identified some of these "idols" which end up competing with God for our allegiance in contemporary evangelical circles in their book *No God But God* (Chicago: Moody, 1992).

9. See Sven Birkerts, *The Gutenberg Elegies: The Fate of Reading in an Electronic Age* (Boston: Faber and Faber, 1994), 80-81.

10. Calvin Miller, *The Finale* (Downers Grove, Ill.: InterVarsity, 1970), 21.

11. I am here drawing on the Latin phrase used by Rudolf Otto, *mysterium tremendum et fascinans* in *The Idea of the Holy*, Trans. John W. Harvey (Oxford: Oxford University Press, 1923; 2nd ed., 1950), from *Das Heilige* (1917).

12. For example, the phrases "remember" and "do not forget" appear repeatedly in Deuteronomy. Jesus told his followers to observe the bread and cup of the Lord's Supper "in remembrance" of him.

13. I intentionally use the gender exclusive term "his" here as a matter of historical accuracy—it is highly unlikely that any of the authors of the Bible were female.

Chapter Two

1. Former Packer player David Hathcock tells this story to Gregg Russell, "On the Right Track," University of Memphis Magazine, Spring, 1999.

2. Italics mine. The full doctrinal statement is: "The Bible alone, and the Bible in its entirety, is the Word of God written and is therefore inerrant in the autographs. God is a Trinity, Father, Son, and Holy Spirit, each an uncreated person, one in essence, equal in power and glory." Simply put, this understanding of the Bible and of God is what distinguishes evangelicals from others.

3. In his book, *Is There a Text in This Class?* (Cambridge: Harvard Univ. Press, 1982), 323, Stanley Fish tells this story. One summer, he taught two classes back to back in the same classroom. The first class concerned itself with English and linguistics. The second class focused on English and religious poetry of the seventeenth century. For the first class, Fish wrote their reading assignment on the board, listed by authors' last name:

Jacobs-Rosenbaum
Levin
Thorne
Hayes
Ohman(?)

Leaving this assignment on the board, Dr. Fish told the next class that what they saw on the blackboard was a religious poem and asked them to interpret it. The students came up with elaborate connections between Jacobs and Jacob's ladder, and how instead of a ladder, the poem was asserting that the way to heaven was through a rose tree (translating the name Rosenbaum as a German noun), a clear reference to Mary. Levin referred to the tribe of Levi as well as to leaven, as in the unleavened bread of the Passover and mass. Thorne was a reference to Jesus' crown of thorns. "Ohman(?)" (Fish inserted the question mark because he was unsure of the spelling of this author's name) was interpreted as either "Oh, man" or a Middle English form of Amen——the proper way to end any good religious poem. Even the shape of the names suggested a cross. Fish's point is to demonstrate how our pre-understanding of the category of literature influences how we see and interpret it. The fact that they were told at the outset that this was a religious poem caused them to see things in the names and even the shape of the list that the previous class would not have seen.

4. "All understanding of verbal meaning is necessarily genre-bound." See E. D. Hirsch, Jr., *Validity in Interpretation* (New Haven, Conn.: Yale, 1967), 76.

5. "Those who are well-read have a greater, more refined reservoir of expectations. Knowing what to expect, they often come away from a story with a greater understanding and appreciation than one who has little idea of what stories are about." See John H. Sailhamer, *The Pentateuch as Narrative: A Biblical-Theological Commentary* (Grand Rapids, Mich.: Zondervan, 1992), 12.

6. C. S. Lewis, *A Preface to Paradise Lost* (London: Oxford, 1959).

7. Walter R. Fisher, a communication theorist, states that "(c)ommunicators intend messages, and all communicators are strategic in their chosen causes, selections of materials, designs of composition, and styles of presentation. Every communicator, in other words, seeks to make the best possible case for his or her position." *Human Communication as Narration: Toward a Philosophy of Reason, Value, and Action* (Columbia, S.C.: Univ. of S. Carolina, 1987, 1989), 117.

8. I realize that some may question who gets to select the literary type for a biblical book——is it God's decision or the human author's? Theologians have chosen the term *inspiration* to describe how the Bible is the product of a kind of dual authorship, where God and the human author are working mutually. God's message is expressed in the way that he intends it, while the uniqueness of each human author is preserved. Evangelical scholars at the International Council on Biblical Inerrancy (1978) drafted a document called the "Chicago Statement on Inerrancy." Article 8 describes this facet of inspiration in this way: "We affirm that God in His Work of inspiration utilized the distinctive personalities and literary styles of the writers whom He had chosen and prepared. We deny that God, in causing these writers to use the

very words that He chose, overrode their personalities."

We should therefore avoid splitting apart the two sources, human and divine, by attributing some properties (like literary category) to one source, and other properties to the other source.

9. "Genres are usually distinguished from literary forms on the basis of length and complexity. Whereas literary forms can be short and structurally simple, (genres) are longer pieces that may themselves contain a number of shorter literary forms." See James L. Bailey and Lyle D. Vander Broek, *Literary Forms in the New Testament: A Handbook* (Louisville, Ky.: Westminster John Knox Press, 1992), 13-14.

Chapter Three

1. Contributed by Nick Hobart to *Reader's Digest's* "Campus Comedy."

2. In *The Pursuit of God*, A. W. Tozer uses a similar illustration to emphasize the centrality of worship within the church.

3. What I am presenting here draws upon an approach to understanding communication called Speech-Act Theory. The chief pioneers of Speech-Act Theory are J. L. Austin, *How to Do Things with Words* (2nd ed. Oxford: Oxford Univ. Press, 1975) and John R. Searle, *Speech Acts: An Essay in the Philosophy of Language* (Cambridge: Cambridge Univ. Press, 1969). The best treatment of the application of Speech-Act Theory to biblical interpretation thus far is in the essays found in *After Pentecost: Language and Biblical Interpretation, Scripture and Hermeneutics Series* Vol. 2 Craig Bartholomew, Colin Green and Karl Möller (eds), (Grand Rapids/London: Zondervan/Paternoster, 2001); see also Kevin J. Vanhoozer, *Is There a Meaning in This Text? The Bible, the Reader, and the Morality of Literary Knowledge.* (Grand Rapids, Mich.: Zondervan, 1998). My own version is an attempt both to simplify and build upon their work.

Chapter Four

1. David C. Steinmetz also uses the metaphor of detective stories to make a different, important, and additional point for theological purposes. According to Steinmetz, the protagonist's second telling of the story corresponds to later passages in the Bible, which retrospectively shed light on the earlier events. For example, Hebrews helps us to interpret many of the people, events, and objects from the Hebrew Bible, helping us to recognize, for example, the

significance of Melchizedek in the larger story (the metanarrative) of the Bible. See David C. Steinmetz, "Uncovering a Second Narrative: Detective Fiction and the Construction of Historical Method," pp. 54-65 in *The Art of Reading Scripture*, ed. by Ellen F. Davis and Richard B. Hays (Grand Rapids, Mich.: Eerdmans, 2003).

2. For more on this, see chapter 8 under characterization.

3. For more on this, see chapter 8 under setting.

4. For more on this, see chapter 8 under setting.

5. (See further on "Stories: Setting")

Chapter Five

1. "The Student, the Fish, and Professor Agassiz," from *American Poems* (3rd ed.; Boston: Houghton, Osgood and Co., 1879), pp. 450-54. This essay first appeared in *Every Saturday* 16 (Apr. 4, 1874), 369-70, under the title "In the Laboratory With Agassiz, By a Former Pupil." It appeared as an appendix in Irving L. Jensen, *Independent Bible Study* (Chicago: Moody Press, 1963), 173-178.

2. The interpretive schools adopting and building on this goal of focusing on the text, called "text immanent" approaches, include New Criticism, Archetypal Analysis, Structuralism, Semiotics, Formalism, and Discourse Analysis (Text Linguistics).

3. William Golding. *Lord of the Flies* (London: Faber and Faber, 1954).

4. For example, this position is represented in the following statement: "Texts, like dead men and women, have no rights, no aims, no interests. They can be used in whatever way readers or interpreters choose." See Robert Morgan and John Barton, *Biblical Interpretation* (Oxford: Oxford Univ. Press, 1988), 7.

5. The scholarly approaches which focus primarily on the reader (and the community with whom the reader identifies) include Reader-Response, Ideological Criticism, Sociological or Political Criticism, Poststructuralism, Deconstuctionism, and New Historicism. Friedrich Nietzsche, Jacques Derrida, Richard Rorty, Stanley Fish, Roland Barthes, and Michel Foucault, among others, all maintain that meaning does not exist as a resident property in the text, but rather that meaning takes place through the experience of reading. A more moderate variation of the focus on the reader, promoted by Robert Jauss and Wolfgang Iser (of the so-called Constance School), says that the reader's own interpretation must conform to standards set within the parameters of a particular reading community, so that any interpretation that falls outside

the consensus of that group is considered to be illegitimate——for that group.

6. According to the studies of Piaget, cited in Ragnar Rommetveit, *On Message Structure: A Framework for the Study of Language and Communication* (New York: John Wiley and Sons, 1974), 42.

7. These proposals represent my hermeneutics, a term that refers to the theoretical principles which determine methods of interpretation.

8. One example of this can be found in David J. A. Clines, who cynically asserts, "There are no universally agreed upon legitimate interpretations . . . . (B)iblical interpreters have to give up the goal of determinate and universally acceptable interpretations, and devote themselves to interpretations they can sell——in whatever mode is called for by the communities they choose to serve. I call this 'customized' interpretation." See "Possibilities and Priorities of Biblical Interpretation in an International Perspective," *Biblical Interpretation* 1.1 (1993), 79-80.

9. For example, there are several word plays in Jesus' dialogue with Nicodemus in John 3:3-8. One of these is with the Greek word *anōthen*, born again or born from above; another is *pneumatos*, for spirit or wind. These are clearly intentional, and Nicodemus' misunderstanding is designed to function as a tool for our own understanding.

10. E. P. Torrance, quoted in Cedric B. Johnson, *The Psychology of Biblical Interpretation* (Grand Rapids, Mich.: Zondervan, 1983), 34.

11. Quoting from Isaiah 40:8. Strictly speaking, it is arguable that "the word of the Lord" here is the written Scriptures——more likely in context it refers to the eternality of God's promises in contrast to the frailty and short-lived nature of humanity. Nevertheless, the point still stands: what God says, whether through words spoken via a prophet or written through inspiration, has an enduring quality that does not change despite human finiteness. (See also Psalm 119:89; Matthew 5:17-18).

12. Let me restate an important point that I made earlier: there is no difference between God's meaning and the human author's meaning. The same message and purposes that the human author intended his writing to convey are precisely what the Holy Spirit communicated to and through him as well (2 Peter 1:20–21).

13. Many biblical interpreters have also recognized the need to maintain a distinction between meaning and reference (or significance). Several of the primary defenders of this position include E. D. Hirsch, *Validity in Interpretation* (New Haven, Conn.: Yale Univ. Press, 1967), Walter C. Kaiser, Jr., *Toward an Exegetical Theology* (Grand Rapids, Mich.: Baker, 1980), and Kevin J. Vanhoozer, *Is There a Meaning in This Text? The Bible, the Reader, and the Morality of Literary Knowledge* (Grand Rapids, Mich.: Zondervan, 1998).

14. A former professor of mine, Ed Goodrick, used to refer to this interpretive disease as "versitis."

15. I would actually take this a step further by arguing that the most reliable guide for how we ought to interpret the Bible is the way that biblical authors use earlier Scripture, seeking to understand and follow their pattern as closely as possible. I fully recognize that this is a controversial position with many facets and which needs careful qualifications. I am indebted to a former professor, Walt Kaiser, for his stimulating teaching on this topic— many of his thoughts can be traced in Walter C. Kaiser, Jr., *The Uses of the Old Testament in the New* (Chicago: Moody, 1985).

16. See, for example, John H. Sailhamer, *The Pentateuch as Narrative: A Biblical Theological Approach* (Grand Rapids, Mich.: Zondervan, 1995).

17. See Proverbs 16:2, 25, and the recurrent theme of everyone doing "what was right in his own eyes."

18. One of the valid insights of Reader-Response critics is their assertion that defining what serves as a legitimate reading is a role of a larger interpretive community. Protestants in particular have been slow to recognize and own up to the fact that church tradition plays a large part in assessing whether or not a given interpretation is acceptable within the bounds of orthodox faith.

19. This issue of undervaluing or disregarding the so-called "Old Testament" (a term which you will not find in the Bible) is brought out more fully in Ray Lubeck, "Dusting Off the Old Testament for a New Millennium," pp. 19-38, in Scott Gibson (ed), *Preaching to a Shifting Culture: 12 Perspectives on Communicating that Connects* (Grand Rapids, Mich.: Baker, 2004).

20. From the Hebrew root word *shûb*.

21. Other communication theorists agree on this point: "*Understanding* means to *meet the interactive/communicative expectations of a communicator*" (Gebhard Rusch, "Comprehension vs. Understanding of Literature" in Steven Tötösy de Zepetnek and Irene Sywenky (eds), *The Systemic and Empirical Approach to Literature and Culture as Theory and Application* (Siegen: Siegen Univ. Press, 1997), 115.

22. Kevin J. Vanhoozer, *Is There a Meaning in This Text? The Bible, the Reader, and the Morality of Literary Knowledge* (Grand Rapids, Mich.: Zondervan, 1998), 401-403.

Chapter Six

1. Reported in William W. Klein, Craig L. Blomberg and Robert L. Hubbard,

Introduction to Biblical Interpretation (Waco, Tex.: Word, 1993), 7.

2. Joanne Carlson Brown and Rebecca Parker, "For God So Loved the World?" In Joanne Carlson Brown and Carol R. Bohn (eds) *Christianity, Patriarchy, and Child Abuse: A Feminist Critique* (New York: Pilgrim, 1989), 26-27.

3. Karen Burton Mains, *Lonely No More* (Waco, Tex.: Word, 1993), 115.

4. http://homeschool.crosswalk.com/farris (9/11/2000).

5. A listing of how people have done so is offered in Jim Hill and Rand Cheadle, *The Bible Tells Me So: Uses and Abuses of Holy Scripture* (New York: Anchor/Doubleday, 1996).

6. For example, see Howard G. Hendricks and William D. Hendricks, *Living by the Book* (Chicago: Moody, 1991); Hans Finzel, *Unlocking the Scriptures: A Fresh, New Look at Inductive Bible Study* (Wheaton, Ill.: Victor, 1986); Jeffrey Arnold, *Discovering the Bible for Yourself* (Downers Grove, Ill.: InterVarsity, 1993); and the classic textbook by Robert A. Traina, *Methodical Bible Study* (repr. Grand Rapids, Mich.: Zondervan, 2002, originally published in 1952). Traina does add a fourth step, correlation, that seeks to connect the relationships between the passage under study and the larger context.

7. William S. Kurz, *Reading Luke-Acts: Dynamics of Biblical Narrative* (Louisville, Ky.: Westminster John Knox Press, 1993), 174-175.

8. Vanhoozer states: "The absorption of a text . . . into the Old or New Testament does indeed affect how it is read, namely, by expanding the context of interpretation beyond the original historical and literary contexts." See Kevin J. Vanhoozer, *Is There a Meaning in This Text? The Bible, the Reader, and the Morality of Literary Knowledge* (Grand Rapids, Mich.: Zondervan, 1998), 380. See also George W. Knight III, "The Scriptures Were Written for Our Instruction" *Journal of the Evangelical Theological Society* 39/1 (1996), 3-13.

9. This relatively recent rediscovery has been called "canon(ical) criticism." The pioneering figure here is Brevard S. Childs, *Introduction to the Old Testament as Scripture* (Philadelphia: Fortress, 1979) and *The New Testament as Canon: An Introduction* (Philadelphia: Fortress, 1984).

10. He continues: "The contingent situations affect how Paul articulates his thoughts, but those thoughts are basically not ad hoc in character. . . . Contingency has to do by and large with the mode of expression, not the matter expressed." See Ben Witherington III, *Paul's Narrative Thought World: The Tapestry of Tragedy and Triumph* (Louisville, Ky.: Westminster John Knox Press, 1994), 3-4. See also N. R. Petersen, *Rediscovering Paul: Philemon and the Sociology of Paul's Narrative World* (Philadelphia: Fortress, 1985), 135. Kurtz continues in the same vein: "The presence of (books) within the canon of the Christian Bible therefore relativizes the importance of the original implied readers . . . . As components of the New Testament, . . . (they) are

now meant to be read by Christians of virtually all ages and cultures, not just by first-century Christians proficient in Greek . . . . Once (they) are part of the New Testament of the Christian Bible, their life setting reaches beyond the original one to include all the contemporary Christian uses of Scripture." See William S. Kurz, *Reading Luke-Acts: Dynamics of Biblical Narrative* (Louisville, Ky.: Westminster John Knox Press, 1993), 160-161.

And Francis Watson adds: "The canon converts poetry and prose, narrative, law, prophecy and epistles alike into 'holy Scripture.' Genre is determined not only by a text's intrinsic characteristics but also by its communal usage. It is arbitrary to claim that a text is 'really' a mere letter or poem and that its role as holy Scripture was imposed on it later——as it were, against the grain. That view supposes that texts are wholly limited and confined by their immediate circumstances of origin, and that as soon as they stray from their appointed time and place they will be 'misread.' . . . Yet . . . the possibility that writing will transcend the time and place envisaged by its author is therefore part of its structure from the very beginning." See *Text, Church and World: Biblical Interpretation in Theological Perspective* (Grand Rapids, Mich.: Eerdmans, 1994), 4.

11. See, for example, J. Scott Duvall and J. Daniel Hays, *Grasping God's Word* (Grand Rapids, Mich.: Zondervan, 2001), 22-25.

12. "For many, the literary modes of expression are just so much wrapping paper to be torn off in one's haste to get the proposition inside the package." See Kevin J. Vanhoozer, "From Canon to Concept: 'Same' and 'Other' in the Relation Between Biblical and Systematic Theology," *Scottish Bulletin of Theology* 12/2 (1994), 101.

13. See Paul Ricoeur, *Conflict of Interpretations* (Evanston, Ill.: Northwestern Univ. Press, 1974), 281.

14. Cited in Os Guinness, "Sounding Out the Idols of Church Growth" in Os Guinness and John Seel (eds.), *No God But God* (Chicago: Moody, 1992), 169.

Chapter Seven

1. Hans Christian Andersen, *The Emperor's New Clothes*. Trans. R. Lanning (New York: North-South Books, 2000).

2. Neil Postman, *Amusing Ourselves to Death: Public Discourse in an Age of Show Business* (New York: Viking, 1985); see also Postman and Steve Powers, *How to Watch TV News* (New York: Penguin, 1992).

3. Ibid., 99-100.

4. Referred to by Os Guinness, *Fit, Bodies, Fat Minds: Why Evangelicals Don't Think and What to Do About It* (Grand Rapids, Mich.: Baker, 1994), 146.

5. Richard Kearney, lecturer in the Department of Metaphysics at University College, Dublin, says, "[I]magination lays claim to a certain analogical relation of unity through resemblance." See Richard Kearney, *The Wake of Imagination* (Minneapolis, Minn.: Univ. of Minnesota Press, 1988), 16.

6. Paul Ricoeur shares this perspective: "[T]o make metaphors well is to have an insight into resemblance. This insight into resemblance allows one to read resemblance where one did not see it." See "Arts, Language and Hermeneutic Aesthetics (herméneutique esthétique), An Interview with Paul Ricoeur" by Jean-Marie Brohm and Magali Uhl, September 20, 1996, Trans. by R. D. Sweeney; http://www.philagora.net/philo-fac/ricoeur-e.htm.

7. Francis Schaeffer, *Art and the Bible* (Downers Grove, Ill.: InterVarsity, 1973).

8. See John Goldingay, *Approaches to Old Testament Interpretation* (Downers Grove, Ill.: InterVarsity, 1981), 39-40.

9. Mary Warrnock, *Imagination* (Berkeley: Univ. of California, 1976), 182.

10. This often quoted line is attributed to journalist Henry Louis Mencken (1880–1956), although his original words were, "There is always an easy solution to every human problem——neat, plausible, and wrong." See "The Divine Afflatus," chap. 25 in *A Mencken Chrestomathy* (1949), 443, originally published in the *New York Evening Mail*, November 16, 1917 (see http://www.bartleby.com/73/1736.html).

11. Also quoted by Jesus during his temptation by Satan in the wilderness (Matt. 4:10 and parallels). See also Jesus' rebuke of the Pharisees when they demanded a sign (Matt. 12:39).

12. Daniel M. Doriani, *Putting the Truth to Work: The Theory and Practice of Biblical Application* (Phillipsburg: P&R, 2001), 19.

13. I'm paraphrasing the great preacher Haddon Robinson here.

Chapter Eight

1. Mark Turner, *The Literary Mind* (New York: Oxford Univ. Press, 1996), v (italics his).

2. Alasdair MacIntyre, *After Virtue: A Study in Moral Theory*, 2nd ed (South Bend, Ind.: Univ. of Notre Dame Press, 1983), 197.

3. "We dream in narrative, we day-dream in narrative, remember, anticipate, hope, despair, believe, doubt, plan, revise, criticize, construct, gossip, learn, hate and love by narrative." See Barbara Hardy, "Toward a Poetics of Fiction: An Approach through Narrative," *Novel* 2 (1968), 5.

4. Lesslie Newbigin, *The Open Secret: An Introduction to the Theology of Mission* (Grand Rapids, Mich.: Eerdmans, 1995), 82.

5. I do want to clarify at this point that I am not dismissing or minimizing the factuality of the recorded events of the Bible. The literary category of "story" includes both nonfiction as well as fiction, and I stand firmly with those who insist that it tells historical truth. Meir Sternberg spells out what is at stake here: "Were the narrative written or read as fiction, then God would turn from the Lord of history into a creature of imagination, with the most disastrous results. The shape of time, the rationale of monotheism, the foundations of conduct, the national sense of identity, the very right to the land of Israel and the hope of deliverance to come: all hang in the generic balance. Hence the Bible's determination to sanctify and compel literal belief in the past." See *The Poetics of Biblical Narrative: Ideological Literature and the Drama of Reading* (Bloomington, Ind.: Indiana Univ., 1985), 32. See also Herbert Chanan Brichto, *Toward a Grammar of Biblical Poetics* (New York: Oxford Univ. Press, 1992), 90.

6. "To relate a part of our story to another person is not only to tell what happened but also to reveal how we make sense of life, how and what we decide is important and not important, and how we respond to the ethical decisions arising from events." See Thomas G. Long, *Preaching and the Forms of the Bible* (Philadelphia: Fortress, 1989), 72-73.

7. Communication theorist Walter R. Fisher also develops this same point: "The world as we know it is a set of stories that must be chosen among in order for us to live life." See *Human Communication as Narration: Toward a Philosophy of Reason, Value, and Action* (Columbia, S.C.: Univ. of South Carolina Press, 1987, 1989), 65.

8. See Robert Alter, *The Art of Biblical Narrative* (New York: Basic, 1981).

9. For more information on gapping, see Wolfgang Iser, *The Act of Reading: A Theory of Aesthetic Response* (Baltimore, Md.: John Hopkins Univ. Press, 1978), 170-191, and Meir Sternberg, *The Poetics of Biblical Narrative: Ideological Literature and the Drama of Reading* (Bloomington, IND.: Indiana Univ. Press, 1985), 237f.

10. Edgar V. Roberts states, "We may define character in literature as the author's creation, through the medium of words, of a personality who takes on actions, thoughts, expressions, and attitudes unique and appropriate to that personality and consistent with it." See *Writing Themes about Literature*, 3rd ed. (Englewood Cliffs, NJ: Prentice-Hall, 1973), 45. A character in the biblical story may have been a real person in the real world, but in the story

he is a creation of the narrator in that the storyteller ends up telling us only what he wants us to know about that character: "Every narrator selects and rejects, lengthens, and abbreviates, illuminates and obscures in keeping with his expressive purpose." See Uriel Simon, "Minor Characters in Biblical Narrative," *Journal for the Study of Old Testament* 46 (1990), 13.

11. Descriptions of physical traits (including dress) are fairly rare in the Bible. When they do occur, they always serve an important purpose within the storyline.

12. Adele Berlin also distinguishes a third kind of character, the agent, who has no particular character traits at all, but who merely performs an action necessary to the plot. See *Poetics and Interpretation of Biblical Narrative* (Sheffield, England: Almond, 1983), 23.

13. Conrad Hyers, *And God Created Laughter: The Bible as Divine Comedy* (Atlanta: John Knox Press, 1987), 45.

14. Gordon Fee and Douglas Stuart, *How to Read the Bible for All Its Worth* (Grand Rapids, Mich.: Zondervan, 1985), 25.

15. Douglas Adams, *The Prostitute in the Family Tree: Discovering Humor and Irony in the Bible* (Louisville, Ky.: Westminster John Knox Press, 1997).

16. "Perhaps the damaging misconception about the Bible is the prejudicial belief that its characters are all straitlaced, tedious saints whose stories demonstrate a steadfast—and boring—piety." See John H. Gottcent, *The Bible: A Literary Study* (Boston: Twayne, 1986), xxvi.

17. According to Danna Nolan Fewell and David Miller Gunn, "Character construction (by readers), like plot construction, is inevitably a search for consistency." See *Compromising Redemption: Relating Characters in the Book of Ruth* (Louisville, Ky.: Westminster John Knox Press, 1990), 15.

18. "The most important causality in stories, then, does not lie simply in the sequence of events, but rather in how the sequence of events stimulates a sequence of emotion in the reader." See Kieran Egan, "What Is a Plot?" *New Literary History* 9 (1978), cited by R. Alan Culpepper, *Anatomy of the Fourth Gospel: A Study in Literary Design* (Philadelphia: Fortress, 1983), 78. N. T. Wright adds this comment: "Stories (i.e., plots) are the crucial agents that invest "events" with "meaning." The way the bare facts are described, the point at which the tension or climax occurs, the selection and arrangement of the parts—these all indicate the meaning which the events are believed to possess; and thus what the author means to communicate by telling them to the reader." See *The New Testament and the People of God* (Minneapolis, Minn.: Fortress, 1992), 79.

19. R. Alan Culpepper, *Anatomy of the Fourth Gospel: A Study in Literary Design* (Philadelphia: Fortress, 1983), 85.

20. Very often plots involve simultaneous conflicts. For example, Job is in conflict with God (3:1), with his wife and his "friends" (see 3: 2), with Satan (though unwittingly, 3:3 (see Job 1-2)), with his physical pain (3:4), and with himself in his doubt, grief, and suffering (3:5).

21. See Shimon Bar-Efrat, *Narrative Art in the Bible* (Eng. Trans. Dorothea Shefer-Vanson, Sheffield, England: Almond, 1984), 93.

22. Several biblical names are suggested as being close to tragic figures, but none truly qualify. Samson is heroic in his death, as is King Saul (to a lesser degree), yet in neither case are they commendable examples of virtue facing irresistible odds—they simply get what is coming to them for their sinful behavior. Likewise Judas doesn't fit the virtuous character, and also gets (by his own hand) his just punishment. The character Job does fit the heroic qualifications in the face of tremendous hardship, but, since the story ends happily with him not only restored but doubly blessed, it is actually a comedy. In the case of Jesus, Easter reverses the tragedy of Good Friday, turning the story into comedy. For more on (the absence of) tragedy in the Bible, see J. Cheryl Exum and J. William Whedbee, "Isaac, Samson, and Saul: Reflections on the Comic and Tragic Visions," *Semeia* 32 (1984), 5-40.

23. "[P]lots, and the reading of plots, are goal-oriented: we read to get to the end because the end will make sense of what has gone before. . . . We want to know how order will come from disorder, completeness from incompleteness, and the further we become immersed in the conflict, the obstacles to resolution, the more captured we are by our desire to know how it will all end." See David Gunn and Danna Nolan Fewell, *Narrative in the Hebrew Bible* (New York: Oxford Univ., 1993), 105. As we approach the end of a story, then, we expect a "promise to bestow meaning and significance on the beginning and the middle." See Peter Brooks, *Reading for the Plot: Design and Intention in Narrative* (New York: Vintage, 1985), 19.

24. Reading the Bible as canon (an intratext) militates against viewing any given story within it as a comedy or tragedy in a final sense, since scenes, episodes and stories continue to flow into subsequent narrative units. While there may be denouement in an intermediate sense, the larger, ongoing metanarrative resists closure. In other words, episodic closures are never final, because they are always embedded within a larger narrative framework whose inertia carries these along on greater currents. In light of these considerations, the labels of tragedy and comedy, however useful to describing smaller plot structures, must be used provisionally.

25. Cited by Yehuda T. Radday, "On Missing the Humour in the Bible: An Introduction," in Yehuda T. Radday and Athalya Brenner (eds.), *On Humour and Comic in the Bible* (Sheffield, England: Almond, 1990), 21.

26. For a book length treatment of this feature, see Thomas Jemielity, *Satire and the Hebrew Prophets* (Louisville, Ky.: Westminster John Knox Press, 1992).

27. Wayne Booth asserts that irony "cannot be understood without rejecting what (it) seems to say." See *The Rhetoric of Irony* (Chicago: Univ. of Chicago Press, 1974), 1; see also Wayne C. Booth, "The Pleasures and Pitfalls of Irony: or, Why Don't You Say What You Mean?" in Don M. Burks (ed.), *Rhetoric, Philosophy and Literature: An Exploration* (West Lafayette, Ind.: Purdue Univ. Press, 1978), 1-13.

28. An example of implicit clues might be Luke-Acts. Luke does not begin by saying, "I, Luke, . . ." However, since both Luke and Acts are written in the same style to the same person (Theophilus), they reflect the same author. Furthermore, in Acts the author uses the third person (they/them) to describe Paul and his companions except at those times when Luke is with them, at which points in the text it uses the first person (we/us). We conclude, then, that Luke is the implied author.

29. Most of the New Testament epistles identify the implied author in the opening of the letter. Old Testament examples where the text identifies its author include Nehemiah, superscriptions to various Psalms and Proverbs, Ecclesiastes, Song of Songs, and most of the prophets.

30. Use of the first person is found primarily in Ezekiel; Amos 7-9; Habakkuk; Zechariah 1-8, 11; Psalms; the speeches of Job and Song of Songs; Ecclesiastes; Lamentations 3; Daniel 7-12; Nehemiah; Acts 20-28; Romans; Philemon; James; 1 and 2 Peter; Jude, and Revelation.

31. "In the case of biblical narrative, the narrator has a potentially omniscient perceptual point of view. He can be anywhere and everywhere, even inside the minds of the characters. The reader's perception is formed by what the narrator reveals of his omniscience and the way it is revealed. Thus, although the narrator potentially knows more than the reader, for practical purposes the perceptual viewpoints of the narrator and the reader coincide—the reader comes to see what the narrator sees." See Adele Berlin, *Poetics and Interpretation of Biblical Narrative* (Sheffield, England: Almond, 1983), 52.

32. Brent Curtis and John Eldridge, *The Sacred Romance: Drawing Closer to the Heart of God* (Nashville: Thomas Nelson, 1997), 35.

Chapter Nine

1. Laurence Perrine, *Sound and Sense: An Introduction to Poetry*, 2nd ed. (New York: Harcourt, Brace and World, 1963), 3-4.

2. http://www.britannica.com/eb/article?tocId=9110446andquery=poetryand ct. Accessed November 3, 2004.

3. Thomas G. Long, *Preaching and the Literary Forms of the Bible* (Philadelphia: Fortress, 1989), 45.

4. The distinction between synonymous and synthetic parallelism is not always clear. Strictly speaking, even in synonymous parallelism, there is always some change in perspective or emphasis. As James Kugel has pointed out, there is some advance movement from the first line to the second: "A is so, and what's more, B is so.... B typically supports A, carries it further, backs it up, completes it, goes beyond it." See *The Idea of Biblical Poetry* (New Haven, Conn.: Yale, 1981), 8, 52.

5. "The ways of parallelism are numerous and varied, and the intensity of the semantic parallelism established between clauses might be said to range from 'zero perceivable correspondence' to 'near-zero perceivable differentiation' (i.e., just short of word-for-word repetition." See Kugel, *The Idea of Biblical Poetry*.

6. In the last line, we can see the equivalence of meaning between "ascribe (glory to) Yahweh" and "worship Yahweh," and the terms "glory" and "splendor" are also parallel, yet "holiness" is a distinctive element. It is in situations like this where the categories of synonymous parallelism and synthetic become blurred. Our chief interest, however, is not in giving labels, but in recognizing how parallelism works.

7. In 1 Timothy 3:16, Paul uses three pairs of opposites which reflect merism: body/spirit; angels (highest rational creatures)/nations (pagan gentiles, lowest of rational creatures); world (earth)/glory (heaven).

Chapter Ten

1. Some, including many dispensationalists, may have additional, theological reasons for preferring a focus on the Epistles. For example, John MacArthur, Jr. urges using the Hebrew Bible (Old Testament) merely to illustrate "New Testament" teaching. His reason is that he feels compelled to herald the new covenant, which he believes is done most clearly (only?) in the Epistles ("Frequently Asked Questions about Expository Preaching," in *Rediscovering Expository Preaching*, ed. John MacArthur, Jr. (Dallas: Word, 1992), 341-342. This was driven home to me in an advanced elective course I took in seminary called "Hermeneutics and Homiletics." Each student was to select a passage, work through the hermeneutical and exegetical issues, and then give a brief sermon to the rest of the class based on that text. One classmate of mine attempted to preach from a narrative, but did it very poorly—a point apparent to everyone, including the student. In the ensuing class discussion, he confessed, "I grew up in a church where the only preaching I ever heard was always based on the New Testament epistles. I really don't even know

how to preach anything else except them!"

2. In using the term "the Lord," I understand Paul to be referring here specifically to Jesus, during his earthly ministry. The context here is not about divine inspiration of Paul's writing. Instead the issue is whether the divine source is the Holy Spirit or a reference back to something that Jesus already said during his incarnation.

3. This form of literary structure is called a diatribe (see Appendix).

4. For further study on relationships, particularly in epistolary literature, see Thomas R. Schreiner, *Interpreting the Pauline Epistles* (Grand Rapids, Mich.: Baker, 1990), 97-126; and Robert H. Stein, *A Basic Guide to Interpreting the Bible: Playing By the Rules* (Grand Rapids, Mich.: Baker, 1994), 178-184.

Chapter Eleven

1. For more on characterization in Ruth, see Danna Nolan Fewell and David Miller Gunn, *Compromising Redemption: Relating Characters in the Book of Ruth* (Louisville, Ky.: Westminster John Knox Press, 1990).

2. The NIV, unfortunately in my opinion, obscures this fact by inserting her name where it does not appear in the Hebrew text.

3. The genealogy of Ruth 4 reads, "Amminadab the father of Nahshon, Nahshon the father of Salmon, Salmon the father of Boaz, Boaz the father of Obed...." See vv. 20-21. Nahshon was over the age of twenty as the Israelites came out of Egypt (Numbers 1:3, 7) and was the designated leader of the tribe of Judah at the time (Numbers 3:2; 7:10-17). Since that generation died in the wilderness (Numbers 14:29-30), Salmon was the oldest of his line able to enter the promised land, and Moses' words would most likely have been heard by Salmon (constituting the first generation). Boaz (the second generation) may have been the first of his line actually born in the promised land. If Boaz and Elimelech belonged to the same generation (e.g., were cousins), a probable inference based upon the difference in ages between Boaz and Ruth (Ruth 3:10), then Mahlon and Kilion would have been the third generation. Even if my calculations may be off by a generation, or even two, it is still much less than the required ten generation waiting period of Deuteronomy 23:3-6: "No Ammonite or Moabite or any of his descendants may enter the assembly of Yahweh, even down to the tenth generation. For they did not come to meet you with bread and water on your way when you came out of Egypt, and they hired Balaam son of Beor from Pethor in Aram Naharaim to pronounce a curse on you.... Do not seek a treaty of friendship with them as long as you live."

4. The Hebrew word for return occurs in Ruth 1:6, 7, 8, 10, 11, 12, 15 (twice),

16, 21, 22 (twice); 2:6; 4:3, 15.

5. I take Proverbs 31:10-31 to describe the same lady wisdom as seen elsewhere in Proverbs. Thus I don't think that this passage is a "women's" passage per se. It is wisdom itself that is personified, not just qualities to look for in a wife.

6. The importance of returning to God——and the land——would have had special bearing in post-captivity Israel, encouraging them to experience redemption from their loss, just as Naomi had.

7. The Hebrew root word here again is *šûb*, to give or turn back / to return / to repent.

Chapter Twelve

1. The translation is my own, and its somewhat awkward wording is because of my desire to follow the form of the Hebrew text as closely as possible. However, all of the steps I am recommending here would also work in common English translations.

2. Perhaps you are wondering how Hannah would have known about a royal, coming Messiah, since she lived decades before Israel ever had its first king, before David in particular became king, and long before Yahweh made this covenant with David. Yet from long ago, God had made it clear that his intent was ultimately to raise up a royal son who would rule his people. Because of this, several passages which Hannah would have known anticipate a hope for salvation from their enemies coming through a future king (Genesis 49:10; Numbers 24:7-9, 17-19; Deuteronomy 17:14-20).

Chapter Thirteen

1. The translation here is the New International Version, with a few revisions.

2. The Greek word for "loves to be first" is *philoprôteurôn*, based on *phileô* rather than *agape*.

3. In both of the cases in this verse, the term for "loved ones" (see NIV "friends") is derived from the Greek word *phileô*. In all other cases except in verse 9, noted above, the root Greek word is *agape*.

Epilogue

1. Neil Postman, "Defending Against the Indefensible" in *Conscientious Objections* (New York: Vintage, 1988), 26-27.

2. Conrad Hyers, *And God Created Laughter: The Bible as Divine Comedy* (Atlanta: John Knox Press, 1987), 89.

Appendix

1. Many scholars also consider certain other portions of Scripture as apocalyptic: Isaiah 24-27; Ezekiel 37-39; Matthew 24-25 and its parallels in Mark 13 and Luke 21.

2. Though prophecy and apocalyptic have different emphases, apocalyptic came from prophecy and can actually be considered a particular kind of prophecy. Ronald Youngblood remarks, "Apocalyptic, then, is prophecy continued, prophecy developed, prophecy adapted to new needs in new situations." See "A Holistic Typology of Prophecy and Apocalyptic" in Avraham Gileadi (ed.), *Israel's Apostasy and Restoration* (Grand Rapids, Mich.: Baker, 1988), 216.

3. For further study on apocalyptic, see Paul Hanson, *The Dawn of Apocalyptic* (Philadelphia: Fortress, 1975); Grant R. Osborne, *The Hermeneutical Spiral: A Comprehensive Introduction to Biblical Literature* (Downers Grove, Ill.: InterVarsity, 1991), 221-234; and Leland Ryken, *Words of Delight: A Literary Introduction to the Bible* (rev. ed. Grand Rapids, Mich.: Baker, 1992), 477-505.

4. The same may be said about end-times charts. The value of these charts is arguable, but at the least it must be recognized that this interest is an entirely different undertaking than trying to follow the main ideas that the authors are seeking to develop. These passages were simply not intended for chronological purposes: "The apocalyptic genre, much like the prophetic, presents the truth of God not consecutively or logically, but multidimensionally." See Willem A. Van Gemeren, *Interpreting the Prophetic Word* (Grand Rapids, Mich.: Zondervan, 1990), 411.

5. Mark Strom offers good advice: "The great danger lies not in isolated bizarre events or individuals, but in the diabolical way in which every society, culture and nation promotes the original lie that humans control their own destiny and can solve their own problems. In other words, the institutions, events and trends of ordinary life conspire to make us believe that we are gods." See *The Symphony of Scripture* (Downers Grove, Ill.: InterVarsity, 1990), 263 (emphasis his).

6. For further study in reading epistles, see Gordon D. Fee and Douglas Stuart, *How to Read the Bible for All Its Worth* (Grand Rapids, Mich.: Zondervan, 1982), 43-71; Michael Goulder, "The Pauline Epistles" in Robert Alter and Frank Kermode (eds), *The Literary Guide to the Bible* (Cambridge: Harvard, 1987), 479-502; and Sidney Greidanus, *The Modern Preacher and the Ancient Text: Interpreting and Preaching Biblical Literature* (Grand Rapids, Mich.: Eerdmans, 1988), 311-341.

7. For further study on forms in the epistles, see James L. Bailey and Lyle D. Vander Broek, *Literary Forms in the New Testament* (Louisville, Ky.: Westminster John Knox Press, 1992), 21-87, 191-201.

8. Walter Liefeld says that these patterns of repetition "running through a passage...give a sense of direction like tire tracks running across wet cement. Following the imprint provides continuity." See *New Testament Exposition: From Text to Sermon* (Grand Rapids, Mich.: Zondervan, 1984), 32.

9. "(T)he end of most biblical narratives were known beforehand (e.g., Jesus' resurrection), so that plot interest pertains more to how the story is told than to suspense." See William S. Kurz, *Reading Luke-Acts: Dynamics of Biblical Narrative* (Louisville, Ky.: Westminster John Knox Press, 1993), 171.

10. There are other books also bearing the name "gospel": from Nag Hammadi (*Gospel of Truth, Gospel of Thomas, Gospel of Philip, Gospel of the Egyptians, and Gospel of Mary*) and other apocryphal books from the second century. These, however, are clearly recognized as being different in both content and form by biblical scholars of all theological persuasions. (See Robert Guelich, "The Gospel Genre" in Peter Stuhlmacher (ed), *The Gospel and the Gospels* (Grand Rapids, Mich.: Eerdmans, 1991), 175, 204-205. The term for saying that the four canonical gospels are a category unto themselves is *sui generis*.

11. It is understandable for readers to assume that the book of Acts is not a gospel because it doesn't describe the earthly ministry of Jesus. However, recently, many scholars have recognized that Luke and Acts cannot be studied in isolation from one another but present a single, unified narrative. Examples include William S. Kurz, *Reading Luke-Acts: Dynamics of Biblical Narrative* (Louisville, Ky.: Westminster John Knox Press, 1993); I. Howard Marshall, "Luke and His 'Gospel'" in Peter Stuhlmacher (ed), *The Gospel and the Gospels* (Grand Rapids, Mich.: Eerdmans, 1991), 273-292; Robert F. O'Toole, *The Unity of Luke's Theology: An Analysis of Luke-Acts* (Wilmington: Michael Glazier, 1984); and Robert C. Tannehill, *The Narrative Unity of Luke-Acts: A Literary Interpretation* (2 vols, Philadelphia: Fortress, 1986).

12. The genre of gospel as a "multifaceted narrative about Jesus relates to the larger framework of biblical history, because the life of Jesus not only emerges from that history but also transforms and transcends it." See James L. Bailey and Lyle D. Vander Broek, *Literary Forms in the New Testament: a*

Handbook (Louisville, Ky.: Westminster John Knox Press, 1992), 91.

13. This is not to say that they altered the truth—only that they felt freedom to organize and structure the story and dialogue in a way that highlights the points they are trying to make. Their chief interest was not to present a chronologically-governed account of Jesus' life, but one according to theological motives. James Barr is helpful here: "Genre mistakes cause the wrong kind of truth values to be attached to biblical sentences." See *The Bible in the Modern World* (London: SCM, 1973), 125.

14. For a good literary approach to Matthew's gospel, see Jack Dean Kingsbury, *Matthew as Story* (Philadelphia: Fortress, 1986).

15. A good literary reading of Mark may be found in David Rhoads and Donald Michie, *Mark as Story: An Introduction to the Narrative of a Gospel* (Philadelphia: Fortress, 1982).

16. Luke employs the "journey" motif as the structuring device behind both Luke and Acts, with many parallels between Jesus' life (Luke) and those of his followers (Acts).

17. Helpful here is Jack Dean Kingsbury, *Conflict in Luke: Jesus, Authorities, Disciples* (Minneapolis, Minn.: Fortress, 1991); William S. Kurz, *Reading Luke-Acts: Dynamics of Biblical Narrative* (Louisville, Ky.: Westminster John Knox Press, 1993); and Robert C. Tannehill, *The Literary Unity of Luke-Acts: A Literary Interpretation, Vol. 1 Luke, Vol. 2 Acts* (Minneapolis, Minn.: Fortress, 1990).

18. John especially employs three narrative devices: (1) legal and courtroom terminology, (e.g., forensic imagery); (2) irony, (characters saying things much more real or profound than they realize), (4:19; 8:53; 9:40; 11:49-50; 19:14, 19) or the reader's awareness of deeper meanings than what appears on the surface (2:19-22; 12:12-16); (3) numerous symbols and metaphors, some of which are deliberately ambiguous (light, bread, born from above/born again, water, "children" of Abraham, etc.).

19. Gordon Fee and Douglas Stuart, *How to Read the Bible for All Its Worth* (Grand Rapids, Mich.: Zondervan, 1982), 113 (emphasis mine).

20. "The overwhelming conclusion of the prophetic corpus is that God will save all who repent." See Paul R. House, *The Unity of the Twelve* (Sheffield, England: Almond, 1990), 120.

21. Walter C. Kaiser, Jr. has made a good case for understanding the New Covenant as a Renewed Covenant. See *Toward an Old Testament Theology* (Grand Rapids, Mich.: Zondervan, 1978), 231-235, and "The Old Promise and the New Covenant" *Journal of the Evangelical Theological Society* 15 (1972), 11-23.

22. Thomas Jemielity, *Satire in the Hebrew Prophets* (Louisville, Ky.: Westminster John Knox Press, 1992), 41. This book is an excellent presentation of biblical satire in general and prophetic satire in particular. For further study, see: R. P. Carroll, "Is Humour Also Among the Prophets?" in Yehuda T. Radday and Athalya Brenner (eds.), *On Humour and Comic in the Hebrew Bible* (Sheffield, England: Almond, 1990), 167-189.

23. In addition to the forms listed, there are many others. Also helpful here is Claus Westermann, *Basic Forms of Prophetic Speech* (repr. Louisville, Ky.: Westminster John Knox Press, 1967, 1991), and Sidney Greidanus, *The Modern Preacher and the Ancient Text: Interpreting and Preaching Biblical Literature* (Grand Rapids, Mich.: Eerdmans, 1988), 228-255.

24. C. S. Lewis, *Reflections on the Psalms* (repr. Glasgow: Collins/Fontana, 1961, 1976), 10.

25. For more on reading the book of Psalms as an entire literary unit, see Michael Wilcock, *The Message of the Psalms*, 2 vols. (Downers Grove, Ill.: InterVarsity, 2001); J. Clinton McCann, *A Theological Introduction to the Book of Psalms* (Nashville: Abingdon, 1993); and J. Clinton McCann (ed), *The Shape and Shaping of the Psalter* (Sheffield, England: JSOT Press, 1993).

26. James L. Crenshaw identified these Psalms as 37, 39, 49, and 73 in *OT Wisdom: An Introduction* (Atlanta: John Knox Press , 1981). Others add Psalms 1, 15, 32, 34, 111, 112, 127, 128, and 133; see John H Hayes, *OT Form Criticism* (San Antonio: Trinity Univ. Press, 1977), 249-250.

27. Walter Brueggemann, *The Creative Word: Canon as a Model for Biblical Education* (Philadelphia: Fortress, 1982), 84 (emphasis his).

28. Ibid., 70.

29. The fear of Yahweh is "a commitment to the LORD by following his instruction. It is a response of faithful obedience to the LORD by subjection to his revealed will." See Albert H. Baylis, *On the Way to Jesus: A Journey Through the Bible* (Portland, Oreg.: Multnomah, 1986), 237. R. E. Clements defines the "fear of Yahweh" as "an attitude of mind, a respect for the role of piety and faith, and also a strong determination to 'do the right thing,' even when it may be costly and difficult to do so." See *Wisdom in Theology* (Grand Rapids, Mich.: Eerdmans, 1992), 61.

30. C. H. Dodd, *The Parables of the Kingdom* (London: Fontana, 1961), 16.

Printed in Great Britain
by Amazon

49728070R00163